First World War
and Army of Occupation
War Diary
France, Belgium and Germany

32 DIVISION
14 Infantry Brigade
Manchester Regiment
2nd Battalion
1 January 1916 - 31 January 1918

WO95/2392/2

The Naval & Military Press Ltd
www.nmarchive.com
Published in association with The National Archives

Published by

The Naval & Military Press Ltd

Unit 10 Ridgewood Industrial Park,

Uckfield, East Sussex,

TN22 5QE England

Tel: +44 (0) 1825 749494

www.naval-military-press.com

www.nmarchive.com

This diary has been reprinted in facsimile from the original. Any imperfections are inevitably reproduced and the quality may fall short of modern type and cartographic standards.

© **Crown Copyright**
Images reproduced by permission of The National Archives, London, England, 2015.

Contents

Document type	Place/Title	Date From	Date To
Heading	WO95/2392/2		
Heading	32nd Division 14th Infy Bde 2nd Bn Manchester Regt Jan 1916-Jan 1918 From 5 Div 14 Bde To 96 Bde 32 Div		
Heading	14th Brigade. 32nd Division. 2nd Battalion The Manchester Regiment January 1916		
War Diary	Sailly Lorette	01/01/1916	03/01/1916
War Diary	Henencourt	04/01/1916	10/01/1916
War Diary	Authville	11/01/1916	18/01/1916
War Diary	Henencourt	19/01/1916	26/01/1916
War Diary	Martinsart	27/01/1916	31/01/1916
Miscellaneous	Report on Oil Drum Bomb	11/01/1916	11/01/1916
Diagram etc	Sketch Shewing demensions and details of Oil Drum Bomb	11/01/1916	11/01/1916
Miscellaneous	A Form. Messages And Signals.		
Miscellaneous	Intelligence Report.	15/01/1916	15/01/1916
Miscellaneous	A Form. Messages And Signals.		
Miscellaneous	Intelligence Report	16/01/1916	16/01/1916
Miscellaneous	A Form. Messages And Signals.		
Heading	14th Brigade. 32nd Division. 2nd Battalion The Manchester Regiment February 1916		
War Diary	Henencourt	01/02/1916	01/02/1916
War Diary	Authville	02/02/1916	06/02/1916
War Diary	Henencourt	07/02/1916	13/02/1916
War Diary	St. Gratien	14/02/1916	28/02/1916
War Diary	Henencourt	29/02/1916	29/02/1916
Heading	14th Brigade. 32nd Division. 2nd Battalion The Manchester Regiment March 1916		
War Diary		01/03/1916	08/03/1916
War Diary	Millencourt	09/03/1916	21/03/1916
War Diary	Albert Aveluy	22/03/1916	31/03/1916
War Diary	Albert Aveluy	28/03/1916	28/03/1916
Miscellaneous Map			
Miscellaneous	2nd Bn The Manchester Regiment.		
Miscellaneous	Fighting Strength etc. in Trenches.	09/03/1916	09/03/1916
Miscellaneous	Messages And Signals.		
Miscellaneous	Return Of Man Employed Away From Battalion 2nd Bn Manchester Regiment.	08/03/1916	08/03/1916
Miscellaneous	2nd Battalion The Manchester Regt.	08/03/1916	08/03/1916
Miscellaneous	Fighting Strength etc.		
Heading	14th Brigade. 32nd Division. 2nd Battalion The Manchester Regiment. May 1916		
War Diary	Pierregot	01/05/1916	05/05/1916
War Diary	Warloy	06/05/1916	06/05/1916
War Diary	Aveluy	07/05/1916	10/05/1916
War Diary	Authville	11/05/1916	14/05/1916
War Diary	Aveluy	15/05/1916	18/05/1916
War Diary	Warloy	19/05/1916	24/05/1916
War Diary	Bouzincourt Aveluy	25/05/1916	29/05/1916

War Diary	Contay	30/05/1916	31/05/1916
Miscellaneous	A Form. Messages And Signals.		
Miscellaneous	Intelligence Report.		
Miscellaneous	Intelligence Report.	10/05/1916	10/05/1916
Miscellaneous	A Form. Messages And Signals.		
Miscellaneous	Intelligence Report		
Miscellaneous	A Form. Messages And Signals.		
Miscellaneous	Intelligence Report	13/05/1916	13/05/1916
Miscellaneous	A Form. Messages And Signals.		
Heading	14th Brigade. 32nd Division. 2nd Battalion The Manchester Regiment April 1916		
War Diary		01/04/1916	04/04/1916
War Diary	Aveluy	05/04/1916	09/04/1916
War Diary	Authville	10/04/1916	12/04/1916
War Diary	Bouzincourt	13/04/1916	17/04/1916
War Diary	Authville	18/04/1916	22/04/1916
War Diary	Aveluy	22/04/1916	24/04/1916
War Diary	Contay	25/04/1916	30/04/1916
Heading	14th Brigade. 32nd Division. 2nd Battalion The Manchester Regiment June 1916		
War Diary		01/06/1916	30/06/1916
Miscellaneous	Battalion Orders By Lieut Col N. Luxmoore Commanding The 2nd Bn Manchester Regiment.	11/06/1916	11/06/1916
Operation(al) Order(s)	Operation Orders By Lieut Col N. Luxmoore Commanding 2nd Bn Manchester Regiment.	11/06/1916	11/06/1916
Heading	14th Inf. Bde. 32nd Div. War Diary 2nd Battn. The Manchester Regiment. July 1916		
War Diary	Senlis	01/07/1916	04/07/1916
War Diary	Forceville	05/07/1916	06/07/1916
War Diary	Senlis	07/07/1916	07/07/1916
War Diary	Bouzincourt	07/07/1916	08/07/1916
War Diary	Ovillers	08/07/1916	11/07/1916
War Diary	Bouzincourt	12/07/1916	14/07/1916
War Diary	Ovillers	15/07/1916	15/07/1916
War Diary	Senlis	16/07/1916	16/07/1916
War Diary	Halloy	17/07/1916	17/07/1916
War Diary	Le Souich	18/07/1916	18/07/1916
War Diary	Marquay	20/07/1916	20/07/1916
War Diary	St Pierre	21/07/1916	25/07/1916
War Diary	Haillicourt	26/07/1916	29/07/1916
War Diary	Le Preol	30/07/1916	31/07/1916
Heading	Report On Operations		
Miscellaneous			
Miscellaneous	Operations During The Great Advance.	16/07/1916	16/07/1916
Miscellaneous	Operations During The Great Advance Phase.		
Map			
Heading	14th Brigade. 32nd Division. 2nd Battalion The Manchester Regiment. August 1916		
War Diary	Le Preol Annequin	01/08/1916	02/08/1916
War Diary	Le Preol	03/08/1916	05/08/1916
War Diary	Cambrin	06/08/1916	11/08/1916
War Diary	Cuinchy	12/08/1916	16/08/1916
War Diary	Le Quesnoy	17/08/1916	23/08/1916
War Diary	Cuinchy	24/08/1916	29/08/1916
War Diary	Cambrin	30/08/1916	31/08/1916

Heading	14th Brigade. 32nd Division. 2nd Battalion The Manchester Regiment September 1916		
War Diary	Cambrin	01/09/1916	04/09/1916
War Diary	Cuinchy	05/09/1916	08/09/1916
War Diary	Annezin	09/09/1916	18/09/1916
War Diary	Cambrin	19/09/1916	22/09/1916
War Diary	Annequin	22/09/1916	26/09/1916
War Diary	Cambrin	27/09/1916	30/09/1916
Heading	Details of Raid as Carried Out on the Night 28/29th September 1916		
Miscellaneous	Moving Up To Trenches.		
Miscellaneous	Details of Raid by 2nd. Manchester Regiment on Enemy Trenches from Point A. 28.c. 55/55 to Point A 28.c. 7/4. on the night of September 1916		
Miscellaneous	Details of Raid By 2nd Battalion the Manchester Regiment.		
Miscellaneous	Reference Map. Trench Map To 36 NW And Attached Sketch.		
Map			
Miscellaneous	Appendix N.		
Miscellaneous	Programme of Artillery of Front Appendix F.		
Map			
Map	Attached Map C		
Map			
Heading	14th Brigade. 32nd Division. 2nd Battalion The Manchester Regiment October 1916		
War Diary	Cambrin	01/10/1916	03/10/1916
War Diary	Bethune	04/10/1916	09/10/1916
War Diary	Busnes	10/10/1916	14/10/1916
War Diary	Auchy a la Tours	15/10/1916	15/10/1916
War Diary	Ternas	16/10/1916	16/10/1916
War Diary	Canettemont & Honval	16/10/1916	17/10/1916
War Diary	Beauval	18/10/1916	20/10/1916
War Diary	Warloy Baillon	21/10/1916	22/10/1916
War Diary	Brickfields Area. (Albert)	22/10/1916	25/10/1916
War Diary	Contay	26/10/1916	31/10/1916
Heading	14th Brigade. 32nd Division. 2nd Battalion The Manchester Regiment November 1916		
War Diary	Contay	01/11/1916	12/11/1916
War Diary	Bouzincourt	13/11/1916	14/11/1916
War Diary	Mailly Maillet	15/11/1916	15/11/1916
War Diary	Trenches	16/11/1916	20/11/1916
War Diary	Mailly Maillet	21/11/1916	21/11/1916
War Diary	Trenches	21/11/1916	23/11/1916
War Diary	Terramesnil	24/11/1916	24/11/1916
War Diary	Doullens	25/11/1916	25/11/1916
War Diary	Halloy L Pernois	26/11/1916	30/11/1916
Miscellaneous	Operations Undertaken By 2nd. Battalion The Manchester Regiment.		
Miscellaneous	Lessons to be learnt from recent operations.		
Heading	14th Brigade. 32nd Division. 2nd Battalion The Manchester Regiment December 1916		
War Diary	Halloy Les Pernois	01/12/1916	31/12/1916
War Diary	Pernois-Les-Halloy	01/01/1917	05/01/1917
War Diary	Beauval	06/01/1917	07/01/1917
War Diary	Bertrancourt & Bus Courcelles	08/01/1917	08/01/1917

Type	Location/Description	From	To
War Diary	Courcelles	09/01/1917	11/01/1917
War Diary	Courcelles & Trenches	12/01/1917	14/01/1917
War Diary	Courcelles	15/01/1917	17/01/1917
War Diary	Courcelles & Trenches	17/01/1917	20/01/1917
War Diary	Bus	21/01/1917	21/01/1917
War Diary	Bolton Camp	22/01/1917	22/01/1917
War Diary	Trenches	23/01/1917	26/01/1917
War Diary	Bertrancourt	27/01/1917	30/01/1917
War Diary	Trenches	31/01/1917	31/01/1917
Miscellaneous	Battalion Defence Scheme.	17/01/1917	17/01/1917
War Diary	Trenches	01/02/1917	03/02/1917
War Diary	Bertrancourt	04/02/1917	05/02/1917
War Diary	Trenches	06/02/1917	08/02/1917
War Diary	Bertrancourt	09/02/1917	10/02/1917
War Diary	Trenches	11/02/1917	12/02/1917
War Diary	Mailly Maillet	13/02/1917	14/02/1917
War Diary	Louvencourt	15/02/1917	15/02/1917
War Diary	Contay	16/02/1917	20/02/1917
War Diary	Villers Bocage	21/02/1917	21/02/1917
War Diary	Rivery	22/02/1917	22/02/1917
War Diary	Thennes	23/02/1917	23/02/1917
War Diary	Fresnoy	24/02/1917	24/02/1917
War Diary	Dugouts Bouchoir	25/02/1917	28/02/1917
War Diary	Bouchoir	01/03/1917	07/03/1917
War Diary	Beaufort	08/03/1917	13/03/1917
War Diary	Trenches	14/03/1917	17/03/1917
War Diary	Wancourt	18/03/1917	18/03/1917
War Diary	Mesnil St Nichaise	19/03/1917	20/03/1917
War Diary	Voyennes	21/03/1917	26/03/1917
War Diary	Lanchy	27/03/1917	27/03/1917
War Diary	Beauvois	28/03/1917	31/03/1917
Miscellaneous	Addendum To 14th Infantry Brigade Operation Order No. 120		
Operation(al) Order(s)	2nd Battalion The Manchester Regiment Operation Order No. 1	13/03/1917	13/03/1917
War Diary		01/04/1917	30/04/1917
Miscellaneous	Capture Of A German 77, MM, Battery. Francilly-Selency. April. 2nd. 1917	02/04/1917	02/04/1917
Miscellaneous	Names Of Officers & Warrant Officers Who Were In Action April 2nd 1917		
Miscellaneous			
Miscellaneous	2nd Battalion The Manchester Regt.		
Miscellaneous	Movement Of The Battalion During The Period April 12th To April 29th 1917		
Miscellaneous	14th Infantry Brigade Training Programme	23/04/1917	23/04/1917
Miscellaneous	14th Infantry Brigade Training Programme	26/04/1917	26/04/1917
Miscellaneous	14th Infantry Brigade.	23/04/1917	23/04/1917
Miscellaneous			
Miscellaneous	14th Infantry Brigade Training Programme	29/04/1917	29/04/1917
Miscellaneous	14th Infantry Brigade.		
Miscellaneous	14th Infantry Brigade (Bombers And Rifle Grenadiers).		
Miscellaneous	14th Infantry Brigade (Training of Signallers)		
War Diary	Quivieres	01/05/1917	14/05/1917
War Diary	Voyennes	15/05/1917	15/05/1917
War Diary	Hattencourt	16/05/1917	16/05/1917
War Diary	Le. Quesnel	17/05/1917	29/05/1917

War Diary	Demuin	30/05/1917	31/05/1917
Miscellaneous	2nd. Battalion The Manchester Regiment. Appendix A	02/05/1917	02/05/1917
Miscellaneous	14th Infantry Brigade Training Programme (from 30th April To 5th May Inclusive) Appendix B	30/04/1917	30/04/1917
Miscellaneous	2nd Bn The Manchester Rgt Instructions No. 1 Appendix C	02/05/1917	02/05/1917
Miscellaneous	2nd Battalion The Manchester Regiment. Major. Appendix D	02/05/1917	02/05/1917
Miscellaneous	14th Infantry Brigade (Training of Signallers.) Appendix E		
Miscellaneous	2nd Battalion The Manchester Regiment.	04/05/1917	04/05/1917
Miscellaneous	Operation Orders By Major J.F. Dempster Commanding 2nd Battalion. The Manchester Regiment Appendix G	19/05/1917	19/05/1917
Miscellaneous	Fourth Army No. G.S. 702 Appendix 1	22/05/1917	22/05/1917
Heading	D.A.G. G.H.Q. 3rd Echelon Divisional War Diary DMS. Second Army June 1917		
Miscellaneous	2 Manchester Rgt Vol 35		
War Diary	Demuin	01/06/1917	01/06/1917
War Diary	Bailleul	02/06/1917	12/06/1917
War Diary	Tergedhem	13/06/1917	14/06/1917
War Diary	Teterghem	15/06/1917	16/06/1917
War Diary	Nieuport	17/06/1917	30/06/1917
Miscellaneous	2nd Battalion The Manchester Regiment. Appendix No. 1	03/06/1917	03/06/1917
Miscellaneous	2nd Battalion The Manchester Regiment. Appendix No. 2	03/06/1917	03/06/1917
Miscellaneous	2nd. Battalion The Manchester Regiment.	03/06/1917	03/06/1917
Heading	C.O HD Officer		
Miscellaneous	2nd Battalion The Manchester Regiment. Appendix No. 3	04/06/1917	04/06/1917
Miscellaneous	After Orders By Lieut. Colonel J.F. Dempster Commanding 2nd. Battalion The Manchester Regiment. Appendix No. 4	04/06/1917	04/06/1917
Miscellaneous	2nd Battalion The Manchester Regiment. Appendix No. 5	05/06/1917	05/06/1917
Heading	C.O. & HG Officers.		
Miscellaneous	After Orders By Lieut Colonel J.F Dempster, Commanding 2nd Battalion The Manchester Regiment. Appendix 6	06/06/1917	06/06/1917
Operation(al) Order(s)	Preliminary Operation Orders No. 1. Appendix 7	06/06/1917	06/06/1917
Miscellaneous	2nd Battalion The Manchester Regiment. Appendix 8	06/06/1917	06/06/1917
Miscellaneous	2nd Battalion The Manchester Regiment. Appendix No 9	07/06/1917	07/06/1917
Miscellaneous	2nd Battalion The Manchester Regiment. Appendix No 10	10/06/1917	10/06/1917
Miscellaneous	Extract from 32nd. Divisional Routine Orders. Appendix No. 11	10/06/1917	10/06/1917
Miscellaneous	2nd Battalion The Manchester Regiment. Appendix No. 12	22/06/1917	22/06/1917
Miscellaneous	2nd Battalion The Manchester Regiment. Appendix No. 13	21/06/1917	21/06/1917
Miscellaneous	2nd Battalion The Manchester Regiment. Appendix No. 14	22/06/1917	22/06/1917
Map			
Miscellaneous	2nd Battalion The Manchester Regiment. Appendix 15	21/06/1917	21/06/1917

Type	Description	Start	End
Miscellaneous	2nd. Battalion The Manchester Regiment. Appendix No. 16	26/06/1917	26/06/1917
Miscellaneous	2nd Battalion The Manchester Regiment. Appendix 17	29/06/1917	29/06/1917
Miscellaneous	Appendix A To Scheme C Dated 29.6.17	29/06/1917	29/06/1917
Miscellaneous	2nd Battalion The Manchester Regiment. Appendix 18	29/06/1917	29/06/1917
Operation(al) Order(s)	2nd. Bn The Manchester Regiment. Operation Orders No. 107. Appendix 19	18/06/1917	18/06/1917
Operation(al) Order(s)	2nd. Battalion The Manchester Regiment. Operation Orders No. 108 Appendix No. 20	20/06/1917	20/06/1917
Operation(al) Order(s)	2nd. Battalion The Manchester Regiment. Operation Orders No. 110 Appendix No. 21	23/06/1917	23/06/1917
Operation(al) Order(s)	2nd Battalion The Manchester Regiment. Operation Orders No. 111 Appendix No. 22	25/06/1917	25/06/1917
Operation(al) Order(s)	2nd Battalion The Manchester Regiment. Operation Orders No. 115 Appendix No. 23	29/06/1917	29/06/1917
Operation(al) Order(s)	2nd Battalion The Manchester Regiment Operation Orders No. 114 Appendix No. 24	28/06/1917	28/06/1917
Operation(al) Order(s)	2nd Battalion The Manchester Regiment Operation Orders No. 116 Appendix No. 25	30/06/1917	30/06/1917
Operation(al) Order(s)	2nd Battalion The Manchester Regiment. Operation Orders No. 117 Appendix No. 26	30/06/1917	30/06/1917
War Diary	Nieuport	01/07/1917	01/07/1917
War Diary	Camp Rabillet	02/07/1917	03/07/1917
War Diary	Ghyvelde	04/07/1917	10/07/1917
War Diary	Jeanbart Camp	11/07/1917	11/07/1917
War Diary	Nieuport	12/07/1917	18/07/1917
War Diary	Zuydecoote	19/07/1917	31/07/1917
Operation(al) Order(s)	2nd Battalion The Manchester Regiment. Operation Orders No. 118 Appendix No 1	01/07/1917	01/07/1917
Miscellaneous	2nd Battalion The Manchester Regiment. Appendix No. 2	05/07/1917	05/07/1917
Miscellaneous	Programme of Training From 7th To 16th July Inclusive.	05/07/1917	05/07/1917
Miscellaneous	2nd Battalion The Manchester Regiment. Appendix 3	27/07/1917	27/07/1917
Miscellaneous	2nd Battalion The Manchester Regiment.	27/07/1917	27/07/1917
War Diary	Zuydecoote	01/08/1917	01/08/1917
War Diary	Oust-Dunkerque	02/08/1917	03/08/1917
War Diary	La. Panne	04/08/1917	27/08/1917
War Diary	Nieuport	28/08/1917	01/09/1917
War Diary	Right Sub Sector	02/09/1917	02/09/1917
War Diary	Lombartzyde Sector	03/09/1917	12/09/1917
War Diary	Coxyde	13/09/1917	24/09/1917
War Diary	Oost-Dunkerke	25/09/1917	30/09/1917
War Diary	Nieuport	01/10/1917	05/10/1917
War Diary	Coxyde	06/10/1917	06/10/1917
War Diary	Adinkerke	07/10/1917	07/10/1917
War Diary	Petite Synthe	08/10/1917	25/10/1917
War Diary	Petite Synthe & L'Erkelsbrugge	25/10/1917	26/10/1917
War Diary	Arneke	26/10/1917	11/11/1917
War Diary	Oudezeele	12/11/1917	12/11/1917
War Diary	Tunnelling Camp Poperinghe	13/11/1917	24/11/1917
War Diary	Canal Bank	25/11/1917	30/11/1917
War Diary	Yser Canal	01/12/1917	01/12/1917
War Diary	Irish Farm	02/12/1917	02/12/1917
War Diary	Belle Vue	03/12/1917	03/12/1917
War Diary	Left Sub-Sector	04/12/1917	05/12/1917

War Diary	Belle Vue	06/12/1917	09/12/1917
War Diary	Yser Canal	10/12/1917	10/12/1917
War Diary	Hospital Farm	11/12/1917	17/12/1917
War Diary	Canal Bank	18/12/1917	23/12/1917
War Diary	Right Sub-Sector	24/12/1917	27/12/1917
War Diary	Corps Line & Albert	28/12/1917	30/12/1917
War Diary	Canal Bank	31/12/1917	01/01/1918
War Diary	Listergaux	02/01/1917	22/01/1917
War Diary	Dirty Bucket Camp	23/01/1917	30/01/1917
War Diary	Emile Camp	31/01/1918	31/01/1918

WD 96 / 2392 (2)

WD 96 / 2392 (2)

32ND DIVISION
14TH INFY BDE

2ND BN MANCHESTER REGT
JAN 1916 – JAN 1918

FROM 5 DIV 14 BDE

To 96 BDE 32 DIV

14th Brigade.

32nd Division.

2nd BATTALION

THE MANCHESTER REGIMENT

JANUARY 1 9 1 6

Appendices attached:-

Report on Oil Drum Bomb.

Intelligence Summaries

1 Batt. The Manchester Regiment

WAR DIARY
or
INTELLIGENCE SUMMARY
(Erase heading not required). Sheet No. I

Army Form C 2118.

Instructions regarding War Diaries and Intelligence Summaries are contained in F.S. Regs., Part II and the Staff Manual respectively. Title Pages will be prepared in manuscript.

Place.	Date	Hour	Summary of Events and Information.	Remarks and references to Appendices
SAILLY-LORETTE	January 1916 1st.		Battalion in billets at SAILLY-LORETTE	
"	2nd.		Battalion in billets	
"	3rd.		Battalion left SAILLY-LORETTE at 9-45 a.m. en route for HENENCOURT 10-5 a.m. up with 95th Bde 32nd Division. Marched past Major General V.H. Ffrench before entering HENENCOURT. Took over billets from 1/4 King's Own Lancaster Regt.	
HENENCOURT.	4th		Battalion in billets.	
HENENCOURT.	5th		Battalion in billets. Commanding Officer inspected Battalion at Pass...	
"	6th		Battalion in billets	
"	7th		Battalion in billets. Route march for Battalion at 9-15 a.m.	
"	8th		Battalion in billets	
"	9th		Battalion in billets	

Army Form C 2118.

WAR DIARY
or
INTELLIGENCE SUMMARY
(Erase heading not required). Sheet No. 2.

Instructions regarding War Diaries and Intelligence Summaries are contained in F.S. Regs., Part II and the Staff Manual respectively. Title Pages will be prepared in manuscript.

Place.	Date	Hour	Summary of Events and Information.	Remarks and references to Appendices
HENENCOURT.	10th		Battalion left HENENCOURT at 4 pm en route for AUTHUILLE is take over from 15th Lancashire Fusiliers. Battalion arrived at AUTHUILLE about 8-0 pm. One platoon at Gordon Castle, One Officer and 26 men at "A" Kep, One Officer and 25 men. "B" Kep. One N.C.O. and 20 men at Mill Post. "C" Coy to furnish garrison at AUTHUILLE. "D" Coy on left section of defences of AUTHUILLE. "C" Coy on Reserve Aug. cut off by RIVER ANCRE South of Cemetery.	
AUTHUILLE.	11th		Battalion in AUTHUILLE Defences. Casualties. Two men wounded.	
"	12th		Battalion in AUTHUILLE Defences.	
"	13th	.010		
"	14th		Battalion relieved 1st Bn Dorset Regt in sector. L.1. (Trenches 14++ to 150). Relief commenced at 8 pm. "B" Coy on the Right, "C" Coy Centre, "D" on the Left, and "A" Coy in Battalion Reserve On our Right, 16th Bn H.L.I. on our Right the 9th Bn Lancashire Fusiliers.	

Stationery Services Press, X 8. 5,000 7/15

Army Form C 2118.

WAR DIARY
or
INTELLIGENCE SUMMARY
(Erase heading not required). Sheet No 3.

Instructions regarding War Diaries and Intelligence Summaries are contained in F.S. Regs., Part II and the Staff Manual respectively. Title Pages will be prepared in manuscript.

Place.	Date	Hour	Summary of Events and Information.	Remarks and references to Appendices
AUTHUILLE	15th		Battalion in the trenches. Casualties Nil. 2/Lt. Hirst and one man wounded. Capt. J.A. Guyther and Capt. O.J. Alves awarded the Military Cross. The following N.C.O's and men were awarded the Distinguished Conduct Medal. No 6968 CSM. Harrison, 898 CSM Grout, 301 Pte. Ward J. and 8673 Pte. McQuillan. Medal ribbons were presented by Brig General C.W. Compton Comdg: 14th Infy Bde	
"	16th		Battalion in the trenches	
"	17th		"	
"	18th		Casualty. One man wounded.	
"	18th		Battalion relieved by the 15th Bn Lancashire Fusiliers. The relief was completed by 9.pm and Battalion marched to billets at HENENCOURT.	
HENENCOURT	19th		Battalion in Billets.	
"	20th		do	
"	21st		do	
"	22nd		do	

Army Form C 2118.

WAR DIARY
or
INTELLIGENCE SUMMARY

(Erase heading not required). Sheet No 14.

Instructions regarding War Diaries and Intelligence Summaries are contained in F.S. Regs., Part II and the Staff Manual respectively. Title Pages will be prepared in manuscript.

Place.	Date	Hour	Summary of Events and Information.	Remarks and references to Appendices
HENENCOURT	23rd		Battalion in Billets.	
"	24th		do	
"	25th		do	
"	26th		Battalion marched to MARTINSART to relieve the 15th Bn Lancashire Fusiliers who were in Brigade Reserve. "D" Coy proceeded to AUTHUILLE to relieve one company of the 10th Lancashire Fusiliers who were in AUTHUILLE Town Defence.	
MARTINSART	27th		"A" "B" and "C" Coys in billets at MARTINSART. "D" Coy in AUTHUILLE Defence.	
"	28th		Casualty. One man wounded in "D" Coy	
"	29th		do	
"	30th		"A" "B" and "C" Coys in billets at MARTINSART. "D" Coy in AUTHUILLE Defence.	
"	31st		"A" "B" and "C" Coys in billets at MARTINSART. "D" Coy in AUTHUILLE Defence.	

N. Luxmoore Lieut Col.
Comdg. 2nd Bn Manchester Regt.

2nd Manchester Regt — Intelligence Report — 11.1.16

Report on Oil Drum Bomb

An unexploded bomb of this type was opened up on the 11th January 1916.

This consisted of a circular iron drum stopped at both ends with thick wooden plugs. Through the bottom plug the fuse for the detonator was inserted. Through a 3½ inch circular disc screwed on to the bottom plug.

A flat metal handle is screwed on to the upper plug. The wooden plugs are screwed into place by screws through the cylinder and covered round the edges with resin to render watertight.

Upon the removal of the fuse it was found that the detonator was left behind in the drum, and the top plug was therefore taken out.

On the removal of the upper plug it was found that the cylinder was filled with a yellowish powder resembling sawdust. This powder was emptied out and buried in it were found bolts, nuts and scrapiron. The details of the contents are given as these were comparatively few considering the amount of powder and were as

follows :- Bolts and nuts - 3 (2 half inch, 1 quarter inch)
　　　　　　Bolts - 16 (mostly ½ inch)
　　　　　　Nuts - 2 (½ inch)
　　　　　　Nails - 1 (3 inch)
　　　　　　Washers - 1
　　　　　　Scrap iron - 32 pieces (mostly triangular
　　　　　　　　　of ½ inch sides and ⅛" thick)

All the bolts and nuts etc were covered with varnish, presumably to prevent the acid of the explosive corroding the iron. The detonator was a copper cylinder, 1¾"×¼" very similar to our Mark 7.

The fuse was fired and judged to be a 10 second fuse.

The powder would not ignite or explode when subjected to a lighted match. Part of this powder was put in a tin and exploded with a detonator and off went off with considerable force. The powder on the upper part of the cylinder was wet.

The bomb did not explode on account of the fuse having gone out.

The attached sketch gives the dimensions and details of the cylinder.

In the field 11.1.16.

H. Humphries, Lieut
Intelligence Officer
2nd Manchester Regt.

N. Luxmoore, Lieut Colonel
Commanding Officer
2nd Manchester Regt.

Sketch showing dimensions and details of Oil Drum Bomb

→ Upper wooden plug

→ Cylindrical drum made of 1/8" iron or steel.

→ Space filled with explosive and shrapnel

→ detonator

→ lower wooden plug
→ metal wings 3" long

→ fuse

15" 10" 1½" ¼" 1½" 1¾" 9½"

In the field
11-1-16.

H. J. Gwyther Lieut.
Intelligence Officer
2nd Manchester Regt.

N. Luxmoore. Lieut Colonel
Commanding Officer
2nd Manchester Regt

"A" Form. Army Form C. 2121.
MESSAGES AND SIGNALS.

TO: Staff Captain 14th Infy Bde

Sender's Number: MB 9 484
Day of Month: 15-1-16.
AAA

Situation Report: 14th - 15th. Artillery has been quiet on both sides. Enemy fired a few shots about 5.45 pm 14th inst which were answered by 12 pounder Howitzer guns. Six Patrols went out from Sector G1 at times varying from 8 P.M. to 1 AM 15th inst. and encountered no hostile patrols. Forty to fifty rifle grenades were thrown at left Coy between 4 pm and 5 pm, and were answered by our Trench Mortars and West Grenade Throwers.

N. Luxmoore Lieut Colonel
Comdg 2nd Bn The Manchester Regt

Intelligence Report.   15th January 1916

2nd Bn The Monokshete Regt. — Sector G,

Patrols :— (a) Patrol under Sgt Farrington proceeded from Sap in 144 A trench to reconnoitre the hedge running from this sap to the enemy's trench. Patrol set out at 9.15 p.m and returned at 11.30 p.m reporting all clear and no hostile patrols.

(b) Patrol under ~~xxxxxxx~~ 2 Lieut Robertson patrolled the front of Nos 145 and 146 Trenches and encountered no hostile patrol. Patrol set out at 8 p.m and returned at 9 p.m.

(c) Patrol under 2 Lieut Price set out at 10 p.m. to reconnoitre the front of Nos 146 and 147 Trenches. Patrol returned at 11 p.m. reporting that no hostile patrols had been encountered and all was quiet in front.

(d) Patrol under 2 Lieut Levick set out at midnight from Sap 15 No 149 Trench to reconnoitre enemy's sap opposite. Patrol returned at 1 a.m reporting that the enemy's sap was manned by two men and had practically no wire in front of it. Patrol also reported that there was practically no wire in front of our own sap and for that reason did not bomb the enemy.

(e) Patrol under 2 Lieut Johnson reconnoitred the front of 149 and 150 Trench. Patrol set out at 3 a.m. and returned at 4 am reporting that there were no enemy patrols or wiring parties out.

(f) Patrol under 2 Lieut Sorrell whilst covering a wiring party in front of No 148 trench investigated the enemy's wire and trench in front, and reported that the enemy appeared to have a sentry about every 100 yds and a visiting patrol between them. Patrol also reported that the enemy's wire was very scrappy

Hostilities:- About 40 ~~rifle~~ grenades were thrown at Trenches No 144 and 145 between 4 pm and 8 pm. No damage and no casualties were caused.
About 12 rifle grenades were thrown at No 149 Trenches at 4 p.m. Our heavy trench mortar fired 5 rounds and the West bomb battery 20 rounds, and silenced the enemy's grenade firing.

No 149 Trench was shelled by light HE from a N.E direction at 5.30 pm. This was answered by 12 rounds from our field guns

Signals At 8.45 pm five red lights were sent up from the right of our sector by the enemy. This was immediately followed by machine gun fire and light HE shells on Authuille Wood. A green light was sent up by the enemy and the firing ceased.

In the field
15.1.16.

H.J. Geoffer Lieut N. Lusmoore. Lt Col.
Intellegence Officer Commanding
2nd Manchester Regt. 2nd Manchester Regt.

Intelligence Report.   15th / 16th January 1916

2nd Bn The Manchester Regt —   Sector G.

Patrols
(a) Patrol under Cpl Davies reconnoitred the front of Nos 149 and 150 Trenches from 3.15 a.m — 3.45 a.m and reported all quiet and no hostile patrols out.

(b) Patrol under 2 Lieut Sorrell reconnoitred the front of No 148 Trench from 3.30 a.m to 4.0 a.m and reported all quiet

Hostilities
Light H.E were very active on the head of Thiepval Avenue and the left subsector between 6 p.m and 10 p.m. Slight damage was done to No 148 Trench.

Wiring party in front of No 144 Trench were fired at by the enemy at about 11.30 p.m.

Wiring parties in front of No 148 Trench were fired at by the enemy at about 3 a.m and an officer was hit.

Enemy rifle grenaded the left subsector at 11.30 a.m (16th inst). The majority of these fell round Bisset Trench and apparently were searching for our Trench mortar and West Bomb batteries. This was answered by the West Bomb batteries but not by the Trench Mortars on account of lack of ammunition (except for 3 rounds).

Mining — Hostile mining is suspected in the left subsector. Tapping can be heard from M.G. emplacement at the head of Shipod Avenue.

Signals — A red light was fired from the enemy's trench in front of No 147 Trench at 8.30 p.m. This light was fired backward towards ~~enemy's~~ support lines and hostile artillery immediately opened on Authuille Village and Davaar Avenue.

In the field
16.1.16

H J Gwyther Capt
Intelligence Officer
2nd Manchester Regt

N. Luxmoore Lt Colonel
2nd Manchester Regt

"A" Form. Army Form C. 2121.
MESSAGES AND SIGNALS.

TO: 14th Infy Bde

Sender's Number: MRa+93. Day of Month: 16-1-16. AAA

Situation Report 15th /16th.
Enemy shelled top of THIEPVAL Avenue between 6.30 pm and 10 pm with "Whizz bangs" and light H.E. At 10-30 pm 15th and at 1 AM 16th enemy also shelled Battalion Headquarters and Reserve Coy Shelters with shrapnel and a few H.E. Our guns were very slow in answering. Working party of one Platoon of Dorsets was engaged in repairing shelters in right coy trenches on 15th inst. This party deepened and improved TOBERMORY Avenue this morning. Excavations are now prepared for French Shelters at Battalion Headquarters and in TOBERMORY Avenue. If these shelters could be supplied to Battalion their erection could be proceeded with immediately. Additional accommodation is urgently needed at Battalion Headquarters. Wiring of Fire Trenches is being proceeded with as

"A" Form.
MESSAGES AND SIGNALS.
Army Form C. 2121.

fast as supply of necessary material permits. 2/Lt H.G. LEVICK was wounded by a rifle bullet while superintending wiring of 148 Fire Trench. Trench Mortors were hampered in their reply to enemy rifle grenades to day by shortage of ammunition.

N. Luxmoore. Lieut Colonel
Comdg 2nd Bn The Manchester Regt.

Intellegence Report — 16th 17th January

2nd Bn The Manchester Regt — Sector G.1

Patrols
(1) Patrol under 2 Lieut R.C. Ossenhigh set out from the right of No 144 Trench at 8.30 p.m. to reconnoitre the enemy's trench in front and to try and estimate its strength. Patrol worked forward to the enemy's wire and then along their trench to the left. Opposite the centre of No 144 Trench patrol was fired at from the right. A bomb was thrown at this point. Fire ceased from this point but opened up again on the left. A bomb was thrown at this point and the firing ceased. A light was then sent up from in front and single shots fired. A bomb was thrown at this point also. Patrol then returned. Patrol considered that the line in front was thinly held with three sentry groups in 150 yds. Patrol returned at 10.15 pm.

(2) 2 Lieut Peck reconnoitred enemy's sap in front of 144 A Trench at 4.45 a.m. There appeared to be two men in the sap head.

(3) Patrol under Sgt Coward reconnoitred the fronts of Nos 146, 147 and 148 Trenches from 10.0 p.m. – 11.30 p.m. Our wire was found to be badly damaged and the ground covered with shell holes. No hostile patrols were encountered.

(4) Covering parties for wiring parties in the left subsector reported no hostile patrols between 5.0 a.m. and 6.30 a.m.

Hostilities Our wiring parties in front of right, centre and left sectors were fired up by the enemy.

Enemy was active with rifle grenades in the left subsector between 11.a.m and 2 p.m. (16th inst). These were answered by the West Bomb batteries.

Our Trench Mortars and West Bomb batteries opened on the enemy's trenches at 11.a.m (17th inst) and were answered by whiz bangs on Thiepval Avenue.

Working Parties An hostile working party was observed at R.31.a.3.2 at 9.30 p.m. This was fired up and dispersed.

Sniping A man was observed at R.31.a.3.2, apparently working on the wire at 6.30 a.m. This man was fired at and hit by Pte King and was seen to be dragged in by two men.

H.J. Humphreys, Capt
Intelligence Officer

H.S.I name Lt u/ Adj
for O.C. 2nd Manchester Regt

"A" Form. Army Form C. 2121.
MESSAGES AND SIGNALS.

TO: 14 Infy Bde

Sender's Number: M Ra 508
Day of Month: 17-1-16
AAA

Situation Report 16th-17th. Artillery quiet on both sides up till 2-30 pm 17th. Our guns fired in retaliation to rifle grenades at 9-30 am 17th. Enemy answered our Trench Mortars and West Bomb Throwers in left Coy subsector at 11 am 17th inst by shelling THIEPVAL AVENUE with 77mm. Enemy shelled AUTHUILLE at 2-30-3 pm with salvoes of 4 guns. Wiring of front trenches is being continued. Our wiring parties were fired on by the enemy last night. New entanglements are being erected well in advance of present lines and about 40 yards from the front trenches. In this work since the night of the 14th-15th 27½ coils of barbed wire and 14 rolls of French wire have been used. Many coils of wire and iron stakes are still required to complete the work however.

"A" Form.
MESSAGES AND SIGNALS.
Army Form C. 2121.

	Code m.	Words	Charge	This message is on a/c of:	Recd. at m.
Office of Origin and Service Instructions.		Sent			Date
		At m.		Service.	From
		To			
		By		(Signature of "Franking Officer.")	By

TO {					

*	Sender's Number	Day of Month	In reply to Number	**A A A**

A Fleet of 23 of our Aeroplanes passed over Sector this morning about 10-am flying in a North Easterly direction. [support trench]

Work by day (1) Improvement of TOBERMORY Street
(2) General revetting of front trenches.
(3) Repairing of Fire Steps.
Work by night. (1) Wiring (2) Building of bridge traverses in right subsector.
(3) Improvement of shelter roofs.
(4) New emplacement dug for West Spring Gun.

N. Luanmore. Lieut Colonel
Commanding 2nd Bn The Manchester Regt

From			
Place			
Time			

The above may be forwarded as now corrected. (Z)

Censor. Signature of Addressor or person authorised to telegraph in his name.

* This line should be erased if not required.

"A" Form.   Army Form C. 2121.
MESSAGES AND SIGNALS.   No. of Message_____

Prefix.......Code.......m.	Words	Charge	This message is on a/c of:	Recd. at........m.
Of....of Origin and Service Instructions.				
	Sent		.............Service.	Date..........
..............At..............m.				From
..............To..............				
..............By..............			(Signature of "Franking Officer.")	By..........

TO { 14th Infy Bde

Sender's Number	Day of Month	In reply to Number	AAA
* MRa 528	18-1-16		

Situation Report :- 17th/18th
No 145 Front Trench was heavily shelled by rifle grenades about 9.25am 18th inst. Our field guns replied successfully. Our trench Artillery succeeded in silencing enemy rifle grenade battery which opened again on right Coy sub sector about 10-am.
Patrol under 2/Lt S. SORRELL reconnoitred and entered enemy sap opposite S15 in No 150 Trench. Full report has been forwarded on this subject. Four other patrols covered front of the Sector but encountered no hostile parties. Wiring was continued again last night. Working party of 50 men of 1st Dorset Regt was distributed this morning 18th amongst three subsectors, and put at disposal of Subsector Commanders. Good progress has been made

From			
Place			
Time			

"A" Form.
MESSAGES AND SIGNALS.

Army Form C. 2121.

Prefix	Code	m.	Words	Charge	This message is on a/c of:	Recd. at	m.
Office of Origin and Service Instructions.			Sent			Date	
			At	m.	Service.	From	
			To			By	
			By		(Signature of "Franking Officer.")		

TO

Sender's Number	Day of Month	In reply to Number	
			AAA

with repair of two long shelters in right subsector. These will soon be ready for use Battn Sappers have excavation completed at Battn Head Qrs for 10 widths of Tubular French Shelter. New French latrine for men has also been constructed at Battn Hd Qrs. 16 Coils barbed wire and 7 Rolls French wire put out in front of Sector. Damage done by rifle grenades in right subsector repaired. Parapet raised in 144 Front Trench. Battn Grenadier Officer reports that "since taking over Sector G1 our Grenadiers have gained the upper hand of the enemy and in all subsectors have effectively silenced the Enemy Grenadiers on every occasion up on which they opened fire. My men were greatly assisted on the left by the French Mortar batteries"

From: N. Luxmoore. Lieut Colonel
Place: Commanding 2nd Bn The Manchester Regt
Time:

The above may be forwarded as now corrected.   (Z)

Censor.   Signature of Addressor or person authorised to telegraph in his name.

* This line should be erased if not required.

14th Brigade.
32nd Division.

2nd BATTALION

THE MANCHESTER REGIMENT

FEBRUARY 1916

Army Form C. 2118

WAR DIARY
or
INTELLIGENCE SUMMARY
(Erase heading not required.)

Instructions regarding War Diaries and Intelligence Summaries are contained in F.S. Regs., Part II. and the Staff Manual respectively. Title Pages will be prepared in manuscript.

Place	Date	Hour	Summary of Events and Information	Remarks and references to Appendices
HENENCOURT	February 1st		Battalion marched to AUTHUILLE. Trenches and relieved 1st Bn Dorset Regt. "A" Coy on right. "B" Coy centre. "C" Coy left. "D" Coy Reserve. Dug outs. (G1.144 - 150) On our right 1/6th Bn H.L.I., on our left 19th Bn Lancashire Fusiliers.	
AUTHUILLE	2nd		Battalion in Trenches.	
"	3rd		Battalion in Trenches. 8 men wounded. "B" Coy. 1 man died of wounds.	
"	4th		Enemy shelled AUTHUILLE heavily with 8 in H.E.	
"	5th		Battalion in Trenches. Enemy shelled AUTHUILLE.	
"	6th		Battalion in Trenches. One man killed. Two men wounded. Battalion relieved by 2nd Bn Royal Inniskilling Fusiliers; relief commenced at 8 p.m., completed by 1 a.m. Took over Billets from 15th Bn Lancashire Fusiliers at HENENCOURT.	
HENENCOURT	7th		Battalion in Billets.	
"	8th		Battalion in Billets.	
"	9th		Battalion in Billets.	
"	10th		Battalion in Billets.	
"	11th		Battalion in Billets.	
"	12th		Battalion in Billets.	
"	13th		Battalion left HENENCOURT en route for ST GRATIEN. Battalion left HENENCOURT 10 am arrived at 2.15 pm at ST GRATIEN. Took over Billets from 5th Bn Gordons.	

ns regarding War Diaries and Intelligence
Summaries are contained in F.S. Regs., Part II.
and the Staff Manual respectively. Title Pages
will be prepared in manuscript.

WAR DIARY
or
INTELLIGENCE SUMMARY
(Erase heading not required.)

Army Form C. 2118

Place	Date	Hour	Summary of Events and Information	Remarks and references to Appendices
ST. GRATIEN	February 14th		Battalion in Billets.	
"	15th		Battalion in Billets.	
"	16th		Battalion in Billets.	
"	17th		Battalion in Billets.	
"	18th		Battalion in Billets.	
"	19th		Battalion in Billets. Brigade Route March.	
"	20th		Battalion in Billets.	
"	21st		Battalion in Billets.	
"	22nd		Battalion in Billets.	
"	23rd		Battalion in Billets.	
"	24th		Battalion in Billets.	
"	25th		Battalion in Billets.	
"	26th		Battalion in Billets.	
"	27th		Battalion in Billets.	
"	28th		Battalion in Billets.	
HENENCOURT.	29th		Battalion left ST. GRATIEN at 9.30 a.m. en route for HENENCOURT. Arrived at HENENCOURT at 1 p.m. handed over Billets by 16th H.L.I.	

C.B. Stapleton
Major for Lt Col
Comdg 2nd Bn The Manchester Regt.

1875 Wt. W593/826 1,000,000 4/15 J.B.C. & A. A.D.S.S./Forms/C. 2118.

14th Brigade.
32nd Division.

2nd BATTALION

THE MANCHESTER REGIMENT

MARCH 1 9 1 6

Appendices attached:-

    Map shewing distribution of Battalion.
    Strengths.

Army Form C. 2118

WAR DIARY
or
INTELLIGENCE SUMMARY

(Erase heading not required.)

2nd Battn. The Manchester Regiment

Instructions regarding War Diaries and Intelligence Summaries are contained in F.S. Regs., Part II. and the Staff Manual respectively. Title Pages will be prepared in manuscript.

Place	Date	Hour	Summary of Events and Information	Remarks and references to Appendices
	MARCH 1st		Battalion in Trenches, relieved 8th Norfolk Regt. in Sector E3, and were relieved by 10th K.O.Y.L.I. & 2nd K.O.Y.L.I., on our right 19th Lanc. Fusiliers. (Casualties three men wounded)	
	2nd		Battalion in Trenches Sector E3. (2 Lieut. A. Robertson & one man wounded.)	
	3rd		Battalion in Trenches Sector E3. (one man wounded.)	
	4th		Battalion in Trenches Sector E3 (two men wounded, no news slid of wounds)	
	5th		Battalion in Trenches Sector E3.	
	6th		Battalion in Trenches — — (one man wounded)	
	7th		Battalion in Trenches — —	
	8th		Battalion in Trenches — —	
MILLENCOURT	9th		Battalion relieved by 1st Dorset Regt. and went into billets from 1.30 p.m.	
"	10th		Battalion in billets, Bombardment of ALBERT & trenches, Battalion stood to arms, lasting two hours, all then finished.	
"	11th		Battalion in billets.	
"	12th		Battalion in billets.	
"	14th		Battalion in billets, G.O.C.'s Inspection (by Major-Genl M.H. Grogh C.B. C.M.G.)	
"	15th		Battalion relieved 1st Dorset Regt in Sector E3, relief completed by 8 p.m. on our right 16th H.L.I., on our left 15th H.L.I.	
	16th		Battalion in Trenches Sector E3. (one man seriously wounded)	

WAR DIARY or INTELLIGENCE SUMMARY

(Erase heading not required.) 2nd Battn. The Manchester Regiment

Army Form C. 2118

Place	Date	Hour	Summary of Events and Information	Remarks and references to Appendices
	March 17th		Battalion in Trenches Sector E3. Enemy shelled ALBERT & trenches heavily, two men wounded	
	18th		Battalion in Trenches Sector E3.	
	19th		Battalion in Trenches Sector E3. (one man wounded)	
	20th		Battalion in Trenches Sector E3. (three men wounded) Enemy exploded 2 mines at 3 p.m. destroying 4 posts – Coys B & S.	
	21st		Battalion in Trenches, relieved by 1st Dorset Regt, relief commencing at 7 p.m., completed by 8.30 p.m. Took over billets from 1st Dorset Regt A & D Coys, Rouen Barracks, Signallers at ALBERT, B, C Coys and Batn HQrs depots at AVELUY. (Casualties one killed and three men wounded.)	
ALBERT AVELUY	22nd		Battalion in Billets (casualties one killed, four men wounded.)	
"	23rd		Battalion in Billets	
"	24th		Battalion in Billets	
"	25th		Battalion in Billets	
"	26th		Battalion in Billets	
	27th		Battalion relieved 1st Dorset Regiment in Trenches Sector E3. F.S. previous night Sector E2. 2nd K.O.Y.L.I., Left Sectr F1 15th H.L.I.	
	28th		Battalion in Trenches Sector E3 relief commencing at 4 p.m., completed by 8.30 p.m. on 28th night Sector E2. 2nd K.O.Y.L.I., Left Sectr F1 15th H.L.I.	
	29th		Battalion in Trenches Sector E3. (Casualties four wounded)	
	30th		Battalion in Trenches Sector E3.	
	31st		Battalion in Trenches Sector E3.	

N. Luxmoore. Lieut Colonel.
Commdg 2nd Bn. The Manchester Regiment

WAR DIARY
or
INTELLIGENCE SUMMARY

(2nd Bn The Manchester Regiment)

Place	Date	Hour	Summary of Events and Information	Remarks and references to Appendices
	28.3.16		On the morning of the 28th inst at 11 A.M. Corporal J. KEELAN, 2nd Bn THE MANCHESTER REGT. left X.13/1 trench, to recover a body observed lying close to the German wire, leaving our trench from point X.13.D 4.3/0.4, he proceeded round the edges of ILOT and MANGIN CRATERS and located the body about point X.13.D 5/3. CORPORAL J. KEELAN then dragged the body back between MANGIN CRATER and MANGIN SORTEN, who had been waiting in our trench. The three men carried the body back to our trenches from this point across the open.	

N. Luxmoore. Lieut Colonel
Comdg 2nd Bn The Manchester Regt

Prefix......Code......m.	Words	Charge	This message is on a/c of:	Recd. at......m.
Office of Origin and Service Instructions.	Sent		......Service.	Date......
	At......m.			From......
	To......			
	By......		(Signature of "Franking Officer.")	By......

TO { 14⁰ Inf Bde

Sender's Number.	Day of Month.	In reply to Number.	
* MRa 942	8-3-16		A A A

Herewith map shewing distribution of
Battalion in Section E.3.

Apsulley Cyclist/Orpt
for OC 2 Manchester Regt

[Stamp: HEADQUARTERS 14th INFANTRY BRIGADE SG 103/1 9 MAR 1916]

From
Place
Time

The above may be forwarded as now corrected. (Z)

2nd Bn The Manchester Regiment

Distribution	Officers	W. Officers Staff & Qr.	Sergts.	Corpls.	Bugles	Privates	Total	Remarks
A. Company	3/4	1	9	8	14	117	149	No establishment given but shown.
B. "	4	2	6	8	15	111	142	Authority dispatches signal Horse Guards for Brigade
C. "	3	1	7	8	10	114	140	One Lance Corporal for discipline
D. "	N/4 3/4	1	5	6	10	116	141	1 Orderly for HQ & 2 per Coy in case telephone system fails
Lieut. Gunners	1	—	1	—	3	46	50	
Shepherd (Battalion)	1	1	—	—	3	21	24	Owing to Correspondence, & when in Reserves keeping two orderly rooms.
Stretcher Bearers	—	—	—	—	1	16	17	
Hd. Qr. Orderlies	—	—	1	1	1	8	9	
Orderly Room	—	—	1	1	1	1	4	
Officer Mess	—	—	—	—	1	4	6	
Regt. Bombers	1	—	1	—	—	14	15	
Signallers	—	—	1	1	3	20	24	over & due to the number of telephones furnished in the trenches and upkeep of wires.
Pioneers & Sanitary	—	—	1	—	1	10	12	
Police	—	—	1/1	—	3/1	3	6	
Drummers	—	—	—	1	1	7	—	Company Cooks, Headquarters Cooks.
Cooks	—	—	—	1	1	11	13	Includes Intelligence Officer.
Hd. Qr. Officers	4	—	—	1	—	—	4	
Hd. Qr. Servants	—	1	—	—	—	7	7	
Transport	1	—	1	—	5	47	53	Includes grooms, harness cleaners, saddlers, wheelers, drivers.
Qr. Mr. Stores	1	1	1	—	2	2	5	Bicycle Supplies & Storeman when 2 Qr. Mr. Stores are necessary
Shoemakers & Tailors	—	1	—	1	3	4	7	Labor on Advanced Base. To carry out necessary repairs.
	234	5	37	35	44/47	688/5	838	
Details	4	—	1	—	1	5	134	
R.A.M.C.	1	—	—	—	1	—	5	
P.O.C	—	—	—	—	—	—	1	
Chaplain	1	—	—	—	—	—		
Total	30	5	38	35	44	693	948	

N. Luxmoore Lieut. Col.
Comdg. 2nd Bn Manchester Regiment

Fighting Strength etc. in trenches.

2/Manchester Regt.

    Fighting Strength (vide   967.
    Fighting Strength Return.)
    Less, Personnel with
        Transport Echelon. 88
        Details Detached. 147
                    235 235.
    Balance in Trenches.   732.

    This figure is made up as follows :-
        Front Line Coys (2). 266.
        *Counter Attack Coy. 125.
        Reserve Coy.   147.
                      538.   538.
    Hd. Qrs.   127.
    Bombers.   14.
    Lewis Detachment.   53.
    Total.   732.

    * USNA REDOUBT.

15/H.L.I.

    Fighting Strength (vide   968.
    Fighting Strength Return)
    Less, Personnel with
        Transport Echelon. 88.
        Details Detached. 100.
                    188. 188.
    Balance in Trenches.   780.
    This figure is made up as follows :-
        Front Line Coys (3). 508.
        Reserve Coy.   169.
                      677.   677.
    Hd. Qrs.   64.
    Lewis Detachment.   39.
    Total.   780.

9/3/16.

                                  Br. General,
                              Comdg., 14th Inf. Bde.

MESSAGES AND SIGNALS.

TO		14th Mf Bde	

Sender's Number.	Day of Month.	In reply to Number.	
* MRa 941	8-3-16		A A A

Herewith distribution list of Battalion. There are two Coys in the Front line.

A J Scully Capt. a/adjt.
for O.C 2nd Manchester Regt.

(Z)

Return of Men Employed away from Battalion
2nd Bn Manchester Regiment.

How Employed.	Officers	O. Ranks.	Remarks
81st T. Mortar Battery		10	
32nd Division Employ		8.	
Assistant Miners		28.	
Tunnelling Coy 253rd		4.	
14th Infy Bde Employ		10	
10th Corps H. Qrs.		5.	
Railhead (MARICOURT)		17	
135th A. Troop. Coy		1	
Woodcutters (BEHENCOURT.)		2	
10th Corps Signals.		2	
5th Division Employ		2.	
102 Coy A.S.C.		2	
Sick in Divisional Area		41	
32nd Div. Amm. Column.	1		2/Lieut G.B. Griffin
14th Infy Bde	2		Lieut K.S. Torrance. Captain C.C Johnson.
Town Major ALBERT.		10	
Supplies		5.	
Total.	3.	147.	N. Luxmoore. Lt Colonel 8.3.16. 2/Manchester Reg

2nd Battalion The Manchester Regt.

	Officers	O. Ranks	Remarks
Front Line Coys	6	266	
Counter Attack Coy.	3	125	
Reserve Coy.	3	147	
Lewis Gunners	1	53	
Sappers	1	29	
Stretcher Bearers		17	In the Trenches.
H.Qr Orderlies		9	
Orderly Room		4 ※	
Officers Mess		6 ※	
Regtl Bombers	1	14	
Signallers		24	
Pioneers & Sanitary		12	
Police		7	
Cooks		12	
H.Qr Servants		7 ※	
H.Qr Officers	4		
Total.	19	732	
R A M C		5	
Transport	1	63	In Billets
Qr Mr Stores	1	12 ※	
Shoemakers & Tailors		7	ALBERT.
R.C. Chaplain	1	1	
Total.	22	820	

8.3.16.

N. Luxmoore Lieut. Col.
Comdg. 2nd Bn Manchester Regiment

Fighting Strength etc.

2/Manchester Regt.

(1) Fighting Strength in Trenches :- 732

(2) Fighting Strength out of Trenches :-

    (a) Transport Echelon.
Transport	53	
Q.M.Stores	5	
Coy.Q.M.Employ	12	
Shoemakers and Tailors	7	
* R.A.M.C.	5	
* Chaplain	1	
3 Servants and 2 Grooms	5	
	88	88

    (b) Details detached.
81 T.M.Batty	10	
32/Divl Employ	8	
Asst. Miners	28	
253 Tunnelling Coy.	4	
14/Inf.Bde.H.Q.	10	
10/Corps H.Q.	5	
Railhead	17	
135/Army Troops Coy.	1	
Woodcutters	2	
10/Corps Signals	2	
5/Divl H.Q.	2	
2/Coy. A.S.C.	2	
Sick Divl Area	41	
Town Major ALBERT	10	
Supplies	5	
	147	147

Total   235   235

                     Total Fighting Strength   967

* Should not have been included in "Fighting Strength"

14th Brigade.

32nd Division.

2nd BATTALION

THE MANCHESTER REGIMENT

M A Y 1 9 1 6

WAR DIARY
or
INTELLIGENCE SUMMARY

(Erase heading not required.)

Army Form C. 2118

2 Manchester R

Vol 22

Place	Date	Hour	Summary of Events and Information	Remarks and references to Appendices
PIERREGOT	May 1st		Battalion in billets PIERREGOT. Took part in tactical scheme under Divisional Commander. Major C.A. ANDERSON to Hospital.	
PIERREGOT	2nd		Battalion in Billets.	
PIERREGOT	3rd		Battalion in Billets.	
PIERREGOT	4th		Battalion in Billets. Took part in tactical scheme under Divisional Commander.	
PIERREGOT	5th		Battalion marched to WARLOY. Left PIERREGOT at 2pm and arrived at WARLOY about 8pm. Billets vacated by 16th Bn H.L.I. were taken over.	
WARLOY	6th		Battalion left WARLOY 8pm en route for AVELUY and took over billets from 16th Bn Northumberland Fusiliers about midnight. "A" and "C" Coys in the dugouts at CRUCIFIX CORNER.	
AVELUY	7th		Battalion at AVELUY. "B" and "D" Coys in billets AVELUY, "A" and "C" Coys in the dugouts at CRUCIFIX CORNER. 2/Lieut J.W. CURLEY joined Battalion.	
AVELUY	8th		Battalion at AVELUY "B" and "D" Coys in billets AVELUY, "A" and "C" Coy in the dugouts at CRUCIFIX CORNER. Enemy shelled AVELUY, casualties one man wounded by Shrapnel (slight).	

Army Form C. 2118

WAR DIARY
or
INTELLIGENCE SUMMARY

(Erase heading not required.)

Place	Date	Hour	Summary of Events and Information	Remarks and references to Appendices
	May			
AVELUY	9th		Battalion at AVELUY and CRUCIFIX CORNER.	
AVELUY	10th		Battalion at AVELUY and CRUCIFIX CORNER. Relieved 19th Bn. Lancashire Fusiliers in AUTHUILLE (sub-sector) relief commencing at 8pm. A party under Lt. N.R. Tomblin reconnoitred the ground in front of our trenches between 11 and 12 pm.	
AUTHUILLE	11th		Battalion in the Trenches. During the early hours of the morning our trenches were subjected to a heavy bombardment by the enemy. Casualties 7 men killed and 12 men wounded. Lieut A.E. PARRY wounded.	
AUTHUILLE	12th		Battalion in the trenches. Casualties one man wounded. During the night patrols under Lt. Whitfield, L/Cpl Holt and L/Cpl Trivett reconnoitred the front of our trenches.	
AUTHUILLE	13th		Battalion in the Trenches. Casualties one man and Lieut E. TANNER wounded. During the night 13th/14th patrols under Cpl McGrane, Cpl Morgan and L/Cpl Trivett reconnoitred the front of AUTHUILLE subsector from 8.30 pm till 2 am.	

WAR DIARY or INTELLIGENCE SUMMARY

Army Form C. 2118

Place	Date	Hour	Summary of Events and Information	Remarks and references to Appendices
AUTHUILLE	May 14th		Battalion in the Trenches. Relieved by 19th Bn Lancashire Fusiliers, relief commencing at 8 p.m. "A" and "C" Coys in AVELUY, "B" and "D" Coys at CRUCIFIX CORNER. Battalion complete in billets AVELUY and dugouts CRUCIFIX CORNER 11.35 p.m.	
AVELUY	15th		30 other ranks reinforcements joined. "A" and "C" Coys in billets at AVELUY. "B" and "D" Coys dugouts at CRUCIFIX CORNER.	
AVELUY	16th		"A" and "C" Coys in billets at AVELUY. "B" and "D" Coys in dugouts at CRUCIFIX CORNER.	
AVELUY	17th		"A" and "C" Coys in billets at AVELUY. "B" and "D" Coys in dugouts at CRUCIFIX CORNER. Casualties 2 men wounded.	
AVELUY	18th		"A" and "C" Coys in billets at AVELUY. "B" and "D" Coys in dugouts at CRUCIFIX CORNER. Battalion left AVELUY en route for WARLOY and took over billets vacated by 19th Bn H.L.I. arriving in billets at 3 am 19th inst.	

Army Form C. 2118

WAR DIARY
or
INTELLIGENCE SUMMARY
(Erase heading not required.)

Instructions regarding War Diaries and Intelligence Summaries are contained in F.S. Regs., Part II. and the Staff Manual respectively. Title Pages will be prepared in manuscript.

Place	Date	Hour	Summary of Events and Information	Remarks and references to Appendices
WARLOY	May 19th		Battalion in billets. Lieut S.J. Norman re-joined from 4th Bn Manchester Regt.	
WARLOY	20th		Battalion in billets.	
WARLOY	21st		Battalion in billets.	
WARLOY	22nd		Battalion in billets. Battalion took part in scheme.- Contact between aeroplane and troops on the ground. Lieut Col. W. Tupmoore, commanding Battalion, observed operations from an aeroplane.	
WARLOY	23rd		Battalion in billets. Reinforcements 39 other ranks joined.	
WARLOY	24th		Battalion in billets. Relieved by 1st Bn Dorset Regt at 7pm and marched to BOUZINCOURT. Relieved 19th Bn Lancashire Fusiliers; two companies at BOUZINCOURT, two companies at AVELUY. Relief completed at 11:30 /pm.	
BOUZINCOURT AVELUY	25th		"A" and "B" coys in huts BOUZINCOURT. "C" and "D" coys in billets AVELUY.	

Army Form C. 2118

WAR DIARY
or
INTELLIGENCE SUMMARY
(Erase heading not required.)

Instructions regarding War Diaries and Intelligence Summaries are contained in F. S. Regs., Part II. and the Staff Manual respectively. Title Pages will be prepared in manuscript.

Place	Date	Hour	Summary of Events and Information	Remarks and references to Appendices
	May			
BOUZINCOURT AVELUY	26th		"A" and "B" Coys in huts. 38 other ranks reinforcement joined. "C" and "D" Coys in billets.	
BOUZINCOURT AVELUY	27th		"A" and "B" Coys in huts. "C" and "D" Coys in billets.	
BOUZINCOURT AVELUY	28th		"A" and "B" Coys in huts. "C" and "D" Coys in billets.	
BOUZINCOURT AVELUY	29th		"A" and "B" Coys in huts. "C" and "D" Coys in billets. Battalion relieved by 15th Bn Lancashire Fusiliers at 7pm and march to CONTAY WOOD. Relieved the 2nd Bn Royal Inniskilling Fusiliers in huts; relief complete at 11pm.	
CONTAY	30th		Battalion in huts CONTAY WOOD.	
CONTAY	31st		Battalion in huts CONTAY WOOD.	

N. Lusmore, Lieut Col.,
Comdg 2nd Bn The Manchester Regiment.

"A" Form.				Army Form C. 2121.
MESSAGES AND SIGNALS.				No. of Message

Prefix	Code	m.	Words	Charge	This message is on a/c of:	Recd. at	m.
Office of Origin and Service Instructions.							
			Sent			Date	
			At	m.	Service.		
			To			From	
			By		(Signature of "Franking Officer.")	By	

TO		Situation	14th Inf Bde

Sender's Number.	Day of Month	In reply to Number	
* M.R. 515	12-5-16		A A A

Situation Report At about 9.45 pm 11-5-16 Enemy shelled the new trench in W.61. DAVAAR Ave Durham Street and Y.17 with artillery and Trench mortars. Some heavy howitzer shells estimated at 21 c.m. were fired from the direction of POZIERES. Otherwise nothing to report and quite a quiet night.

Work Done. Repair of trenches where damaged and strengthening of wire along the whole front.

Work to be Done. Continuation of above.

Patrols. See Intelligence Report.

No German telegrams wires discovered.

N. Swanmore. Lieut Col
Cmdg Strandbrokes M.B

From			
Place			
Time			

The above may be forwarded as now corrected.   (Z)

Censor.   Signature of Addressor or person authorised to telegraph in his name.
* This line should be erased if not required.

Intelligence Report.   11th – 12th April

2nd Bn The Manchester Regt – Authuille subsector

<u>Operations</u> (a) Artillery At 3.15 p.m. our 8" Howitzers commenced to register on THIEPVAL.

At 3.45 p.m. the hostile artillery retaliated on THIEPVAL subsector. Our 18 prs replied at 3.55 p.m.

At 7 p.m. the enemy threw shrapnel over the S.W edge of THIEPVAL WOOD. This was probably after a body of troops which had entered the wood 5 minutes before.

At 7 p.m. a few 77 m.m shells fell near Coy HdQr in DAVAAR AV.

At 9.45 p.m. enemy shelled the new trench in W6.1, DAVAAR AV, DURHAM ST, and X14 trench with "oilcans", heavy TMs, 10.5 cms shells and heavy artillery. The heavy howitzers came from the direction of POZIERES and were judged to be of 21 cm calibre. Five casualties were caused and a working party dispersed.

queried.
from 254

<u>Intelligence</u> An hostile working party was dispersed by Lewis gun fire at 12.15 a.m in front of W6.2 trench.

Our wiring party in front of R31.2 tr was twice dispersed by hostile M.G fire at 1.50 a.m.

Patrols. Covering parties for wiring parties out along our whole front reported no hostile activities between 10 pm and 2 a.m.

General. Hostile M.G. fire was active throughout the night.

H J Humphries Capt
Intelligence Officer
2nd Bn The Manchester Regt.

A J Buckley Capt for Lieut Colonel
Commanding
2nd Bn The Manchester Regt

Intelligence Report　　　　10th – 14th May 1916
2nd Bn The 1st Manchester Regt　　Authuille Subsector

Operations (a) Artillery At 1.40 a.m. our artillery opened fire covering the raid on our right. Within 3 minutes the enemy had established a barrage with T.M^s, Minnenwerfers, torpedoes and oilcans on trenches X1.3.4.5. Within 5 minutes the hostile artillery had joined and created a very intensive bombardment along our whole front. This bombardment was kept up until 3.30 a.m. and was most intensive on trenches X1 3 4.5 which were heavily shelled with 6" howitzers and very heavy Minnenwerfers (thought to be the new 230 lb bomb). Our trenches were very badly damaged and we suffered heavy casualties. OBAN AV, CAMPBELL AV, DAVAAR AV and DURHAM ST were heavily shelled and damaged.

Patrols A patrol under 2nd Lieut Tomblin reconnoitred the fronts of Nos X1 1 3 and 4 trenches between 11 pm and 12 mn. No hostile activity was encountered.

General An hostile observation balloon was

observed over CONTALMAISON at 9.0 a.m.

Signals   Test signals were sent up from the
           battalion in THIEPVAL subsector at 10.30 p.m.

H.J.Gwyther Capt.   A.J.Scully Capt. for. Lieut Colonel
Intelligence Officer   Commanding
2nd Bn The Manchester Regt.   2nd Bn The Manchester Regt.

"A" Form.
Army Form C. 2121.

MESSAGES AND SIGNALS.

Prefix	Code	m.	Words	Charge	This message is on a/c of:	Recd. at	m.
Office of Origin and Service Instructions.			Sent		Service.	Date	
			At	m.		From	
			To			By	
			By		(Signature of "Franking Officer.")		

TO — 14th Inf Bde

Sender's Number.	Day of Month	In reply to Number	AAA
* M.R 509	11-5-16		

Our Artillery opened fire at 1.54 am to cover a raid being given on our right. About 3 minutes later the enemy opened an intense bombardment along the whole of our front with guns & trench mortars. Machine Guns were also active. The trenches were badly damaged by this fire. The bombardment ceased about 3. am and the situation has been normal since then.

Work Done: Wire strengthened opposite X.1.4 & 5 Kentrs. Repair of trenches where damaged.

Work to be done: Continuation of above

Patrols Sent Orders given Report
No German Telephone & wire discovered

N. Lushmore, Lieut Coy
Army Shorehurst R.B.

From			
Place			
Time		(Z)	

Intelligence Report.   12th – 13th April

2nd Bn The Manchester Regt. – Authuille subsector

Operations. (a) "Oildrums". At 5 p.m. Three (3) oildrums fell in W6.1 trench and at the same time the enemy shelled DURHAM ST with 77 m.m. shells.
(b) Rifle grenades. At 2.40 a.m. four rifle grenades fell in R 31.2 trench. Our rifle grenade batteries replied.
(c) Artillery. At 11.30 p.m. two salvoes of 77 m.m. shells fell in W6.1 trench. Between 4 p.m and 6 p.m the enemy shelled X 1.4 trench with 10.5 cm and 15 cm shells. Between 4 p.m and 4.30 p.m these fell in quick succession. From 4.30 p.m. to 6 p.m the 15 cm guns were evidently registering on X 1.4 trench and Rock St as there was a 4 to 5 minute interval between the shells. At 3.30 a.m. three oildrums fell near W6.1 trench.
At 4.0 a.m. the enemy opened up a bombardment on our sector. Oildrums, TM's 77 mm shells, 10.5 cm shells fell along our whole front. CAMPBELL

POST. CAMPBELL and DAVAAR AVENUES were shelled with 10.5 cm and 77mm shells. The bombardment lasted for about 20 minutes during which time there was considerable M.G. fire.
Our artillery replied with a few 18 pdrs at 4.15 a.m.

Intelligence. M.G. fire was very active during the night along the whole front.
A trench mortar battery has been located at X.2a.1.7 by the Bn on our right.
All the heavier artillery referred to above came from the direction of POZIERES

Patrols. Patrol under Sgt Whitfield covered the front of R31.1 and 2 between 10 pm and 11.30 p.m.
Patrol under L/Cpl Holt covered the front of Q36.1 and 2 between 11.30 pm and 1 a.m.
Patrol under L/Cpl Trivett covered the front of W61 trench between 9.30 pm and 1 a.m.
All these patrols reported no hostile activity in No Mans Land.

H.J.Smyther Capt
Intelligence Officer
2nd Bn The Manchester Regt.

A.J.Daily Capt for Lieut Colonel
Commanding
2nd Bn The Manchester Regt

"A" Form.   Army Form C. 2121.
MESSAGES AND SIGNALS.   No. of Message _____

Prefix......Code......m.	Words	Charge	This message is on a/c of:	Recd. at _____ m.
Office of Origin and Service Instr......ns.	Sent			Date _____
	At _____ m.		_____ Service.	From _____
	To _____			
	By _____		(Signature of "Franking Officer.")	By _____

TO: 14th Inf. Bde.

| Sender's Number. | Day of Month | In reply to Number | |
| * M.R.580 | 1 - 5 -16. | | A A A |

<u>Situation</u> Two vilcans and a few rifle grenades fell near W6.1 and R31.2 trenches at 5.15p.m. Between 5pm and 6pm X.1.3 and 4 trenches and ROCK ST were shelled with 10.5 cm and 15 cm shells. The latter appeared to be registering. At 4 a.m. the enemy opened up a bombardment on our front line and main communication trenches. This lasted for 20 minutes and was not very intensive. Enemy M.G.s were active during the night. Q36.1 and W6.1 trenches and DAVAAR AV were shelled at mid day with 77mm and 10.5 cm shells. Patrols see intelligence report.

<u>Work done</u> Repair of trenches where damaged and strengthening of wire

<u>Work to be done</u> Continuation of above.

From _____
Place _____
Time _____

The above may be forwarded as now corrected.   (Z)

Censor.   Signature of Addressor or person authorised to telegraph in his name.
* This line should be erased if not required.

Intelligence Report   13th–14th May.

2nd Bn The Manchester Regt — Authuille subsector

Operations (a) Artillery. At 12.15 pm the enemy sent over several 77 m.m shells over R 31.2 trench and DAVAAR Av. Our artillery replied. At 4pm the enemy sent 10.5 cm shells and TMs into X.1.4 trench doing considerable damage. Our TMs replied apparently with good effect as much debris was sent flying.

Intelligence. The Bn on our right reported a large hostile patrol in front of the NAB at 11pm. A patrol at the same place was reported the previous night.

The hostile M.G. fire was considerably less on our right but increased over the THIEPVAL sector.

Patrols Patrol under Sgt McGrane covered the fronts of R 31.1 and 2 and Q 36.1 and 2 between 9pm and 12.30 a.m.
Patrol under Cpl Morgan covered the front of X.1.4 between 10pm and 2am.
Patrol under L/Cpl Trivett covered the front of W.6.1 between 8.30pm and 1a.m.
Patrol under Sgt Lynch covered the left of W.6.1 trench between 9pm and 10pm.

All these patrols report no hostile activities in
N. Man's Land.

General. The Lewis Guns of our right company
and the Bn on our right kept up a
continuous cross fire across the front of
the NAB throughout the night.

H J Huyshe Capt   N. Luxmoore, Lieut Colonel
Intelligence Officer   Commanding
2nd Bn The Manchester Regt.   2nd Bn The Manchesters

"A" Form.
Army Form C. 2121.

MESSAGES AND SIGNALS.

No. of Message_____

Prefix_____ Code_____ m. | Words | Charge | This message is on a/c of: | Recd. at_____ m.
Office of Origin and Service Instructions | Sent | | Service. | Date_____
_____ | At_____ m. | | | From_____
_____ | To_____ | | (Signature of "Franking Officer.") | By_____
_____ | By | | |

TO 16ᵗʰ Inf Bde

Sender's Number: MR 545
Day of Month: 14-5-16
In reply to Number:
AAA

Situation Report. A very quiet night & day. At about 4 pm the enemy shelled just behind R.31.1 + 2 trenches with about 12 77 m. shells and at 5 pm shelled X 14 trench. Otherwise no activity to report.

Work Done. Repair of trenches where damaged & strengthening of wire along the whole front.

Work to be done. Continuation of above.

Patrols. See Intelligence Report.

No German telephone wires discovered.

A Spedy Capt + Adjt
for O.C. Manchester Bn

From_____
Place_____
Time_____

The above may be forwarded as now corrected.   (Z)

_____ Censor. | Signature of Addressor or person authorised to telegraph in his name.
* This line should be erased if not required.

(4198) Wt. W14042—M44. 300000 Pads. 12/15. Sir J. C. & S.

14th Brigade.

32nd Division.

2nd BATTALION

THE MANCHESTER REGIMENT

APRIL 1916

Army Form C. 2118

WAR DIARY
or
INTELLIGENCE SUMMARY
(Erase heading not required.)

Instructions regarding War Diaries and Intelligence Summaries are contained in F. S. Regs., Part II. and the Staff Manual respectively. Title Pages will be prepared in manuscript.

Place	Date	Hour	Summary of Events and Information	Remarks and references to Appendices
	April 1st		Battalion in the trenches. Sector E.3.	
	2nd		Battalion in the trenches. Sector E.3.	
	3rd		Battalion in the trenches. Sector E.3. Casualties 2 men killed, 1 wounded.	
	4th		Battalion relieved by the 2nd Bn Yorkshire Regt (23rd Infy Bde) Relief commenced at 7 p.m. marched to AVELUY and took over billets from the 15th Bn 49 L.I.	
AVELUY	5th		In billets.	
"	6th		In billets.	
"	7th		In billets.	
"	8th		In billets.	
"	9th		Battalion relieved the 19th Bn Lancashires in AUTHUILLE trenches. Relief commenced at 5 p.m. On our right 8th Bn K.O.Y.L.I. On our left the 15th Bn 49 L.I.	
AUTHUILLE	10th		In the trenches. Reinforcement, one officer and one other ranks. Lieut A.E. PARRY from 11th Bn Manchester Regt.	
	11th		Battalion in the trenches.	

1875 Wt. W593/826 1,000,000 4/15 J.B.C. & A. A.D.S.S./Forms/C. 2118.

WAR DIARY
or
INTELLIGENCE SUMMARY

(Erase heading not required.)

Army Form C. 2118

Instructions regarding War Diaries and Intelligence Summaries are contained in F. S. Regs., Part II. and the Staff Manual respectively. Title Pages will be prepared in manuscript.

Place	Date	Hour	Summary of Events and Information	Remarks and references to Appendices
AUTHUILLE	12th		Battalion in the trenches. Relieved by the 19th 49. L.I. commenced at 9.30pm. marched to BOUZINCOURT and billeted in the huts. vacated by the 17th 19. L.I.	
BOUZINCOURT	13th		Billeted in the huts. "B" Coy at AVELUY	
"	14th		Billeted in the huts. "B" Coy at AVELUY	
"	15th		Billeted in the huts. "B"	
"	16th		Billeted in the huts. "B"	
"	17th		The battalion marched to AUTHUILLE to relieve the 19th Bn. 9.L.I. in AUTHUILLE Sub-sector. Relief commenced at 8 pm. Bn attached to 97th Infy Bde. 8th Bn. K.O.Y.L.I. on our right, and 2nd Bn. K.O.Y.L.I. on our left.	
AUTHUILLE	18th		Battalion in the trenches	
"	19th		Battalion in the trenches. Capt B.L. ERSKINE joined.	
"	20th		Battalion in the trenches. Casualty one man shell shock.	
"	21st		Battalion in the trenches. Casualty five men shell shock. Relieved by 19th Bn 9.L.I. marched to AVELUY and took over billets vacated by the 19th Bn 19. L. I.	
AVELUY	22nd		In billets.	
	23rd		In billets.	

1875 Wt. W593/826 1,000,000 4/15 J.R.C. & A. A.D.S.S./Forms/C. 2118.

WAR DIARY or INTELLIGENCE SUMMARY

(Erase heading not required.)

Place	Date	Hour	Summary of Events and Information	Remarks and references to Appendices
AVELUY.	24th		Battalion relieved by the 15th Bn Lancashire Fus. commencing at 10.30 pm and marched to CONTAY arrived in billets about 4.30 A.M	
CONTAY	25th		Battalion in billets.	
"	26th		Battalion in billets.	
"	27th		Battalion in billets. Bn took part in tactical scheme under direction of Brigade Divisional General.	
"	28th		Battalion in billets.	
"	29th		Battalion in billets.	
"	30th		Bn changed stations with 1st Bn Dorset Regt at PIERREGOT. Moved off from CONTAY at 5.30 pm, arrived at PIERREGOT about 8 pm.	

N. Fraser, Lieut Col.
Comdg. 2nd Bn Manchester Regiment

14th Brigade.

32nd Division

2nd BATTALION

THE MANCHESTER REGIMENT

JUNE 1916

Battalion Orders attached.

WAR DIARY or INTELLIGENCE SUMMARY

Army Form C. 2118

2 Manchester Regt

1923

(Erase heading not required.)

Instructions regarding War Diaries and Intelligence Summaries are contained in F.S. Regs., Part II. and the Staff Manual respectively. Title Pages will be prepared in manuscript.

Place	Date 1916	Hour	Summary of Events and Information	Remarks and references to Appendices
	June 1st		The Battalion encamped in huts Contay Wood. The B'n took part in a Tactical Exercise in conjunction with the 3rd Corps. Practised communication between Rifle Battn + Aeroplane.	
	" 2		In huts Contay wood. Took part in Counter Attack scheme from Behencourt road by day and night. Bivouaced in the wood.	
	" 3		In huts Contay Wood	
	" 4		In huts Contay Wood. United Services hired to Brigade in Contay football ground	
	" 5		In huts Contay Wood	
	" 6		In huts Contay Wood. Battalion route march combined with Reconnaissance scheme	
	" 7		In huts Contay Wood. The Battalion held Sports on Contay football ground (See supplement for results)	
	" 8		In huts Contay Wood. The B'n took part the day in a Practical Exercise on Behencourt — Bayonet Training Ground	

WAR DIARY
or
INTELLIGENCE SUMMARY
(Erase heading not required.)

No 2

Army Form C. 2118

Place	Date 1916	Hour	Summary of Events and Information	Remarks and references to Appendices
	June 9		In huts Contay Wood. Brigade Sports and Assault at Arms was held this day on Contay grounds. Bruma. The Bn taking part in them.	
	10		In huts Contay Wood.	
	11		In huts Contay Wood.	
	12		The Battalion moved to Henlis and took over billets vacated by the 11th Border Regt. Also took part in a retrenchment before taking over billets.	
	13		"A" "B" "D" Coys in the Trenches. "C" Coy in reserve in billets at Aveluy. A B & D Coys took over Trenches from 16th Lanc: Fusiliers during 9 p.m.	
	14		On relief of the 16th Lanc. F. was completed 1 o'clock am this day. Casualties nil.	
	15		In Trenches as above. Casualties 1 killed 1 wounded by accidental premature bursting of a rifle grenade.	

Army Form C. 2118

WAR DIARY
or
INTELLIGENCE SUMMARY
(Erase heading not required.)

No 3

Instructions regarding War Diaries and Intelligence Summaries are contained in F. S. Regs., Part II. and the Staff Manual respectively. Title Pages will be prepared in manuscript.

Place	Date 1916	Hour	Summary of Events and Information	Remarks and references to Appendices
	June 16		In trenches. Casualties 1 Accidently wounded 2 Shell shock. Relieved by 19th Lanc Fus: Relief commenced 10 P.M	Extending the front good work in anticipation of the advance
	17		Relief by 19th Lanc & 2nd Rs completed 4.35 A.M. A & D Boys in Bucket Looney St, Crucifix Corner. "C" boy in Billets Aveluy	Practically working day and night on improvement front trenches etc.
	18		A B & D boy in Billets Looney St Crucifix Corner. "C" boy in Billets Aveluy	
	19		-do-	
	20		-do- Battalion relieved 19th Lanc Fus: in Authuille Subsector. Relief commenced 10 P.M	
	21		Relief of 19th Lanc Fus: completed 2-30 A.M. Casualty 1 man wounded (Self Inflicted) Batt on our left 15 H.L.I. Batt on our right 9th Royal Scots Rifles	
	22		Batt in trenches Casualties. 2 men wounded	

Army Form C. 2118

WAR DIARY
or
INTELLIGENCE SUMMARY
(Erase heading not required.)

Instructions regarding War Diaries and Intelligence Summaries are contained in F. S. Regs., Part II. and the Staff Manual respectively. Title Pages will be prepared in manuscript.

Place	Date 1916	Hour	Summary of Events and Information	Remarks and references to Appendices
	June 23	10.45 pm	Battalion relieved by 11th Battn Border Regt in the Authuille Subsector commencing 1.45 A.M. (24th inst) Relief completed Casualties:- 2 men wounded. Reinforcement 6 men	
	24		Battn in Billets in Bouzincourt	
	25		Battn in Billets in Bouzincourt	
	26		Battn in Billets in Bouzincourt	
	27	1 A.M.	Battn moved to Aveluy Wood preparatory to going into action on the morning of the 28th. Operations were however postponed until further notice	
	28	11.30 pm	Battn returned to Billets in Senlis. Took over Billets	
	29		Battn in Billets in Senlis.	
	30		Battn in Billets in Senlis	

N. Luxmoore
2nd Lt. O.C.
2nd Bn the Manchester Regt

Army Form C. 2118

WAR DIARY
or
INTELLIGENCE SUMMARY
(Erase heading not required.)

Place	Date	Hour	Summary of Events and Information	Remarks and references to Appendices
	1916 June 4th		Battalion Sports Results - Supplement. Snackrace — 1st L/Cpl Young — A 100yds for men — 1st Pte Brewer — A 40 years & over Tug of War — won by — A 100 yds — 1st Pte Summers — C — 2nd Sgt Day — C 220 yds — 1st R/O Summers — C Officers Race — 1st Lieut W.W. Smith — A 100 yds 440 yds — 1st L/C Young — D Sergeants Race — 1st RSM Hulewell — B (Mile Open) — 1st Sgt Gray 1st Dorset Regt Boxing: - 6 round contest between L/C Yarwood and L/C McDonagh Result L/C Yarwood K.O. L/C McDonagh in 4th round. N. Luxmoore O.C. 2nd Batt. The Manchester Regt	

Battalion Orders by Lieut Col N. Lawrence
Commanding the 2nd/5th Manchester Regiment
Ref Map 1/40000 57D & 62D   11.6.16.

(1) **Detail**:- Orderly Officer tomorrow 2/Lt G.N. Carey.

(2) **Reinforcements** No 9726 Cpl Kelly "B" Coy reverts to private at his own request from 10th inst. No 2215 A/C Sgt Somm "C" Coy reverts to private at his own request from 15th inst.

"C" Coy No 2349 Cpl Lindup: back "A" Coy. No 5921 Pte Gulliver "A" Coy are attached to Convalescent Camp. No 2662 Pte Jones "C" Coy evacuated sick 5.6.16.

(4) **Promotions**:- No 9249 L/Cpl J. Egglesden "B" Coy is promoted to the substantive rank of Corpl from the 20.5.15. No 9902 L/Cpl T. Bowling "A" Coy and No 9249 L/Cpl J. Egglesden "B" Coy are promoted Acting L/Sgts this day.

(5) **Inter Coy Transfer** No 9902 L/Sgt T. Bowling "A" Coy is transferred to "B" Coy this day.

(6) **Tactical Exercise**:- The Battalion will take part in a Divisional Tactical Exercise tomorrow 12th inst in the BEHENCOURT - BAIZIEUX area of 1/10 Inf. Lst. Attached. Starting point Roads & Track Junction U.21.D.6/4. Order of march Signallers, Scouts, Messengers & D.R.B Coys, & Lewis Gunners. That of Column will be:- Starting point at 7.5 AM. Pack Animals (excluding Lewis Gunners will march with the Bn: Rendezvous N.W. Corner of BEHENCOURT Wood. Dinners will be served to the men on the completion of the exercise at Cr.Rds S.W. Corner of BAIZIEUX Wood.
Operation orders will be issued separately.

Lieut Shepard is detailed as 13th Liason Officer and will meet the Div Commander at Point C.25/S/0/5 at 9.30 am
Lieut S. Small is detailed as 13th Liason officer & will report to Br HdQrs on reaching the Rendezvous.

On reaching the Rendezvous Coys will send 2 men to report to Br HdQrs to act as messengers.

Dress:- Fighting order.

(7) On the conclusion of the Tactical Exercise 13th will march direct to Senlis and take over billets vacated by 11th Border Regt. Coy QMS. & 3NCO's under Lieut Raynor will proceed to Senlis in the morning to take over billets.

The Orderly Officer will remain in Camp and will hand over huts to 11th M.R. and will obtain a receipt that huts are handed over clean and complete.

On arrival at Senlis the Bn: will be held in readiness to move at one hours notice.

Officer kits to be at road & track Junction U.24.D.8/3 at 8 A.M. stored in one large heap.

Mens packs will be taken to the same point and stacked by Coys, HdQrs unit, one man per Coy or unit to be left in charge. Limbers to be notified Coys.
Transport to move as ordered in 11th Inf. Bde. Operation Order No 33.

* Officers kits @ 8 A.M. + mens packs @ 6 A.M.

Pully Capt
Adjt. 2nd/5th Manchester Regt.

Operation Orders by Lieut Col. N. Luxmoore
Commanding 2nd Bn Manchester Regiment

11-6-16.

Ref Map 1/40,000 Sheet 62 D.

(1) General and Special ideas as before.

(2) The Battalion will be in Brigade Reserve.

(3) The Battalion will occupy trenches N edge of BEHENCOURT WOOD, REGENT ST. DOVER ST. in the following order from the right, "A" "B" "C" "D" Coys.

(4) At Zero time Smoke commences and Battalion opens fire for 2 minutes. On Dorsets reaching BEHENCOURT WOOD, the Battalion will close in the wood in 2 lines of Coys in fours at 10 paces interval and 10 paces distance. The Battalion will move out of the Wood 200 yards in rear of 19th Lancashire Fus. in Coy Artillery formation of platoons on a frontage of 250 yards and 150 yds between Coys. Coys will move with their right on the BEHENCOURT-FRANVILLERS Road as far as the track (C.22.a.4/4) running to German farm and will then wheel to the left keeping their right on the track. Right of Coys will direct. Touch will be maintained with 3rd Corps on our right.

(5) As soon as 2nd Line is crossed, and 1st Bn Dorset Regt. has its flanks secured, the 19th Bn Lancashire Fus pass through gap cut by 1st Dorsets and will work northwards along enemy's trench and cut a gap about 35 yds broad and 200 yds N of gap through which they entered. On crossing the German line, the Battalion will form to its left and attack the strong point and get in touch with the Division on our left. 15th Bn H.L.I. will move to N of BAIZIEUX WOOD and keep in touch with the Brigade. It will attack as ordered by the Brig-Genl. Commanding. If it is necessary to extend before crossing the German line, Coys will extend in lines of platoons at 50 yds distance. After crossing the German line, Coys will form to the left and attack in lines of 2 platoons at 25 yds distance with 50 yds distance between "A" and "B" Coys. "B" Coy to be prepared to cover right flank of "A" Coy and mop up trenches on the right. "C" and "D" Coys will be in reserve and will move as ordered. "C" Coy will move 100 yds in rear of "B" Coy with "D" Coy 100 yds in rear of "C" Coy. Left of Coys will move on enemy's 2nd Line trench. On gaining the strong point, Coys will move forward and take up a defensive line joining up with the 19th Bn Lancashire Fus: on the right and the Division on our left, and will consolidate strong points.

(6) O.C. "A" "B" and "C" Coys will have bombers ready to clear trenches and dug outs in the strong point.

(7) Each man will carry 220 rounds S.A.A. and 2 bombs (imaginary). Coy Bombing parties to carry 12 bombs. All available magazines will be carried with the Lewis Guns. Coy Comdrs to detail men to help if necessary.

(8) S.A.A. Ponies will move 500 yds in rear of "D" Coy and reduce the distance whenever possible. Coys to detail 4 men as ammunition carriers and 2 men as bomb carriers. The supply of Ammunition and Bombs to be practised.

(9) Stretcher Bearers will be with "D" Coy.

(10) Attention is called to the alteration in the time table vide para 2. 14th Infy Bde S.G. 151/1. Care must be taken that troops do not approach to near the Barrage.

(11) Zero time 10. am. All troops to be in position by 9.30. am.

(12) Bn. Hd Quarters will be in front of "D" Coy.

A. J. Bentley Captain + Adjt
2nd Bn Manchester Regt

14th Inf.Bde.
32nd Div.

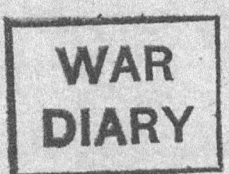

2nd BATTN. THE MANCHESTER REGIMENT.

J U L Y

1 9 1 6

Attached:

Reports on Operations.

Army Form C. 2118

WAR DIARY
or
INTELLIGENCE SUMMARY
(Erase heading not required.)

Instructions regarding War Diaries and Intelligence Summaries are contained in F.S. Regs., Part II. and the Staff Manual respectively. Title Pages will be prepared in manuscript.

Place	Date 1916	Hour	Summary of Events and Information	Remarks and references to Appendices
Senlis	July 1		The Bn. left Senlis on the evening of the 30th ult. proceeding to Authuille Wood preparatory to going into action on the morning of the 1st July. A verbal report of the Bn's movements in attached covering the 2nd & 3rd of July. The Bn. manoeuvred on the evening of the 3rd July and proceeded to billets at Senlis	
Senlis	" 2		Bn. in billets at Senlis. Moved to Toutencourt on the evening of this day	
Toutencourt	" 5		In billets Toutencourt	
Toutencourt	" 6		"	
Senlis	" 7		Bn. moved to Senlis. Bn. in billets in Senlis	
Bouzincourt	" 8		On the morning of 9th Bn. moved to billets at Bouzincourt. Orders were received that Bn. was to proceed to trenches and left at 10 p.m.	
Ovillers	" 9		Bn. in trenches. See attached report	
— " —	" 10		"	
— " —	" 11		Bn. relieved by 16th Northumberland Fus. Relief completed 9.30 pm. Bn. complete in billets at Bouzincourt by 10.15 pm	

Army Form C. 2118

WAR DIARY
or
INTELLIGENCE SUMMARY
(Erase heading not required.)

Instructions regarding War Diaries and Intelligence Summaries are contained in F. S. Regs., Part II. and the Staff Manual respectively. Title Pages will be prepared in manuscript.

M-2

Place	Date 1916	Hour	Summary of Events and Information	Remarks and references to Appendices
Bouzincourt	July 12		Bn in billets at Bouzincourt	
Bouzincourt	13		— " —	
Bouzincourt	14		Bn moved to Trenches 10 pm this day	
Ovillers	15		Bn in Trenches (see Separate report) by O R Reinforcements joined Bn	
Ovillers			Bn relieved by 11th Worcester Regt relief completed 9 pm. moved to billets at Senlis	
Senlis	16		Bn in billets Senlis	
Hallay	17		Bn moved to Hallay	
LeSouich	18		Bn moved to Le Souich	
Sibiville	19		Bn moved to Sibiville	
Marquay	20		Bn moved to Marquay	
St Pierre	21		Bn moved to St Pierre	
St Pierre	22		Bn in Billets St Pierre	
—	23/25		— " —	

Army Form C. 2118

WAR DIARY
or
INTELLIGENCE SUMMARY
(Erase heading not required.)

No. 3

Instructions regarding War Diaries and Intelligence Summaries are contained in F.S. Regs., Part II. and the Staff Manual respectively. Title Pages will be prepared in manuscript.

Place	Date	Hour	Summary of Events and Information	Remarks and references to Appendices
Haillicourt	July 26th 1916		Bn moved to Haillicourt	
—"—	27th		Bn in Billets Haillicourt. Inspection by Brigade General Compton	
—"—	28th		—"—	
—"—	29th		Inspection by Army Commander Lt. Gen. C.C. Munro KCB	
Le Preol	30th		Bn moved to Le Preol	
—"—	31st	10am	Bn in billets Le Preol. Providing working parties at Vermeguin North	
		11pm	Bn in billets Le Preol — do —	

N. Luxmoore Lt Col
Commanding 2nd Bn The Manchester Regt

REPORTS ON OPERATIONS.

1st. July. At 7.30 A.M. the Battalion left CRUCIFIX CORNER (AVELUY) and proceeded towards DUMBARTON TRACK (ATHUILLE WOOD) Upon reaching TRAMWAY CORNER it was found that the 1st. Dorsets and 19th. L.Fus. were not yet clear and the Bn. halted in the road. During this halt information was received from the batteries that the first line trenches had been taken, and from the wounded coming down that the 2nd. line trenches (support) had been taken and that the troops were moving on to the third line. At 9.0 A.M. the Bn. moved forward again up DUMBARTON TRACK in column of fours with 10 paces distance between Coys. Half way through AUTHUILLE WOOD the column was again halted (9.15 A.M.). Here information was received from the front that the Dorsets had gone over and that the 19th. L.F. were just following. Also that a Machine Gun was playing on the edge of the wood and this part would have to be rushed. At 9.30. A. M. orders were received from the 14th Inf Bde. not to move forward until further orders. At the same time information was received from Capt. W.W. Smith who had been with his Coy in ROCK ST. that the 11th. Borderers 1st Dorsets and ½ the 19th. L.F. had been mown down on leaving the Wood by a hostile Machine Gun. He suggested moving forward to our trenches through ROCK ST. and BURY AVE. instead of across the open. This information and suggestion was forwarded to the Brigade. The way up ROCK ST. and BURY AVE. was reconnoitred and found to be clear and passable. It was also found that our front line was full of 1st. Dorsets and 19th. L.F. and Borderers who were under the impression that they were in the enemys line.
On the return journey from BURY AVE. the remaining Coy of the 19th. L.F. was met making its way to the front trench. This information was passed on to the Brigade. The enemy had in the meanwhile commenced to heavily shell the Wood with 10.5 C. and 15Cm. shells, and Lachrymatory shells, and the Bn moved to the Assembly Trenches in the Wood. At 10.30 A.M. the Colonel was sent for to the Brigade, and an attempt was made to re-organise the Bn., and attached units in the assemble Trenches. At 12.15 P.M. the Colonel returned, and a conference of Coy Commanders was held. At this conference the Colonel informed us that the 8th. Division on our immediate right had failed to reach the enemys trenches, and had been badly cut up, that the 96th. and 97th. Bdes held portions of the enemys front line. He informed us that we were to be attached to the 97th Bde who held the NAZE and the LEIPZIG LINE and were expecting a counter attack. We were to move at once to reinforce and to bomb our way up the trenches towards the ed HINDENBURG REDOUBT. An Artillery Barrage had been established on this Redoubt and would be kept on till 1 P.M. As it was impossible to get the Coys up in time a message was sent asking for the barrage to remain on until 1.30. P.M. A and B Coys were ordered to proceed up ROCK ST. to the front line and on to SANDA ST., and to advance across the open to the S.W. face of the NAZE RECTANGLE. The remaining two Coys were to remain in ROCK ST. Two Machine Guns were to go forward with A & B Coys, and the remainder of the attached units and B. Headquarters to wait in the Assembly Trenches. Headquarters then moved forward to take up a position at the head of SANDA St. ROCK ST. was

-2-

found to be blocked with troops and it was therefore decided to go down BURY AVE. and along HOUGH ST. to OBAN AVE. this route was found to be clear. B Coy had been disorganised in the Wood and only 2 platoons were found in ROCK ST. As the time was pressing these 2 platoons were taken along with Hd Qrs. and instructions left for the remainder to follow on These two platoons were sent over the top at the point X1a3.5 at 1.45 P.M. ~~Unfortunately the point at which these platoons~~ and reinforced the 17th H.L.I. in the NAZE at 1.45 P.M. Unfortunately the point at which these platoons went over was rather too far South, and the platoons came under Machine Gun fire. Only a few casualties however, resulted. these two platoons when reaching the NAZE were directed to the left flank and within 10 minutes had bombed forward, established bombing posts, held back the enemys advance, and captured 19 prisoners. These platoons went over under 2/Lieut Culley.

The trenches at the NAZE were found to be packed with 17th H.L.I. 2nd K.O.Y.L.I. 1st Dorsets and 11th Borderers and 19th L.F. Only 4 officers were present and the whole were in a complete state of demoralisation.

At 3.15 P.M. A Coy was sent over to reinforce followed at 3.30 P.M. by the remaining 2 platoons of B Coy., and at 3.45 P.M. by C Coy. D Coy was held in reserve in our original front line, and utilised for carrying forward bombs.

At this time an effort was made to find out exactly how much of the enemys trench we actually held, the information that we had received being evidently wrong. The trenches however, were so packed with troops that it was impossible to move about or to locate the position of our own neighbouring bombing posts. Information was however, received that we had none of our own troops on either of our own flanks

At 3.45 P.M. two Machine Guns were sent forward which established themselves in the enemys original front line. Our men had by this time established a steady bombing barrage which broke the enemys attack and forced him slowly back.

At 6.0. P.M. the Bn was ordered to take over the NAZE and release the 17th H.L.I. and odd troops keeping only 90 men of the K.O.Y.L.I.

At 6.30 Pm. Bn H.Q. Moved forward. When the trenches had been cleared of superflour troops a German map of the trenches was found, and we were able to realise the position we actuallyheld. It was found that we occupied the Western corner of the salient through points R21c44-- R31c 52.15-- X1a 52.87 and that the enemy occupied the LEIPZIG LINE. Consolidation of this line was then commenced.

At 8 P.M. orders were received to dig trenches from TYNDRUM ST. and LIME ST. to join the salient with our originalline, 1 section R.E. and a part of 17th NF were to assist in this work. C & D Coys were detailed respectively for this work

By this time the RUSSIAN SAP had been opened up and a good deal of the traffic which had originally to go over the top was diverted down this passage. this was fortunate as the overland track had by now been marked down by Machine Guns and snipers, and we were incurring considerable losses. Fourteen more prisoners had by now come through, and five

more wounded ones remained in the enemys trench.
Considerable enjoyment was given to our troops by Lieut.
Robertson who made the prisoners run across the open through
their own Artillery Barrage, upon reaching our line these
men were kept out of our dugouts by the sharp end of a
bayonet.

The work of joining up our new and original lines was
commenced at 10 P.M. but very little work could be done
owing to the enemys Machine Gun fire and Artillery Barrage.
The consolidation of the enemys original line was, however,
carried on.
The evacuation of the wounded was carried on throughout
the night over the open in spite of the Machine Gun fire and
snipers. This evacuation was done by Coys, as our Streatcher
Bearers were all occupied throughout the whole night bringing
in and collecting the wounded of the Borderers, Dorsets, and
19th L.Fs. from the front of AUTHUILLE WOO to WOOD POST.
too much praise cannot be given to the heroic efforts of all
these men

2nd July   At 3 A.M. the enemy launched bombing attacks on our position
at points R3.c4.4--R31c52.15--R31c 5.0. At the two latter
points the attacks were driven off by our bombers and Lewis
Guns and at the former point the enemy drove in our post
for about 100 yards. Our bombers and Lewis Gunners
however got out into the open and drove the enemy back with
bombs, whilst the Lewis Gunners engaged the enemys
Machine Guns and kept back enemys reinforcements from coming
across the open, and our snipers engaged the enemy bombers
when they exposed themselves to bombs. The enemy was driven
back for 150 yards leaving us in possession of an extra
50 yards which secured for us the left flank of the Quarry.
Considerable casualties occurred on both sides during this
attack, but the enemy received considerable the worst of mt
matters Whilst leading a bombing attack at this point Lieut
Goldston, Sgt Whitfield and Pte Ward were wounded. The
method of attack described above was found to be very
advantageous. At this point it was found that we were
running short of bombs. A portion of C & D Coys was therefore
used to form a chain of carriers through the Russian Sap
and parties for carrying bombs from all available stores.
By this means a considerable number of bombs were brought
up and by 9 A.M. bomb stores had been established at each
bomb post, each Co HdQrs Bn Hdqrs and at either end of
the Sap.
Throughout the day the work of consolidation and building
of barricades was continued. The work was much hampered by
our own Artillery, which, despite urgent messages would
continued the barrage on our own front line causing many
casualties
Capt W.W. Smith reconnoitred the enemys trenches as far
as the points R31c62.12--R31c8.0--X1a 85515 and found no
signs of the enemy. These trenches were so situated that n
neither parties could hold them whilst the respective
main lines wer in present positions. At 7.30.P.M. a patrol
was sent out from our left to ascertain what troops
occupied the trenches to our left, as the aeroplanes
reported our own men present in these trenches. The patrol
however found an enemys bombing post within 40 yards of our

-4-

own. The enemy appeared to have captured some of our shrapnel helmets, and were wearing them.
Early in the afternoon the Colonel had been again sent for to Bde Hdqrs and returned at 8 P.M. with the news that an attack was to be made at 3.15 A.M. on the next morning (3rd) against the LEIPZIG LINE, but as our men had been fighting for the last 40 hours without sleep and could hardly stand, the attack was to be made by the 15th H.L.I. who would relieve us about 11 P.M.. We were to withdraw to AUTHUILLE DE DEFENCES and be in support if required. At 1.30 A.M. the relief commenced and as it was so near to zero time the Bn was ordered to stand by for the attack. Zero time was however, postponed until 6.15 A.M. and the relief was continued being concluded by 3.0 A.M.
At 6.15 A.M. the 15th H.L.I. attacked. At 7.15 A.M. a message was received asking for a Coy in support. A Coy was sent and moved up across the open and took up bombing posts on the left at which point the attack had been held up.
At 7.30 A.M. a second Coy "C" Coy was asked for and sent. This Coy took up posts on the right as the H.L.I. had been forced to retire from the forward positions gained.
At 7.45 A.M. bombs were asked for urgently. B Coy were loaded up with bombs and sent forward. The remaining Coy (D Coy) were then utilised for detonating bombs in the stores and sending forward a continual suppy.
Bn Hdqrs moved forward at 8.15 A.M. to SANDA ST but finding t that they were not required moved back to AUTHUILLE DEFENCES
At 2 A.M. on the 3rd. during the relief of the Bn by the 15th. H.L.I. the enemy had again launched a bombing attack on the Quarry. This however, was driven off by bombs and Lewis Guns

4th July.   At 1 A.M. the enemy again launched a strong bombing attack on the Quarry, at the same time heavily barraging our original line, our communication trenches and AUTHUILLE.
This attack was however, again driven off.
At 2.30 A.M. the Bn was relieved by the 2nd Wiltshire Regt. and withdrawn to SENLIS!
The spirit of the men throughout the whole attack was xxcx excellent, and was bouyed up by the fact that they considered they were giving the Bosche a worse time than the were receiving themselves. Individual efforts and enterprises were so numerous, that they included almost all members of every Company. Every man appeared to know his duty and did it. The organisation and smooth working of all Coys continued throughtout the whole fight without a hitch, and brought out the control and discipline of all ranks.

OPERATIONS DURING THE GREAT ADVANCE.   PHASE 2

2nd. Bn. The Manchester Regiment.

OVILLERS.

4th July. Bn arrived at SENLIS from the Trenches.

5th July. Bn. left SENLIS at 5.30 P.M. for FORCEVILLE.

7th July. Bn left FORCEVILLE for SENLIS at 7 A.M. Left SENLIS for BOUZINCOURT at 2.30.P.M.

7th July At 9.45 P.M. the Bn. was told to move to CRUCIFIX CORNER where guides would be at 10.P.M. Guides were not there at 11.30 p.m. and the Bn was conducted to the Hdqrs of the 36th Brigade in RIBBLE ST. From here the Bn was utilised throughout the night and the following day to carry forward ammunition, bombs and water to the troops in OVILLERS. The night was very wet and the trenches thick with mud which made the task very irksome, disagreeable and tiring for the men who were wet through and very fatigued by the next day.
The 36th Bde were holding OVILLERS with two weak battalions and the remainder of 3 others, and apparently had to retire from part of the village during the night.

8th July At 1 A.M. an attack was made by the 36th Bde with apparently no success. At 8.30. A.M. the Bde reported that they held part of the village and were in touch with the Bde on their right. Our men were instructed to find out all the ways to the front trenches and the general lie of the land.
At 12 noon we were told that we were to take over the trenches from the 36th Bde., and officers were sent forward to reconnoiter the trenches held.
At 6 p.m. the Bn moved forward to take over from the 36th Bde The trenches in OVILLERS were found to be packed with troops of the Sussex, Essex, Middlesex, Royal Fusiliers and East Surreys, all of whom appeared to be in a great hurry to get out.
At 9 P.M. we heard that the 14th Bde was moving forward to take over the whole line. At 10 P.M. the 1st Dorsets arrived to take over from the Essex. We then found that the latter Regt did not hold the forward trenches which we had been informed that they held, and that their men had already been relieved by our men. As the Germans held the trenches which the Dorsets were to take over much confusion arose. This was increased by the Middlesex who were waiting in reserve and by the 15th H.L.I. who were going to take over from the East Surreys, and who were blocked by the forward troops. Order was, however, eventually gained out of confusion, and the Bde settled down to their new trenches Lieut Colonel Luxmoore commanding the 2nd Manchesters was given complete command of all British Troops in OVILLERS, these troops consisting of 3 battalions each about 300 fighting strength.

9th July. 9 A.M. Col Luxmoore received orders from Bde that the troops were to move forward and take the village. Three objectives were worked out and a conference of Commanding Officers held. 2nd Manchester Regt. was to attack on the Northern and Eastern faces whilst the 15th H.L.I. were to attack on the Southern and part eastern face. 1st. Dorset Regt were in support to the Manchesters and the H.L.I. provided one company for their own support. By arrangement with Bde 19th Lanc Fus. who were stationed in our original trenches provided parties

"2"

for carrying forward ammunition bombs and water to a dump on the Sunken Road. From this point R.S.M. Wood 2nd Manchester Regt arranged the distribution to the different units, a party of scouts, police and servants of the 2nd Manchester Regt being provided for this purpose. The 19th Lanc Fus. acted as reserve for the OVILLERS troops.

Zero time was fixed for 11.30 A.M. and Artillery Barrages were arranged accordingly. Zero time was changed to 12Noon for the benefit of the H.L.I. who were not ready.

Distribution of 2nd Manchester Regt for the attack.

"A" Coy held eastern part of Northern defences from which no attack was to be made, with "C" Coy in support.

"B" Coy held remainder of northern defences and part of western defences, from which their first objectives were points 51 and 61.

"D" Coy held the centre of the western defences, their first objective being from point 61 to point 67. Objectives of H.L.I. were points 67, 68 and 77. At 1.30.pm. it was reported that point 51 had been taken and shortly afterwards H L I. reported that they had gained their first objective. At 2 P.M. we were informed that "D" Coy were held up in centre by M.G. fire and sniping. At 3.30. P.M. point 61 was taken and a message was received from Lt. Sheppard commanding "D" Coy saying that the trench along which he had to work to his first objective finished in open ground about 100 yards from the objective, and as an advance across the open ground with no cover, and exposed to M.G. fire would undoubtedly cost more than 50% of the men attempting the crossing, he had ordered the Coy to move up behind "B" Coy, and from there to work along to the right, and so take their objective and gain touch with the H.L.I., and rejoin those few men who had been able to reach the objective across the open earlier in the day.

1st. objective was finally taken at 4 P.M.

The enemys trenches were found to be practically non-existent forming merely a series of large craters, the lips of which were heavily covered by enemys M.G. and snipers, for this reason the advance was slow, and the identification of the exact points gained was very difficult.

Zero time for the advance on the 2nd. objective was fixed for 4.45 P.M. This time was changed to 5.15 P.M. for the benefit of the H.L.I. who were not ready. At 7 P.M. Capt Grindel commanding "B" Coy returned to HQrs with the information that the attack had been hung up in the open some 150 yards in advance of the 1st. objective. The 15th. H.L.I. reported that they were similarly hung up, the troops were unable to advance due to hostile heavy Machine gun fire and sniping, it was therefore decided for the advanced troops to dig themselves in, in their position, with their entrenching tools as far as possible and to await nightfall.

The 1st Dorset Regt was moved up into the first objective which they commenced to consolidate. The advance from the first objective had been carried out by crawling over the open from crater to crater. After dark 1st Dorset Regt. was moved forward to relieve the 2 attacking Coys of the Manchesters who were withdrawn into support. The H.L.I. arranged a regimental relief. 2 sections of the 206th Co. R.E. came up after dark to assist in the work of consolidation. M.G. emplacements were arranged in 1st. objective line and Lewis Gun and Bombing posts in the forward line.

16th July At 5.30. A.M. the Brigadier arrived at H.Q. and informed us that Division had ordered the advance to be continued a 8 A.M that morning. He had however, explained that the troops were tired and worn out with the previous days fighting

and consolidation and could not possibly move forward again before 11 A.M.
Before taking the next objective, it was decided to attack and take the points 65 and 18 thus securing advanced flank positions before advancing in the centre. By this time 4 Stokes guns and 6 Vickers M.G. and 1 2" trench mortar had been brought up with their accompanying ammunition, a scheme for counter-sniping and machine gun firing was arranged. Stokes gun and trench mortar positions were fixed. The choosing of these positions was very difficult, as it was so hard to fix the exact points that we held and to locate the exact positions of the enemy that it was required to smash in. Zero time was arranged for 12 noon.
It was decided to fire on point 65 with one Stokes gun and to concentrate the remaining Stokes guns on point 18 & T.M. The Heavy Artillery were to fire on these points up to Zero time and to keep a slow deliberate fire on our 3rd objective. At 11.40. A.M. it was doubtful whether the Stokes guns would be in action in time, these guns however got into action at 11.55 A.M. and managed to get off all their ammunition with good results by Zero time.
Up to date, the advance had been carried out across craters and ground which resembled ploughed fields under considerable hostile sniping and M.G. firing. The whole was in an unimaginable mass of craters, dead and debris. It had been found best to advance with scattered parties in small rushes. The advance on points 65 and 18 was to be made up the trenches as far as they existed and the points to be carried by bombing. At 12.30 P.M. "C" Coy who was attacking point 65 reported that they had reached point 52, which was withing a few yards of point 65 and that they were surrounded by enemy, who were bombing from 3 directions. For a considerable time, this party managed to hold its post. Reinforcements rushed out of a crater at point 51 and scrambled into the trench at point 52, at 3 p.m. the enemy outranged us with their small disc bombs. Lt Tomblin with the leading party was killed. Lt Robertson with the supporting party was wounded, and our men were forced back to point 51. The Stokes Gun again barraged Point 65 artillery barrage dropped on to this point and a continual bombing barrage was kept up from Point 51 to prevent an enemy counter attack. At 1.20.P.M. the H.L.I. reported that they were held up with 150 yards from point 18 but that 2 platoons with 1 platoon of Dorsets in support had worked up to the church and were consolidating this position. This point was some 200 yards in advance of any other point gained, and the information was afterwards found to be incorrect, the position actually gained being on the same level with the reminder of the H.L.I. forces and 100 yards away from the Church. One prisoner of the 133rd Regt was taken at this point After consolidation of this point, bombing parties were to work North and south and attempt to reach point 18 from a second direction.
At 3.30 P.M. it was decided to move the Dorsets forward in the centre. Parties of this Regt moved forward up the communication trench for 50 yards and then spread out into craters and reported that they were in touch on their left rear with the Manchesters but were not in touch with the H.L.I. on their right. At 5 P.M. the Dorsets reported that they could move no further forward. The H.L.I. reported also that they had reached Point 18 but were driven out again. It was then decided to consolidate the small points gained As all 3 battalions were very weak in strength and exhausted 1 Coy of 19th L.Fus. was asked for in support. This Coy arrived at 6 P.M.
At 5 P.M. 3 officers Royal Inniskilling Fusiliers arrived in the trenches to look over the ground, as their Bn was to

"4"

attack that night through us in a northernly direction. This attack for its 1st objective, was to take the German line immediately in front of our northern face and to include point 63. Their next objective was to take the next German line about 90 yards in advance of their 1st objective. The 1st objective was to be rushed whilst the Artillery barraged the 2nd objective. Bombing parties were to work up the German trenches running North and the 2nd objective rushed under cover of Artillery Barrage. The Bn arrived in our original trenches at 8 P.M. 2 Coys came forward to make the attack and 2 Coys remained in support in our original line. The attack was to commence at 9 P.M. As Col Luxmoore considered that a heavy barrage would be established by the enemy between our present and original lines and that thus the supports would be unable to come up he ordered one platoon 19th L.Fus to move into the trenches on our northern face to act as an immediate reserve to the R.I.F. if required. At 9 P.M. The R.I.F. attacked and gained their 1st objective despite very heavy hostile M.G fire. As anticipated a very heavy barrage was put up by the enemy across the original NO MANS LAND. At 9.30 P.M. The R.I.F. advanced on their 2nd objective. This however they were unable to gain owing to heavy M.G. fire, and a position in the open had to be taken up. From this point a feeble hostile counter attack was easily repulsed. It was eventually found that the R.I.F had to move back from this forward position and held only one small trench 90 yards in length about 40 yards in advance on left of their 1st objective. During this attack the R.I.F. were supplied with ammunition and bombs from our advanced dump. These were carried forward by our carrying parties and a continual stream of ammunition was established. At 10 PM. we moved our left bombing post forward and obtained touch with the R.I.F. The right bombing post of our northern flank also established touch with R.I.F. at point 63 This attack of the R.I.F. considerably eased our position on the northern flank and by obtaining point 62 considerably facilitated my further advance on our part. At 6 P.M. the 19th L.F. relieved the 18th H.L.I. who were withdrawn into support. At 10pm. R.E. came forward to help consolidation. At 10.30.P.M. 2 Vickers M.G. were sent forward to the captured line of R.I.F.

11th July   At 6 A.M. the Brigadier arrived in the trenches and informed us that due to the exhausted state of the troops he did not intend to press any further attack that day. At 9 A.M. "A" Coy relieved "C" Coy and D Coy was put into support to the Dorsets where it had been throughout the previous night. At 10 A.M. a careful reconnaissance of the actual ground occupied was taken and found to be as follows:-

2nd Manchester Regt.   Pt X8c 0595 through pts X8a59-X8aB2
                       From pt X8A0015 through pts X8A4015-
                       X8A50 to pt X8A0690
                       From X8A50 through pts X8A1507-
                       X8A0507 back post pt X8A0600

           Remarks   Trench running through points
                       X8A- ca 58-63 to 95 is smashed in and
                       unoccupied. Pt 63 (5 yds W of Pt 62)
                       is covered by a Lewis Gun from Pt 62
                       The trench running N.W. from pt 63 is
                       blocked by shell fire but has no bombing
                       post. Trenches leading N from Pt X8A
                       1507 and X8A0507 are blocked with bomb-
                       ing posts

1st. Dorsets   From Pt X8A61 to X8A069
                       "   " X8A61 to X8069 100 yards in
                       advance of former trench The trench
                       from pt 61 is completely obliterated.

At 10 A.M. information was received that CONTALMAISON had been taken.

Throughout the whole of the operations the supply of ammunition, bombs, stokes ammunition water and rations was most excellently and capably carried out by R.S.M. Woods 2nd Manchester Regt. Most excellent work was again done by our stretcher bearers who evacuated some 200 wounded men from the trenches. Many of these had been left by former regiments and at least 6 were brought in from off the German wire where they had been lying for 4 days. By the completion of the tour, all wounded men had been evacuated from the trenches.
Salvage parties from behind were sent up, who collected and burried several hundreds of the dead who were lying out along the sunken road and in NO MANS LAND.
When we left the trenches, these parties had commenced to clear the actual trenches, which were littered with dead, and which were fast approaching a very disagreeable state of decomposition.

Discipline and organisation again came to the front during operations. Though wet through, tired and exhausted, the troops again and again went forward to the attack across exceedingly difficult ground, with the utmost vigour of which they were capable. It cannot but be thought that now, due to the most strategical points having been taken, had the Bn been fresh instead of utterly exhausted, the whole of the village might have been comparatively ~~taken~~ easily taken.

16.7.16.

N. Luxmoore. Lt Colonel
2/ Manchester Regt.

OPERATIONS DURING THE GREAT ADVANCE — PHASE "A"

2nd Bn. The Manchester Regt. — OVILLERS continued

July 12th
13th
14th   Bn remained in rest billets at BOUZINCOURT.

July 14th. Bn relieved the Royal Inniskilling Fusiliers and the Northumberland Fusiliers in OVILLERS at 8 p.m. About at the same time relieved the 19th Lf. in the Southern and Eastern trenches of the village. Shortly after the relief information was received that the Brigade on our right were going to attack that night. Details of the attack were as follows: — The 9th Bde were to attack the Southern line of the village from a Southerly direction taking the line from points 31 to 75. (The portion from 31 to 18 had been taken the previous night). This attack was timed for 11 p.m. If the attack was successful a 2nd attack was to be made at about 2 a.m. in which the 7th Bde would take the outer Eastern defences from point 78 to point 16. The 75th Bde would take the Northern defences from point 16 to point the road junction between points 63 and 95. As there would be a gap between our right at point 52 and the left of the 75th Bde it was arranged that the 75th Bde should send up Very lights when their left was established and we moved this patrol forward to obtain touch. During the attack we would maintain heavy M.G. fire in the enemy trenches North of the village.

At 11 p.m. orders were received from the 14th Bde that the Bn was to cooperate with the 75th Bde in their attack by simultaneously attacking points 63, 72, 82 and 92. It was then arranged for the bombs to attack point 72, 82 and 92 and to keep liaison with the 75th Bde. We would attack point 63.
Between 9.30 p.m. and 11 p.m. our heavy artillery continually fell short into our trenches between points 20 and 52.
At 12 midnight a patrol was sent out from point 52. towards point 63 and ascertain whether this point was occupied. The patrol returned at 1.50 a.m. with the information that the tunnel was distinctly connected to and of a series of craters and that no sign of the enemy had been seen for some time or any sending up of Very lights.
Throughout the night the enemy sent up numbers of white and red lights. M.G. and rifle fire was heavy about point 52. a series of bombs and it suggested from the direction of point 45.

At 2.15 a.m. acting upon the report of the aforementioned patrol, bombing parties were sent forward from point 52 to work from towards point 63. This party however came under a heavy bomb barrage very shortly after leaving point 52. Twenty five casualties were sustained and the party had to move back. The post at point 52 was at the same time driven back being completely outranged by the enemy's bombs and grenades. Lieut. Johnson was killed here.

At 2.20 a.m. the enemy bombed our post at point 53 but were driven off with Stokes Guns.

At 2.30 a.m. Information was received from the South Lancs (75th Bde) that their forward troops (3 Borders) were about to advance. This was timed at 3.10 a.m.

A Stokes Gun and 2" T.M. barrage was immediately arranged on points 13 and 46 to keep down hostile MGs from this direction.

At 5 a.m. it was reported that the Dorsets in touch with the 75th Bde had attacked points 72 and 82 but had been driven back by MG fire.

At 6 a.m. it was reported that the 75th Bde held a line running from just East of the Chalet at point 31, and that the Dorsets were digging forward from their advanced position to join up with the 75th Bde.

Point 52 was reoccupied by us at about 3.30 a.m.

July 15th
The day passed quietly.
At 8 p.m. the Brigade was relieved by the 2nd Worcesters and withdrew to SENLIS.

Two days after leaving OVILLERS the village was at last finally taken, the remainder of the garrison (118 men) having put their hands up.

14th Brigade
32nd Division.

2nd BATTALION

THE MANCHESTER REGIMENT

AUGUST 1 9 1 6

Instructions regarding War Diaries and Intelligence Summaries are contained in F.S. Regs., Part II. and the Staff Manual respectively. Title Pages will be prepared in manuscript.

INTELLIGENCE SUMMARY 2nd Manchester Regt.

(Erase heading not required.)

Place	Date	Hour	Summary of Events and Information	Remarks and references to Appendices
	Aug 1916.			
LE PREOL ANNEQUIN	1st		Battalion in billets at LE PREOL & ANNEQUIN. Battalion Headquarters at LE PREOL. 250 Men & Officers attached to Royal Engineers for Working Parties at ANNEQUIN.	N.E.A.M.
--do--	2nd		Battalion in billets at LE PREOL & ANNEQUIN. Battalion Headquarters at LE PREOL. 250 Men & Officers attached to Royal Engineers for Working Parties at Annequin.	N.E.A.M.
LE PREOL	3rd		Battalion in Billets at LE PREOL.	N.E.A.M.
--do--	4th		Battalion in billets at LE PREOL.	N.E.A.M.
--do--	5th		Battalion in billets at LE PREOL. Battalion relieved 1st Bn Worcester Regt in Village Line CAMBRIN from Wilsons Way to LA BASSEE Canal taking over Strong Points. Relief complete 6-10pm. Transport &c remain at LE PREOL.	N.E.A.M.
CAMBRIN	6th		Battalion in Village Line; Headquarters in HARLEY STREET. Working parties & Carrying up parties being supplied. Casualties:- 1 Man Killed. 1 Man Wounded.	N.E.A.M.
--do--	7th		Battalion in Village Line; Headquarters in HARLEY STREET. Working parties & Carrying up parties being supplied.	N.E.A.M.
--do--	8th		Battalion in Village Line; Headquarters in HARLEY STREET. Working parties & Carrying up parties being supplied.	N.E.A.M.
--do--	9th		Battalion in Village Line; Headquarters in HARLEY STREET. Working parties & Carrying up Parties being supplied.	N.E.A.M.
--do--	10th		Battalion in Village Line; Headquarters in HARLEY STREET. Working parties & Carrying up parties being supplied.	N.E.A.M.
--do--	11th		Battalion in Village Line; Headquarters in HARLEY STREET. Battalion moved into Trenches CUINCHY Subsector, and relieved 5/6th Royal Scots; relief	N.E.A.M.

WAR DIARY
or
INTELLIGENCE SUMMARY 2ⁿᵈ Manchester Regt

(Erase heading not required.)

Place	Date	Hour	Summary of Events and Information	Remarks and references to Appendices
CAMBRIN	Aug 1916 11th (Contd)		commencing 6pm. Distribution, No 1 Company Left Company Sector; No 2 Company Right Company sector. 1st Bn Dorset Regt relieved the Battalion in the Village Line.	
CUINCHY	12th		Battalion in Trenches, CUINCHY subsector.	
--do--	13th		--------do--------	
--do--	14th		--------do--------	
--do--	15th		--------do--------	
--do--	16th		Battalion in Trenches, CUINCHY subsector. 5/6th Royal Scots relieved the Battalion; relief commencing at 6 pm. Battalion took over Huts and billets quitted by 5/6th Royal Scots at LE QUESNOY.	
LE QUESNOY.	17th		Battalion in Huts and billets, LE QUESNOY.	
-- do --	18th		--------do--------	
-- do --	19th		--------do--------	
-- do --	20th		--------do--------	
-- do --	21st		--------do--------	
-- do --	22nd		--------do--------	
-- do --	23rd		Battalion in Huts and billets, LE QUESNOY. Battalion relieved 5/6th Royal Scots in CUINCHY subsector; relief complete by 4pm.	
CUINCHY	24th		Battalion in Trenches, CUINCHY Subsector. Casualty, One Man wounded. No Trench Mortar or Artillery activity. Enemy inactive.	

Instructions regarding War Diaries and Intelligence Summaries are contained in F.S. Regs., Part II. and the Staff Manual respectively. Title Pages will be prepared in manuscript.

INTELLIGENCE SUMMARY

2nd Manchester Regt.

(Erase heading not required.)

Place	Date	Hour	Summary of Events and Information	Remarks and references to Appendices
CUINCHY	Aug 1916. 25th		Battalion in Trenches, CUINCHY subsector. Two mines were exploded in front of the Battalion on our right at 8.30pm. Enemy shelled our Right Companys Front at 8.40pm after the exploding of the mines.	
--do--	26th		Battalion in Trenches, CUINCHY subsector. No Hostile artillery or Trench Mortar activity.	
--do--	27th		Battalion in Trenches, CUINCHY subsector. Artillery inactive; slight Trench Mortar activity. A patrol consisting of 2/Lt.P.D.Krolik, Sgt H.Hufton & Pte Ashworth went out & reconnoitred the ground as far as the German Wire.	
--do--	28th		Battalion in the Trenches, CUINCHY subsector. Enemy quiet; our Trench Mortars bombarded their lines but drew no retaliation.	
--do--	29th		Battalion in the Trenches, CUINCHY subsector. 5/6th Royal Scots relieved the Battalion in the trenches; relief commencing at 6pm. Battalion took over Village Line Defences from the 5/6th Royal Scots.	
CAMBRIN	30th		Battalion in Village Line Defences, CAMBRIN.	
--do--	31st		Battalion in Village Line Defences, CAMBRIN.	

N. Luxmoore. Lieut Colonel.,
Commanding 2nd Bn The Manchester Regiment.

14th Brigade.

32nd Division.

2nd BATTALION

THE MANCHESTER REGIMENT

SEPTEMBER 1916

Appendices attached :-

Raid carried out by Bn 28/29th.

Army Form C. 2118.

WAR DIARY
or
INTELLIGENCE SUMMARY

(Erase heading not required.)

Instructions regarding War Diaries and Intelligence Summaries are contained in F.S. Regs., Part II. and the Staff Manual respectively. Title Pages will be prepared in manuscript.

Place	Date	Hour	Summary of Events and Information	Remarks and references to Appendices
CAMBRIN.	Sept 1916. 1st.		Battalion in Village Line Defences, CAMBRIN. Supplied Working and CarryingParties.	N.E. Lieut.Col.
--do--	2nd.		----------do---------- ----------do----------	N.E. Lieut.Col.
--do--	3rd.		----------do---------- ----------do----------	N.E. Lieut.Col.
--do--	4th.		Battalion relieved the 5/6th Royal Scots in the Left Subsection. Distribution, No 1 Company Right Company Sector: No 2 Company, Left Company Sector. Relief commenced at 6 pm after the Village Line had been handed over to the 1st Bn Dorset Regt. Casualty, 1 Man wounded during relief.	N.E. Lieut.Col.
CUINCHY.	5th.		Battalion in trenches, CUINCHY Subsection. Casualty, 1 man wounded.	N.E. Lieut.Col.
--do--	6th.		----------do---------- Heavy bombardment by our Artillery about 12 Midnight followed by a raid on enemy trenches by 5/6th Royal Scots.	N.E. Lieut.Col.
--do--	7th.		Battalion in trenches, CUINCHY Subsection. Relief of 14th Infantry Brigade commenced.	N.E. Lieut.Col.
--do--	8th.		The Battalion relieved by 17th Bn H.L.I. relief commenced at 12 noon and was completed by 2.30 pm. Battalion marched to ANNEZIN taking over billets there.	N.E. Lieut.Col.
ANNEZIN.	9th		Battalion in Billets ANNEZIN.	N.E. Lieut.Col.
--do--	10th.		------do------ Regimental Transport inspected by Brigadier General C.W. COMPTON Commanding 14th Infantry Brigade.	N.E. Lieut.Col.
--do--	11th.		Battalion in billets ANNEZIN. Working parties found at ANNEQUIN.	N.E. Lieut.Col.
--do--	12th.		------do------ The Following Officer and men were awarded decorations as detailed below:- 2/Lieut. (Temporary Captain) W.W.Smith, K.S.L.I., attached 2nd Bn Manchester Regt awarded Military Cross. No 9089 Pte J.Campbell, 2nd Bn The Manchester Regt awarded Military Medal.	N.E. Lieut.Col.

Army Form C. 2118.

WAR DIARY
or
INTELLIGENCE SUMMARY

(Erase heading not required.)

Instructions regarding War Diaries and Intelligence Summaries are contained in F. S. Regs., Part II. and the Staff Manual respectively. Title Pages will be prepared in manuscript.

Place	Date	Hour	Summary of Events and Information	Remarks and references to Appendices
ANNEZIN.	13th.		Battalion in billets ANNEZIN. Working parties supplied. All available officers of the Battalion attended demonstration of explosion of mine, at ANNEZIN.	N.L. Lieut Col
--do--	14th.		Battalion in billets ANNEZIN. One hundred from No 1 & 2 Companies attended G.O.C., Parade at BETHUNE. Distribution of Medal Ribbons.	N.L. Lieut Col
--do--	15th.		Battalion in billets ANNEZIN.	N.L. Lieut Col
--do--	16th.		----do----	N.L. Lieut Col
--do--	17th.		----do----	N.L. Lieut Col
--do--	18th.		Battalion relieved the 16th Bn Lancashire Fusiliers in the Right Subsection CAMBRIN SECTOR. No 1 Company Left Company Subsection: No 2 Company Right Company Subsection. Relief commenced 2pm completed by 4 pm.	N.L. Lieut Col
CAMBRIN.	19th		Battalion in trenches.	N.L. Lieut Col
--do--	20th		----do----	N.L. Lieut Col
--do--	21st		----so----	N.L. Lieut Col
--do--	22nd		Battalion relieved by 1st Bn Dorset Regt and withdrew to billets at ANNEQUIN North. Relief commenced at 2 pm completed by 4 pm. Casualty 1 man killed.	N.L. Lieut Col
ANNEQUIN North.	23rd		Battalion in billets ANNEQUIN North. Working parties provided.	N.L. Lieut Col
--do--	24th.		----do----	N.L. Lieut Col
--do--	25th.		----do----	N.L. Lieut Col
--do--	26th.		Battalion less 1 Company relieved 1st Bn Dorset Regt in Right Subsection CAMBRIN SECTOR, augmented by 1 Company 5/6th Royal Scots.	N.L. Lieut Col

Army Form C. 2118.

WAR DIARY
or
INTELLIGENCE SUMMARY

(Erase heading not required.)

Instructions regarding War Diaries and Intelligence Summaries are contained in F. S. Regs., Part II. and the Staff Manual respectively. Title Pages will be prepared in manuscript.

Place	Date	Hour	Summary of Events and Information	Remarks and references to Appendices
CAMBRIN.	27th.		Battalion in trenches CAMBRIN.	
--do--	28th.		----do---- Company in Reserve carried out a raid on German Trenches.	M.T. Manc. Col.
			see attached report.	M.T. Manc. Col.
--do--	29th.		Battalion in trenches CAMBRIN.	
--do--	30th.		Battalion relieved by 15th H.L.I., in Village Lines relief commencing at 1.30 pm.	

N. Luxmoore. Lieut., Colonel,

Commanding 2nd Bn The Manchester Regiment.

2449 Wt. W14957/M90 750,000 1/16 J.B.C. & A. Forms/C.2118/12.

DETAILS OF RAID AS CARRIED OUT
on the night 28/29th September 1916.

Moving up to Trenches.

Raiding party left ANDECHIN at 5.15. P.M. and proceeded to
CAMBRAI R.E. Stores, where they blacked their faces and were
supplied with Bombs. The party reached Bn Hdqrs., at 7.30. P.M.
From Bn Hdqrs. the party proceeded to the front trenches, and found
the guides previously established, and white arrow marks absolutely
invaluable.

Tape Party.

The tape party left our trenches at 8.45 P.M., and though seen
by the enemy, and fired upon by Machine Guns, managed to lay
the tape to the enemy wire.

Bangalore Party.

The Bangalore Parties left our trenches at 9 P.M. The flank
parties returned by 9.55 p.m., but the centre party found
great difficulty in getting forward, due to the enemy's lights
and Machine Gun fire. By this time 3 enemy Machine Guns were
whipping ENGLAND, one firing from the enemy's front line,
about 50 yards North of point X, and two from the support line.
Eventually this Torpedo was laid with both the electric and
instantaneous fuse. The party returning to our trench at
11.30. P.M. This party was sent out under an Officer.

Raiding Parties. Directly the centre bangalore party had returned
the actual raiding party were sent out. All raiding parties
had moved out by 12.30. A.M. and O.C. Raid moved forward to
his shell hole.

Casualties. Whilst coming up BOYAU 4 the enemy threw several
trench mortars, one of which fell into the BOYAU bursting
a bag of bombs carried by one of the raid. The trench at the
time was full of men moving up, and the explosion caused
five casualties, four killed and one wounded. During the
process of taking out the tape, and the bangalores two men were
wounded. Whilst getting out, the main raiding parties lost
several wounded.
All these casualties caused a slight amount of confusion in
parties, as the casualties had to be replaced. This, however,
was satisfactorily managed, and the raiders managed to get
in position.

Raid.

Despite the fact that the parties going out had been
undoubtedly seen by the enemy, and ENGLAND was being swept
with Machine Gun fire, it was decided to force the raid
through.
The raiding party were all in position by 12.30.A.M. At 12.45 A.M.
word was received at point O from O.C. raid at shell hole 5 to
blow the torpedoes. These were blown. Exactly how many went up
was unknown, as the flash of the centre one covered the flashes
of the flanking ones.
Unfortunately it had never been realised beforehand that the
instantaneous fuse would burn backwards when the electric fuse
was blown. This fuse came flying back with a leap of flame, and
much disturbed the raiding parties, some of whom were lying on top
of it. Immediately the bangalore went off the enemy were heard
to rush back from their trench, and the Machine Gun 50 yards
from point X opened fire. The leading party rushed through the
gap only to find that about two yards of wire was still about.
This party met the Machine Gun fire and was wiped out with the
exception of two men. The leader of the second party and his
second string were both wounded. The leaders of all parties
except 5 had by this time been knocked out.
Realising that the enemys trench had been evacuated, and that the
to force an entry would necessitate a big increase to the already
large number of casualties, the O.C. Raid decided not to force
the raid through further, and therefore blew the signal for
retiring at 1.10.A.M.

Wounded.

All wounded men were brought in and all the dead at 3 A.M.
with the exception of two whose bodies could not be traced. These
men were 30

Wounded
(continued.)
men were 50 yards out from our trenches, and have now been located.

Casualties.

	Killed		Wounded	
	OFFICERS	O.R.	OFFICERS	O.R.
	-	5	1	12

TOTAL. 5 Killed 13 Wounded.

Gallantry.

Extreme gallantry was shown by Sergt McElroy and L/Cpl Eadie. When Sergt Hufton was hit in the leg just in the Bangalore Torpedo shell hole these men remained behind with him after the raiders had withdrawn promising to send out a stretcher. As no stretcher arrived within half an hour, L/Cpl Eadie came back to our trenches to fetch one. He met the stretcher party just leaving our trench, and proceeded with the stretcher and Cpl Holt to the shell hole where Sergt Hufton lay. L/Sgt Sergt McElroy remained with Sergt Hufton until the stretcher arrived, an hour after the raiders had withdrawn and then helped to carry the wounded man back.

LESSONS LEARNT BY RAID.

"a" It is absolutely essential to have an officer with the Bangalore party in order to ensure that the Torpedo is correctly laid.

"b" It is inadvisable to attempt to destroy the enemy's wire with Artillery or Trench Mortars, as this only tends to spread the wire, and when the Bangalore is placed, instead of finding a clear depth, of say, 4 yards of wire, which can easily be blown an additional depth, even up to 10 yards is found, due to the wire having been spread out and scattered, forming an excellent trip wire entanglement.

DETAILS OF RAID BY 22ND. MANCHESTER REGIMENT

ON ENEMY TRENCHES FROM

POINT A.26.c.55/55 to POINT A.26.c.7/4.

on the night of

4h/5th September 1916.

─────────oOo─────────

DETAILS OF RAID BY 2ND BATTALION THE MANCHESTER REGIMENT.

On Enemy Trenches from

Point A.28.c.55.85 to point A.28.c.7.4.

on the night of

/ th. September 1916.

ARRANGEMENTS AND TRAINING PREVIOUS TO RAID.

Reference:----Trench Map CAMBRIN subsection.
Aeroplane photo 25J 435.
Attached sketches "A" and "B".

Septr 23rd. General idea for Raid issued. Scheme proposed that raiders enter enemy trench at point K. (Attached sketch "A"), one party moves North to Sap L to capture prisoners, a second party moves up communication trench M to search dug-outs, a third party moves up AUCH ALLEY for about 80 yards, a further party moves South and blocks the trench at I.

This scheme was discussed, and it was decided that the parties should be 10, 6, 12, and 8 men strong respectively, Officers accompanying the 1st. and 3rd. parties. A support party of 12 men and one Lewis Gun was decided on, to be situated in the shell holes at A, B, and C. A further reserve party and dump were decided upon to be situated at G, the exit point of our own trench.
It was decided to divide the respective parties up in the following manner.

| Parties | Number | | | Composition | | Remarks. |
	OFF	N.C.O.	Men	No	Duties	
A	-	1	3	4	Support	Also Bomb dump.
B	-	1	3	4	Support	"
C	-	1	3	4	Support	"
K-L	1	2	8	4	Blocking	
				3	Clearing	
				3	Taking away	
K-M	-	3	5	4	Blocking	
				2	Clearing	
				2	Taking away	
K-F	1	4	8	4	Blocking	
				2	Clearing	
				2	Taking away	
				4	Support	
K-I	-	3	5	4	Blocking	
				2	Clearing	
				2	Taking away	

continued.

"g"

It was further decided to have two men waiting at point X, to assist prisoners out of the trench and to receive booty, and a further 4 men at the same place to take prisoners back.
Tape party to consist of 2 men.
Bangalore party to consist of 4 men.

A suitable piece of ground under cover from observation and much resembling NO MAN'S LAND was chosen, and the enemys trenches mapped out upon it. The extent of the trench which had to be entered was dug 2'-6" wide and 1' deep the remainder of the area concerned was mapped out with flags.

Septr 24th. After a conference with General RYCROFT it was decided to blow 3 Bangalore Torpedoes one on either flank of the main Torpedo in order to make the enemy converge towards the centre Torpedo.
After a conference with the R.E. it was decided to blow these Torpedoes electrically, the centre one having a separate lead, the two outer ones being fired in parallel. In order to make things absolutely certain, the centre torpedo was to be fitted with an additional time fuse leading back to shell hole 2 (attached map B), and an extra detonator was to be taken with a BROCK lighter.
The matter of Arms to be carried was then entered upon, see General and Special Orders.
It was further decided that the blocking party should carry ladders as they might be needed. Four ladders were decided upon.
Wire cutters were also to be taken in case the wire was not sufficiently blown, or in case wire was encountered in the enemy trench.
In order to assist the marking of the way back, small white flags were indented for.
For identification of the Raiders it was decided to wear a split sandbag over the neck and shoulders.
A list of stores required was then determined, see appendix E.
In a conference with the Artillery, T.M. Officers and Machine Gun Officers, a barrage was worked out, see Appendix F and attached Map B.

Training The Raiders were divided off into their parties, shown the general lie of the enemy's trenches as marked out, and instructed in their particular duties. In order to become thoroughly acquainted with their particular piece of trench, each party was set to work to dig and deepen their piece.

Septr 25th. Map of barrage was got out. The system of communication was gone into. It was decided that a telephone exchange should be established at point G, and that a telephone should be taken forward to shell hole 2, this telephone to be taken forward to K if necessary. Telephones for Artillery and Trench Mortars were also to be established at G, a slit being cut for this purpose. Messengers were to remain with O.C. Raid, and with telephone at G. Messengers to M.G. Coy., and Trench Mortar batteries also to be at G.
Stretcher Bearers and escort for prisoners to be in position in front line trench South of BOYAU 4.

Training Physical Drill. Practice of parties moving into position preparatory to the blowing of the Bangalore Torpedo and subsequently. Lesson on German phrases. Lecture on general performance during the Raid.

Septr 26th Final arrangements made with Artillery, R.E., M.G. Coy., and Trench Mortar Batteries. From a raid by the 8th Division on the previous night it was found that the enemy trenches in front of that Division were unoccupied, except for sentry posts which were wired in. In case of this occuring during the raid it was decided to block at the nearest traverse and then to
continued

move over the open behind the enemy sentry post.

Training Physical Drill. Practice of moving into position before and after the blowing of the Bangalore Torpedoes. Blocking and clearing dugouts practised, as also the taking back of prisoners. Raid practised by night. Revolver shooting and handling of bludgeons practised. During the night of the 25th., and the 26th. parties went out from the front line trench to investigate the ground at 9 P.M., 11 P.M., and 1 A.M..
General and Special Orders issued.

Septr 27th. Decided to mark the way up to the front line for the raiding party with broad white arrows at all corners, and also to establish guides along the route in order that there should be no chance of any party losing their way. The slit at O was started and notice boards painted showing the location of point O and of the telephone offices.
It was decided that the tape party should leave our trenches 3 hours before Zero time. The Bangalore parties 2 hours 40 minutes before Zero time, the shell hole parties 2 hours 20 minutes and the main parties 1 hour 20 minutes before Zero time.
It was also decided that from dusk until the raiding party was in position, a party of Scouts should be lying out between the lines. These Scouts sending in messages every half hour concerning the situation.
It was further decided that an Officers party should be established in OLD BOYAU TRENCH to check the raiding party as they returned in order to estimate casualties. A collecting post for prisoners also to be established at this point.

Training. Physical Drill. Performance of the raid in the presence of Divisional General and the Brigadier. Training in case of eventualities such as hostile M.G. fire and bombing. Raid practised by night. Revolver and Bludgeon practice. Patrols reconnoitring ground at 12 M.N.
Maps showing Artillery barrage in case of necessity, and disposition of parties in ENGLAND produced (see attached maps D and C respectively).

September 28th.

Cutting of slit and telephone shelters completed, telephone lines and instruments placed in position. Ramp at point C cut directly after stand down.
All corners in the Route to be taken by the raiding party marked with a White arrow, and guides established at all corners.
Decided to have 10 Stretcher bearers in front line trench South of BOYAU 4 and 6 in BACK STREET. Evacuation of wounded to take place down FORMAN STREET and WESTERN PARADE.
Four men told off to receive prisoners and booty at point C, and remove these to BACK STREET where the collecting post of six men was to be established.
Store of Bombs and a spare Lewis Gun placed in the bay just North of point C.
All receiving parties warned with regard to taking away of trophies.
An Officers party arranged to be at the junction of RAILWAY ALLEY and OLD BOYAU TRENCH to check the names of the raiding party upon their return.
Arrangements made for an Officer to take an inventory of all documents found on prisoners at La Higre. Also for all documents to be taken off the wounded passing to the dressing station.

Training.

Final practice of Raid. Physical Drill. Further training for unforeseen events happening. All stores drawn and issued. Practice with actual Torpedo both during the day and the previous night.
Practice with revolvers and bludgeons.
It was further arranged for a party of Scouts to go out into NO MANS LAND directly after stand down on the 29th. and to remain there until the raiders were in position, reporting any hostile activity to point C.

REFERENCE MAP. TRENCH MAP No. 36c NW and attached sketch.

The 2nd Bn The Manchester Regiment will carry out a raid on the
German Trenches at A.28.c.70/45 on night Septr 28-29.

GENERAL IDEA. To enter enemy's trench at X.
To move one party N to point L to capture prisoners
or get identifications.
To move one party up communication trench X to search
dug-outs if any.
To move one party up AUDLEY ALLEY X-P block it about
50 yards up.
To move one party S to block trench at point L.

AMMUNITION The Raid will be carried out by a party of 74 O.R.
and one Lewis Gun.
Commander Capt H.H.C. Brown.
Officers 2/Lt D.D.Evelin
         2/Lt J.Cully.
         2/Lt C.N. Anderson.

Parties The party will leave our trenches at point O A.28.c 51/26
in the following order:-
No 1 Party. 2/Lt C.N.Anderson, and 2 O.R.
to lay tape.
This party will leave our trenches at 9.15 P.M.
No 2 party. Commander 2/Lt J.P.N. Evans, and 4 O.R.
To place Bangalore Torpedo in position at X as soon as
the tape party returns.
No 3 party. Commander Corpl Sandy and 1 O.R. to place
Bangalore Torpedo at M.
No 4 party. Commander Sergt Day and 1 O.R. to place
Bangalore Torpedo in position at point W.
No 5 party. Commander Corpl Travis, and 5 O.R. bombers
to proceed to Shell hole A A.28.c.42/51 Also one
Lewis Gun at 10.15 P.M.
No 6 party. Commander L/Cpl Delany and 2 O.R. bombers
to proceed to Shell hole B, A.28.c.45/50. At 10.15 P.M.
they will throw 6 bombs as far down Sap L as possible
as soon as Torpedo explodes.
No 7 party. Commander Cpl Richards, and 2 O.R. P.M.
bombers to proceed to shell hole C A.28.c.51/45 at 10.15
No 8 party. Commander Sergt Whitfield and 7 O.R. to
enter enemy's trench at X immediately Bangalore Torpedo
is blown, and work S down enemy's trench to point L,
where they will establish a block. This party will leave
point O at 10.20. P.M.
No 9 party. Commander 2/Lt C.N. Anderson and 10 O.R.
will simultaneously with party 8 enter trench at X, and
work N to Sap L endeavouring to obtain prisoners, and
will establish a block just N of junction of Sap L with
main trench. This party will leave point O at 10.20 P.M.
No 10 party. Commander 2/Lt D.D. Evelin and 10 O.R.
will follow immediately behind No 8 and 9 parties, enter
trench at X and work up AUDLEY ALLEY about 50 yards and
establish block. They will endeavour to get prisoners
and will search small trenches running S from AUDLEY ALLEY.
This party will leave point O at 10.20. P.M.
No 11 party. Commander 2/Lt J.Cully, and 6 O.R. will
enter simultaneously with No. 10, and will work up
communication trench X - M about 50 yards, and establish
a block. They will examine small trench running N from
trench X - M and endeavour to obtain prisoners. This
party will leave point O at 10.20. P.M.
No 12 party. 2 O.R. will remain at point X to assist
prisoners when getting out of trench. This party will
leave point O at 10.20. P.M.
No 13 party. 4 O.R. at X to remove prisoners and wounded
across NO MANS to point O. This party will leave point O
at 10.20. P.M.

continued.

-2-

Mortars
continued.   Raid Headquarters. O.C. Raid 2 runners and 1 bugler
will be in Shell hole E A.28.c.52/57.

2/Lt Prentice 218 Field Coy. R.E. will arrange
electric leads and fuses so that 3 Bangalore Torpedoes
to be connected at point C. He will arrange for an
ordinary fuse to be attached to Torpedo at point M.
This fuse to lead to O.C. Raid at Shell hole E.
Previous to exploding, he will test all leads. He will
receive orders from O.C. Raid when to explode Torpedoes.

Artillery.   On the explosion of Bangalore Torpedoes, B/155 enfilading
section will open fire on trench A.28.c.8/7 to A.29 d
18/88.
B/155 enfilading section will open fire on communication
trench running U.E. A.20.c.90/62.
D/155 one 4.5 Howitzer will fire on point A.28.c.09/28.
In the case of the raiding party meeting strong re-
inforcements, or for any special reason a heavy barrage
will be requested for.   (Fire)

Trench Mortars   O.C. Right group 52nd. Div. Trench Mortars will arrange
for fire as follows:-
One 2" Trench Mortar will open fire on Machine Gun em-
placement at MAD POINT. A.28.c.81/17.
One 2" Trench Mortar will open fire on Trench Junction
at point A.28.c.38/71.
One 2" Trench Mortar will open fire on Machine Gun
emplacement at point D A.28.c.58/88.
One 2" Stokes Gun will barrage the enemy's front line
from E-D (A.28.c.38/88-A.28.c.59/65).
One 2" Stokes Gun will barrage the enemy's front line
from F-D?? (A.28.c.30/25-A28.c.81/17).
All these guns will open fire immediately the Bangalore
Torpedoes are exploded.
He will also arrange for two 2" Stokes Guns to be ready
to barrage the enemy's support trench on either side
of MAD POINT, if called upon by O.C. Raid.
He will also arrange for Trench Mortar on right and left
to open fire same as last time.

Vickers Guns.   O.C. No 14 Machine Gun Coy., will arrange for a gun to fire
at Machine Gun emplacement at MAD POINT A.28.c. 81/17, and
also for a gun to fire on Machine Gun emplacement at
D. A.28.c.58/88. Each of these guns will fire one belt
when the Bangalore Torpedoes are exploded, and be prepared
to silence any hostile Machine Gun which may open fire
subsequently.

Lewis Guns.   The Lewis Gun Officer will arrange for all remaining
Lewis Guns to open fire on the German parapet from
E.- T. No Lewis Gun to be in position O. of BOYAU 3.
Care must be taken not to fire on shell hole A.

Liaison.   The following will be the system of telephonic communication
Infantry. A direct line will be laid from Bn Headqrs
to point C.
Two lines will be laid as arranged from point C to Raid
Headquarters in shell hole E.
As soon as party No 2? has entered German trench at M,
two lines will be laid forward, and a station established
in the German trench at point M.
Artillery. The artillery will arrange to have a F.O.O.
with telephone at point C. He will be in constant
communication with O.C. Raid.
Trench Mortars. O.C. right group 52nd Div Trench Mortars
will arrange to have a representative with telephone at
point C. He will be in constant communication with O.C.
Raid.

continued.

The following will be the system of communication by messengers.

> Two messengers with O.C. Raid at point E.
> Two messengers at point C to communicate with Bn headquarters.
> Two messengers at point C to communicate with Trench Mortars and Vickers Guns.

Medical. The Medical Officer will arrange for stretcher bearers and dressings at the head of SAP No 4, and will arrange with Field Ambulance for the evacuation of any wounded. If any wounded prisoners, take an inventory of all papers etc., and report at once to Bn. Hdqrs.

Time. All watches will be synchronised at 6 P.M. at Bn. Hdqrs.

Dress. All hands and faces of the raiding party will be darkened. No papers, letters etc., will be carried by the raiding party, and all Regimental badges, Titles etc. will be removed. All the raiding party will wear a split sandbag over the shoulders.

ARMS.

Arms will be carried as per following detail.

Parties	No of men	Rifles	Bayonets	Revolvers	Bludgeons	Bombs Mills	Grenades Gas Att.	Torches
No 1	1 off, 5 O.R.	-	2	1	-	12	-	-
No 2	1 off, 4 O.R.	-	4	1	-	10	-	-
No 3	4 O.R.	-	-	-	-	4	-	-
No 4	2 O.R.	-	2	-	-	4	-	-
No 5	10 O.R.	2	10	2	3	93	-	-1
No 6	4 O.R.	2	4	-	2	94	-	-
No 7	4 O.R.	3	3	-	-	115	-	1
No 8	3 O.R.	4	3	2	4	96	-	2
No 9	1 off, 10 O.R.	4	12	3	6	130	2	2
No 10	1 off, 12 O.R.	6	12	3	6	144	3	3
No 11	1 off, 8 O.R.	4	8	5	4	96	-	3
No 12	4 O.R.	1	1	1	-	54	-	1
No 13	4 O.R.	4	4	-	2	48	-	1
No 14	1 off, 5 O.R.	5	5	1	-	15	-	-

Dump at C. ---------- Bombs 50 Boxes Mk X

Bombs. The chain of supply for Bombs will be as follows:-
> Dump at C. 50 Boxes.
> A party of 4 men under the orders of O.C.B. Debunk will carry Bombs forward to point E, starting 5 minutes after Zero time, where an advanced store of Bombs will be established for use of party in enemy trenches.
> In the event of the support party being called upon, there will be an extra supply of Bombs (4 boxes) at shell hole G. Any party returning to the German trenches will carry Bombs forward from dump at C.

Chain of Command.	O.C. Raid will ensure that there is a chain of command in each party.
Equipment.	O.C. Raid will render a certificate to Bn HQrs. by 6 P.M. on Septr 28th. that all stores, arms etc. as detailed have been issued to parties.
Pass word.	Pass word will be published under separate cover to all concerned.
Duration of Raid.	The raiding party will not remain in the German trenches more than 60 minutes.
Cessation of Raid.	The signal for raiding parties to retire will be "Lights Out" sounded on a bugle. Bugler will take his orders from O.C. Raid at shell hole G. This call will be taken up by another bugler at point C. Bugler at point C will take his orders from ?.?.?. Eubank.
Zero Time.	....
Gas.	A Special party of 1 N.C.O. and 3 men will be detailed by O.C. Raid to search for any trace of Gas cylinders &c.

[signatures]

DISTRIBUTION OF ORDERS.

14th Infantry Brigade.	3 Copies.
Right Group Commander 2nd Div. Artillery. 1 Copy. (MAJOR ???)	
Lieut. Braithwaite, R.A. ??? 2? Bty R.?. (?.A.Moore, Colonel)	1 Copy.
O.C. 14th Machine Gun Coy. (BRUYEN)	1 Copy.
Right Group Commander 2nd ??? Lt. Trench Mortars. (MAJOR MOORE)	1 Copy.
Captain ?.?.?. Green.	5 Copies.
Commanding Officer.	1 Copy.
Adjutant.	1 Copy.
Intelligence Officer.	1 Copy.
O.C. Bombing Company.	1 Copy.
Lewis Gun Officer.	1 Copy.
Bombing Officer.	1 Copy.

APPENDIX B.

Bombs. (Mills).	100 Boxes.
Bomb Bags.	20.
Bludgeons.	25.
Torpedoes Bangalore 2 lengths 10') 2 lengths 5')	4.
Spare detonators for same.	
Torches Electric.	12.
Tape.	200 yards.
Leads for Torpedo	600 yards.
Revolvers 22	12.
Ammunition for Revolvers.	1 Box.
Cup attachments for Grenades.	8.
Ladders.	4.
Small White Flags.	24.
Wire Cutters large.	4.
Wire Cutters mark V.	8.

PROGRAMME OF ARTILLERY SUPPORT.

APPENDIX F.

Normal Support.

On explosion of Bangalore Torpedo, batteries will fire as under:-
B/168 (enfilading section)
   A.28.c.97 to A.28.d. 19.52. Section fire 10' 360 A
B/155.
   One 4.5" Howitzer
   A.28.c.92.95 - Battery fire 20' - 120 HE.

Special support. In the event of the raiding party meeting strong reinforcements, or requiring a heavy barrage for any other reason, batteries will fire when called upon as follows:-
B/155. 1 Gun A.29.c.80/25.
       1 Gun A.29.c.75.35.
A/168. 1 Gun A.28.c.36.12.
       1 Gun A.28.c.62.25.
       1 Gun A.29.c.45.72.
       1 Gun A.28.c.36.90.
       1 Gun A.28.c.29.66.
       1 Gun A.29.c.27.18.
B/168. 1 Gun A.28.c.68.05.
       1 Gun A.28.c.90.41.
       1 Gun A.28.c.97.55.
       1 Gun A.29.c.64.70.
B/168. 2 Guns Frontal.
       1 Gun A.28.d.18.20.
       1 Gun A.28.c.75.61.
B/155. 1 Howitzer, A.29.c.09.95.
       1   "   A.28.d.00.53.
       1   "   A.28.c.85.80.)
       1   "   A.28.c.85.19.) Machine Gun emplacements

B/168 will move a section from F.24.c.60.35 to A.14.d.6.1 for this operation. The rate of fire will be as the situation demands. It is estimated that the maximum expenditure would be 25 30 A and 720 HE. There will be a R.F.A. Officer in close touch with O.C. Raid and he will be connected by telephone with the group, and will call for artillery fire through the group if required.

Distribution.

Copies to:-

   No 1. copy.   32nd Division.
   No 2   "   14th. Infantry Brigade.
   No 3   "   Battalion War Diary.
   No 4   "   Orderly Room.
   No 5   "   Capt. R.H.V.Green.
   No 6   "   Intelligence Officer.
   No 7   "   Spare Copy.

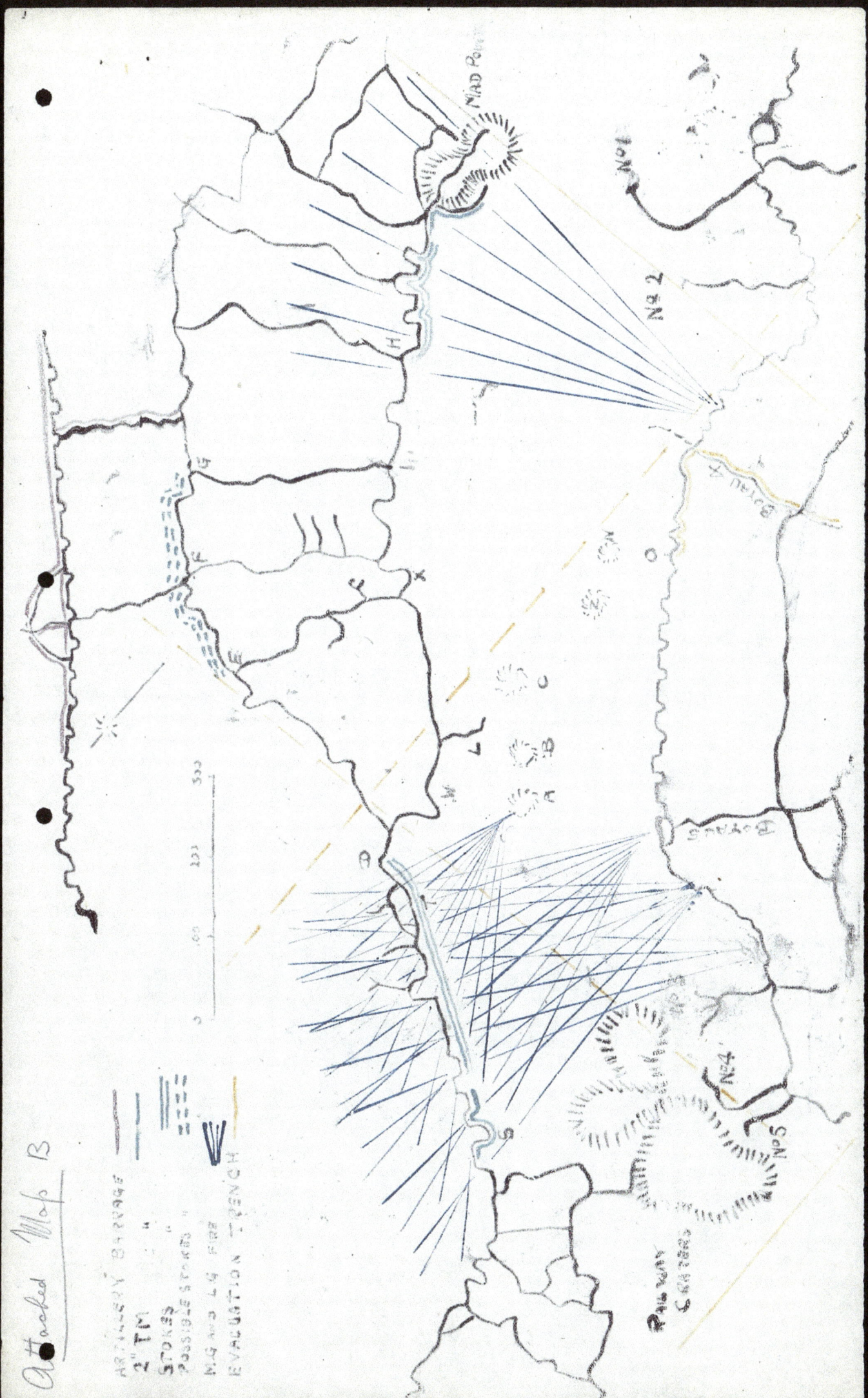

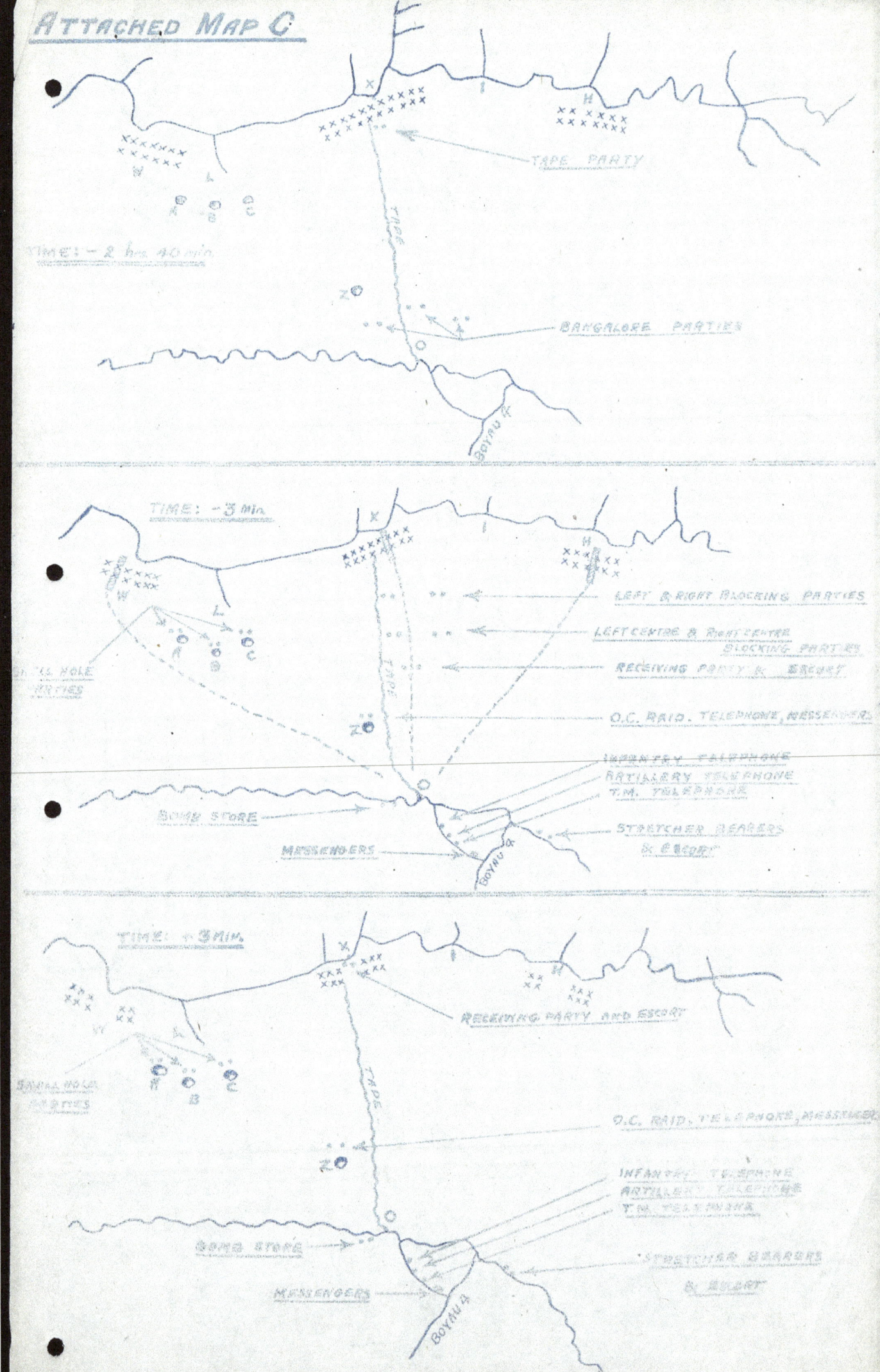

ATTACHED MAP D

Artillery barrage B shown green

14th Brigade.

32nd Division.

2nd BATTALION

THE MANCHESTER REGIMENT

OCTOBER 1 9 1 6

Army Form C. 2118

WAR DIARY
or
INTELLIGENCE SUMMARY

(Erase heading not required.)

Instructions regarding War Diaries and Intelligence Summaries are contained in F. S. Regs., Part II. and the Staff Manual respectively. Title Pages will be prepared in manuscript.

Place	Date 1916	Hour	Summary of Events and Information	Remarks and references to Appendices
CAMBRIN	Oct 1	-	The Battalion in reserve in VILLAGE LINES, CAMBRIN Section.	N.Z.H.M.
-do-	" 2		do	N.Z.H.M.
-do-	" 3		do	N.Z.H.M.
BETHUNE	" 4		The Battalion were relieved by 14th N.F.I. at 2 p.m. and marched to BETHUNE. Complete in Billets 6 p.m.	N.Z.H.M.
-do-	" 5		Battalion in billets BETHUNE. Working parties provided. The B3 took part in a Tactical Exercise.	N.Z.H.M.
-do-	" 6		do Exercise. Signalling to Aeroplanes.	N.Z.H.M.
-do-	" 7		Battalion in billets BETHUNE. do Training etc.	N.Z.H.M.
-do-	" 8		Battalion in billets BETHUNE. -do- Training etc.	N.Z.H.M.
-do-	" 9		Battalion in billets BETHUNE. -do- Training. Crater Drill.	N.Z.H.M.
BUSNES	" 10		Battalion marched to BUSNES. In billets complete 12·45 P.M.	N.Z.H.M.
	" 11		2+ O.R. reinforcements joined Battalion. Battalion in billets BUSNES. Training etc.	N.Z.H.M.
-do-	" 12		Battalion in billets BUSNES Training etc. 2/9 O.R. Reinforcement joined.	N.Z.H.M.
do	" 13		Battalion in billets BUSNES Training etc. Signalling to Aeroplanes.	N.Z.H.M.

Army Form C. 2118

WAR DIARY
or
INTELLIGENCE SUMMARY

(Erase heading not required.)

Instructions regarding War Diaries and Intelligence Summaries are contained in F.S. Regs., Part II and the Staff Manual respectively. Title Pages will be prepared in manuscript.

"2"

Place	Date 1916	Hour	Summary of Events and Information	Remarks and references to Appendices
BUSNES.	Oct 14		Battalion in billets BUSNES. Bn training etc.-	
AUCHY a la TOURS	" 15		Battalion in billets AUCHY a la TOURS. Complete in billets 12-15 P.M.-	
TERNAS.	" 16		Battalion in Billets TERNAS. Complete in billets 3-15 P.M.-	
CANETTEMONT & HONVAL	" 17		Battalion in billets CANETTEMONT & HONVAL.- Complete in billets 5-50 P.M.-	
BEAUVAL	" 18		Battalion in billets BEAUVAL. Complete in Billets 2-20 P.M.-	
do	" 19		Battalion in billets BEAUVAL. Training etc.-	
do	" 20		Battalion in billets BEAUVAL do	
WARLOY BAILLON	" 21		Battalion marched to WARLOY BAILLON. Complete in tents 2-50 P.M.-	
do	" 22		Battalion in tents WARLOY BAILLON. Training etc.-	
BRICKFIELDS AREA (ALBERT.)	" 23		Battalion marched to BRICKFIELDS AREA. (ALBERT) Battalion complete in tents and Bivouacs 3-9 P.M.	
do	" 24		Battalion in tents and Bivouacs BRICKFIELDS AREA (ALBERT.) Training etc.-	
do	" 25		-do-	21 OR Reinforcement joined
CONTAY.	" 26		Battalion marched to CONTAY complete in billets 2-12 P.M.	

WAR DIARY
or
INTELLIGENCE SUMMARY

(Erase heading not required.)

Army Form C. 2118

Instructions regarding War Diaries and Intelligence Summaries are contained in F. S. Regs., Part II. and the Staff Manual respectively. Title Pages will be prepared in manuscript.

"3"

Place	Date 1916	Hour	Summary of Events and Information	Remarks and references to Appendices
CONTAY.	Oct 27		Battalion in billets CONTAY training etc.	N.T.R.
do	28		Battalion in billets CONTAY. do	N.T.R.
do	29		Battalion in billets CONTAY. do Took part in a Tactical Scheme in conjunction with R.H.Q.	N.T.R.
do	30		Battalion in billets CONTAY. do Night operations.	N.T.R.
do	31		Battalion in billets CONTAY. do Took part in a Tactical scheme in conjunction with R.H.Q.	N.T.R.

31/10/16. N. Luxmoore, Lt.Colonel,
       o/ Manchester Regt.

14th Brigade.

32nd Division.

2nd BATTALION

THE MANCHESTER REGIMENT

NOVEMBER 1 9 1 6

Appendices attached:-

    Report on Operations & Lessons Learnt.

Army Form C. 2118

WAR DIARY or INTELLIGENCE SUMMARY

(Erase heading not required.)

"1" of "2" MANCHESTER REGT.   Vol 2 8

Place	Date 1916	Hour	Summary of Events and Information	Remarks and references to Appendices
Contay	Nov 1st to Nov 10th		Battalion in Billets CONTAY. Training etc.	
Contay	Nov 11th		Battalion in Billets CONTAY. Training etc. Working parties provided	
Contay	Nov 12th		Battalion in Billets CONTAY. Training etc.	
Bouzincourt	Nov 13th		Battalion moved to BOUZINCOURT.	
Bouzincourt	Nov 14th		Battalion in tents and huts BOUZINCOURT. 300 men working party provided.	
Mailly Maillet	Nov 15		Battalion moved to Bivouac Field, MAILLY MAILLET Proceeding from there at 11PM to trenches relieving 1st Borders Regt in SERRE Trench. Half R Coy and JHQ in reserve in WHITE CITY, VALLADE and TOURNEA trenches. Relief completed about 7 AM 16th inst	
Trenches	Nov 16		Battalion in trenches as above	

WAR DIARY

INTELLIGENCE SUMMARY

(Erase heading not required.) of 2" MANCHESTER REGT

Army Form C. 2118

Place	Date 1916	Hour	Summary of Events and Information	Remarks and references to Appendices
Trenches	Nov 17		Battalion in trenches to 16th. Bombing attack by the enemy who driven off with casualties. 43" H.Q. (advanced) was taken up in SERRE YARD. Heavy bombardment of our British lines by enemy in reply to our barrage, while an attack took place.	During the two days of the Trenches Casualties were:— Officers: 9 missing, 2 wounded. O.R.: 12 killed, 110 wounded, 252 missing.
Trenches	Nov 18		Bn in trenches. LAGER ALLEY attacked & taken	
Trenches	Nov 19		Battalion in trenches	
Trenches	Nov 20		Battalion relieved by 1st Dorset Regt. moving back to hutts at MAILLY MAILLET.	
MAILLY MAILLET	Nov 21		Battalion in hutts MAILLY MAILLET. Received orders to move to trenches and relieved 1st Dorset Regt in reserve trenches. Moved from MAILLY MAILLET 5 p.m.	
Trenches			Battalion in Trenches	

Army Form C. 2118

WAR DIARY or INTELLIGENCE SUMMARY

(Erase heading not required.) of 2" MANCHESTER REGT

"3"

Instructions regarding War Diaries and Intelligence Summaries are contained in F.S. Regs., Part II. and the Staff Manual respectively. Title Pages will be prepared in manuscript.

Place	Date 1916	Hour	Summary of Events and Information	Remarks and references to Appendices
Francheres	Nov 23rd		Battalion relieved by 2nd Border Regt and moved to billets MAILLY MAILLET. 35 O.R's reinforcements joined Battalion this day.	Appx 1-5
Terramesnil	Nov 24th		Battalion moved to TERRAMESNIL. In billets.	Appx 6
Doullens	Nov 25th		Battalion marched to billets at DOULLENS.	Appx 6
Halloy-L-Pernois	Nov 26		Battalion marched to billets at HALLOY-L-PERNOIS. Training etc	Appx 6
do	Nov 27/30		-do-	Appx 6/10
			360 O.R. Reinforcements joined the Battalion this day. 30 Nov 1916	
			A detailed account of the Battalion's movements from Oct 10th to Nov 27th is attached.	

G. Alfred Thomas Lt & A/adjt for

Capt Commanding 2nd 10. The Manchester Regt.

BATTLE OF THE ANCRE.

OPERATIONS UNDERTAKEN BY 2ND. BATTALION THE MANCHESTER REGIMENT.

Reference attached Maps.

1916.

Octr 10th. Battalion left BETHUNE for the South. Whether the Battalion was for the SOMME or ARRAS was unknown. Arrived BUSNES ON THE 10th. and remained until the 15th.

Octr 15th. to 21st. Battalion marched South to BEAUVAL via RAIMBERT, TERNAS and CANNETTEMENT. On the 19th. the Battalion was due to move from BEAUVAL to WARLOY and billeting parties went forward. Arriving at WARLOY they found that a large attack was due for the 21st inst., and that the Division was to move up in support. This however was postponed later in the day, due to the wet weather, and the Brigade was turned back to BEAUVAL. On the 20th. the move was again postponed for a day and the Brigade moved into WARLOY on the 21st inst. Upon this day it was freezing hard and the Battalion moved into tents.

Octr 23rd to Nov 13th. On the 23rd inst., the Brigade moved to the BRICKFIELD AREA at ALBERT. This area consisted of a stretch of muddy waste on which bivouacs had to be put up. Upon arriving here it was found that the Brigade had to move up the next day to some open ground near OVILLERS where they would bivouac for the night, and that the attack would take place on the 25th. On the evening of the 23rd. the rain commenced again, and the attack was again put off. On the 24th. the ground around OVILLERS and tracks to the valley North of MOUQUET FARM were reconoitred. The ground was found to be completely broken up by shell fire, and thick in mud. Any tracks that existed consisted of single file goat tracks winding in and out and round Craters. It would have been impossible to move a battalion at a greater rate than 1 mile per hour.
On the 25th. the attack was again put off due to the rain.
War Stores had now been collected together on the BRICKFIELDS ready for the attack. On the 26th. it was again decided that by higher authorities that the attack would be postponed for several days, and the Brigade was moved back to the CONTAY area, the Battalion being billeted in CONTAY. On the 30th. the attack was put off indefinitely on the chance of fine weather or frost arriving.
During their stay in CONTAY the Brigade practised their role in the attack.
Scheme of attack.
From previous attacks it had been found that the enemy were often on the run, and that had fresh troops been at hand a far more decisive victory might have been obtained.
It was this particular role that the 32nd. Division was to perform in the general attack.
The main role of the attack was as follows:-
(Reference K-M Map.)
South of the ANCRE the British line ran from SCHWABEN REDOUBT through STUFF REDOUBT, along RESINA Trench to LE SARS.
(RESINA Trench was taken on 21st. inst. as a kicking off trench.)
North of the ANCRE the British were in their original front line.
The 2nd. Corps consisting of the 39th., 19th., 18th., and 4th. Canadian Divisions was to attack South of the Ancre with the 4th. Army.(attacking WARLENCOURT) on their right

continued.

"2"

and the 5th. Corps, attacking North of the ANCRE, on their left.
First objective of the 2nd. Corps was a line running from
R.14.a.55 through R.15.a.and b. to GRANDECOURT trench and along
this trench to CREST TRENCH in R.12.a. From here the 4th.
Canadians were to form a line running through R.12.a, M.7.d.,
M.14.a to M.14.d.4.8.
The second objective consisted of a line just South of the
ANCRE running through R.8.c. and d., R.9.a and b. to the
first objective at R.6.b.5.0.
The second objective of the Canadians was a line from M.7.b.0.0.
through M.8.a. and b. to M.2.d.95.25. at which point they
joined the 4th. Army.
The third objective consisted of a line North of the ANCRE
running through R.8.c.a. and b., R.3.c.and d., R.4.a and b. to
MIRAUMONT, round the outskirts of MIRAUMONT through R.4.b,
L.34.d and b., L.35.a and d., back to R.5.b.5.4.
The fifth Corps by this time were supposed to have reached a
line running from BEAUREGARD DOVECOTE in L.28.c. through
L.27.c and d., L.26.c and d., L.25.c and d., SERRE to LUKE COPSE.
Upon Y night the 32nd Division was to move up to the OVILLERS
area, Divisional H.Q. and the 97th. Brigade being at USNA HILL,
the 14th. and 96th. brigades being bivouaced in the open N.W.
of OVILLERS. Upon the second Corps obtaining their second
objective the 14th. and 96th. Brigades were to move forward
to R.27 and from there up the valley to the ravines in
R.10 and 11. Upon the third objective being gained the 96th.
Brigade were to move forward and take the village of PYS, the
14th. moving to the ravine in R.5.b and d. Upon PYS being
captured the 14th. Brigade move forward and take the village
of IRLES. Upon the village of IRLES being captured the 97th
Brigade were to move forward and take ACHIET-LE-Petit.
TANKS were to operate with the 2nd. and 5th Corps for taking the
first and second objective.

Whilst at rest in CONTAY the method of attacking IRLES and the
artillery formation most advisable were discussed and practised.
The Brigade was to attack in three waves; the 15th H.L.I. forming
the first wave, would take RESURRECTION TRENCH on the outskirts of
IRLES. The 2nd Manchesters and 5th Royal Scots forming the second
wave, would take and mop up the village. The 1st Dorsets forming
the third wave, would pass through the village, and form strong
points N.E. of the village.
Due to the bad ground and to the fact of the dumps being so far
back one Coy from each Battalion would probably have to be
withdrawn for carrying purposes. The attack was to be done under
cover of a "CREEPING BARRAGE" advancing under cover of this barrage
was practiced with the Drums beating the Barrage. It was decided
for the Battalion to attack in four waves, two Coys side by side
in the first two waves, and two Coys side by side in the third
and fourth waves. In Artillery formation each Coy was to move
in a rhomboid formation of platoons. This formation was to be
kept for as long as possible.
It was later decided that as the left flank was so exposed one
Coy. should be taken from the third and fourth waves and be
echeloned on the left as a flank guard.
By the 12th Novr. it had been decided to abandon the general attack
due to the almost impossible ground under the weather conditions,
and to attack small objectives at a time.
Modified Scheme.
In accordance with this new scheme the first objective of the
second Corps was a line running from REGINA TRENCH at R.21.a.5.7.
through R.14.d.o.o. along ANSA LINE through the MILL to the
STATION at Q.18.b.7.4.
The first objective of the Fifth Corps was a line running from
the outskirts of BEAUCOURT in R.7.c along BEAUMONT, FRANKFORT
and MUNICH TRENCH to the outskirts of SERRE and thence along
SERHEB ROAD to our original line at CHASSEURS HEDGE.
ZERO day was chosen for Novr 13th.

* R.10.a, R.4.d round PETIT MIRAUMONT
of R.5.c. a and b.

continued.

"3"

Novr 13th. On the 13th. the Battalion moved to BOUZINCOURT where they were accomodated in tents. During the march in and throughout the day prisoners were seen to be pouring through and it appeared as though the morning attack had been a success. Late in the evening information was received that the second Corps had obtained their objective, the Fifth Corps had taken part of theirs but were held up in front of SERRE. In all 4000 prisoners had been taken.
The objective gained is shown in Red on the attacked Map.

Novr 14th. On the 14th. the village of SERRE was again attacked but without success.
All wounded coming back were full of praise for our "Creeping Barrage"

Novr 15th. Early on the morning of the 15th. it was rumoured that the Battalion was to move to BEAUMONT HAMEL and attack the following morning, the Commanding Officer was sent for to go over the Trenches in front of this village.
During the morning the plans were altered and upon the Commanding Officer's return at 1.30. P.M. he found the Battalion about to move off to ENGLEBELMER where they were to await instruction. The Commanding Officer was then sent for to see the trenches just South of SERRE.
Arriving at ENGLEBELMER the Brigade received instructions to proceed to MAILLY MALLET. The Brigade arrived at this village at 5 P.M. and were bivouaced in a field.
It was by this time dark and very cold and information was received that the Brigade were to rest there for about three hours for hot tea before moving up to the trenches, and that they were to attack at dawn. Hot tea was served up here, and the men attempted to make themselves as comfortable as was possible.
At <u>9 P.M.</u> preliminary instructions were received that guides were to be met at 11 P.M. and the Battalion would move up to LAGER ALLEY. Brigade war stores had not yet arrived from the BRICKFIELDS but were hourly expected.
At <u>11 P.M.</u> the Commanding Officer returned with the news that we were to move at once in rear of the 15th., H.L.I., One Coy of the Dorsets was to move up to our original front line, the remainder of the Dorsets and 5th. Royal Scots were to remain behind.

Novr 16th As no War stores had arrived the Battalion reserve of Bombs was taken from the ammunition carts, and picks and shovels from the tool carts.
Close outside MAILLY the Battalion moved into a communication trench. This trench was close upon 2 miles long and was continually crossed by traffic. As a result of this upon arriving at our original front line it was found that two Coys had lost touch. From this point on the journey had to be made across the open.
As it was now 4 A.M. and would be daylight in an Hour it was essential to push on.
The ground across NO MANS LAND was so broken up with shell fire that it formed a series of crumbling craters. Over this the Battalion had to move in single file. Several other columns were met moving in different directions. Unfortunately at this time the enemy chose to put up a barrage upon NO MANS LAND. Added to these difficulties, the guide was found to be of the type that say they know the way but do not.
Unfortunately a shell bursting in the leading platoon of the middle Coy caused that Coy to lose touch, and also the last. Due to the combination of these circumstances it was discovered upon reaching the enemys original front line that except for the H.Q. Officers only two Officers and 84 men remained. As it was now very near daylight it was essential to move forward to the position occupied by the Berkshires. This position was eventually reached at 5.15. A.M.
As so few men had reached the trench it was only possible

"4"

to relieve half the Berkshires, and the ~~Colonel~~ Commanding Officer and Adjutant moved back to Battalion H.Q. in our original support line. The Berkshires were unable to move out due to it then being daylight.

At 9 A.M. the position of the remaining three and a half Coys. was found. Two platoon of the rear Coy. ("A"Coy) had been stopped in our original front line, the remainder were in the enemy's original lines but were unable to move during daylight. Arrangements were made for the remainder of "B" Coy and "C" Coy. to move up as soon as it became dark to complete the relief of the Berkshires. "D" Coy and half "A" Coy. were to remain where they were until further orders. This information was taken back to Battalion H.Q. The ground was found to be so bad that though H.Q. was little more than 1000 yards back it was impossible, even over the top with a barrage behind you to cover the distance under 1½ hours. During the night of the 16th. a tape was laid ac across NO MANS LAND to indicate the direction of the front line, and an attempt was made to obtain telephonic communication. No sooner however, was a line laid than it was broken by the barrage.

On the morning of the 17th. it was heard that we were to attack on the 18th. On our left would be the 15th. H.L.I. and on our right the 97th Brigade. The 1st. Dorsets who had moved up the night before to the enemys original front line, would be in support.

Accordingly, the ~~Colonel~~ Commanding Officer and Intelligence Officer moved forward to advanced H.Q. in LAGER ALLEY, the trench held by our two Coys, leaving the Adjutant behind at the rear H.Q. to organize supplies.

H.Q. had been informed the previous day that due to heavy shelling "D" Coy and half "A" Coy had moved to another trench with more cover. The location of these Coys was therefore not known. Upon arriving in LAGER ALLEY an attempt was therefore made to find these Coys. Eventually it was discovered that they had not moved. The trench in which these Coys were situated had no cover, and the men had therefore scratched holes in the sides with their entrenching tools. Though subjected to a four hours bombardment directly enfilading them, and though they had suffered 50 casualties, these Coys had removed their wounded to the nearest dressing station and had patiently remained in their exposed position awaiting orders.

These two Coys were moved forward to LAGER ALLEY.

At about 2 P.M. it was discovered, through an Army Intelligence Of Officer and various conflicting incidents, that we did not occupy LAGER ALLEY, but SERRE trench from a point near 39 to point 95 (Redan Map) The 15th. H.L.I. who reported they held the line running N.W. from point 95 were found to be holding a line running N.W. from 83.

At 4 P.M. preliminary orders were received to the effect we were to attack and take the enemy trench running from point 39 to 36 and then send forward a strong post to the point 71. Close touch was to be obtained with the K.O.Y.L.I. on our right who would take MUNICH Trench and then push forward to FRANKFORT TRENCH. The H.L.I. on our left would take first the trench from 17 to 88 with one Coy which would then push forward and prolong our line to the left.

Zero time was fixed for 6.10. A.M. and the creeping barrage would commence at 6 A.M.

We were also informed by a message that 5000 Bombs would come up with rations that night.

Rain had fallen the previous night and the trenches, which before had been very difficult were now almost impassable. The enemy snipers had commenced to range our men crossing the open.

It was found that due to these conditions, and due to losing the way it took from three to six hours to get a message back to the rear H.Q. Very few of these messages went through, and on an average only one messenger out of six returned. Similar condition existed for getting messages to the H.Q. of the H.L.I. and

continued.

"5"

Dorsets which were in the enemys original front line. These messages took from two to four hours.

Nov 18th At 4.30. A.M. the Brigade orders for the attack arrived. Dispite urgent messages, though the rations had arrived, no bombs had arrived. Urgent messages were again sent.
5 A.M. a message was received to draw flares from the H.L.I. H.Q. An officer and six men of "A" Coy were sent at once to draw these. This party eventually reached the H.L.I. H.Q. soon after 6 AM. but were unable to return due to the enemy barrage
At 11 P.M. on the previous night orders were received to take LAGER ALLEY as soon as possible, in order to use it as a pushing off trench.
This was done at 12 midnight, and a bombing post was established close up to MUNICH TRENCH.
At 5.15 A.M. information was received that the enemy had pushed back our bombing post in LAGER ALLEY.
This was immediately taken again.
at 5.30. A.M. the Battalion moved into position in LAGER ALLEY. No bombs had arrived and it was found that the whole Battalion had in all 150 bombs.
The Battalion was to attack in two waves "D" Coy (on the right) "C" Foy and "B" Coy being in line. "A" Coy (20 men all told) was to act as a support to "D" Coy. One platoon of "B" Coy was to attack point 39 from SERRE TRENCH.
At 5.45 A.M. information was received from the officer commanding the Coy of 15th. H.L.I. which had moved up into SERRE TRENCH for the purpose of attacking on our left, that there were some bombs at his old Coy H.Q. The remainder of A Coy was therefore sent at once to try and obtain these bombs.
At 6 A.M. the barrage commenced, the enemy barrage answering within a very few minutes.
at 6.10. A.M. the remainder of ""A" Coy returned with the information that there were no bombs at the H.L.I. Coy H.Q. As it was then too late for these men to join in the attack they were sent to garrison LAGER ALLEY and gain any information of the attack.
At 6.50. A.M. a report came through to H.Q. that our men had entered the enemys trench.
At 7 A.M. and urgent message came down the trench asking for bombs.
At 7.25 A.M. news was received that the H.L.I. had been unable to enater the enemy trench on account of the wire, and that they had withdrawn to SERRE TRENCH.
At 7.40.A.M. information was received that point 39 had been entered and was found to be full of wire. Due to a Machine gun being trained on this point, and to the lack of Bombs, the party were unable to hold the point and had been forced to withdraw. The remainder of our men were reported to be in the enemys lines but it was doubtful whether they would be able to hold out due to the lack of bombs.
At 8 A.M. a message was sent to the K.O.Y.L.I. explaining our position, and asking for Bombs.
At 8.20. A.M. it was rumoured that we were still in the enemy trench, but that point 39 could not be taken. A wounded sergt. of the K.O.Y.L.I. stated that his Regt. was through in some places but held up in others.
At 9.15. A.M. a party was pushed along LAGER TRENCH to attempt to reach MUNICH TRENCH. This party ran up against a strong hostile Bombing party close to MUNICH TRENCH. This party reported sounds of heavy bombing in the enemy trench and signs of a burning Dugout.
At 9.30. A.M. it was reported that the enemy were counter attacking MUNICH TRENCH.
At 9.40..A.M. a bombing block was put in LAGER ALLEY near point 56. The enemy were now reported to be advancing across the open (1 Battalion strong) towards point 39 from the N.N.E.

continued.

"6"

At 9.45 A.M. Urgent reports on the situation were sent to the Brigade via H.L.I. H.Q. and supports asked for, for a third time.
At 10.45 A.M. 2 platoons of the Dorsets arrived with Bombs, and were placed to hold Bombing posts in LAGER ALLEY, and so defend SERRE TRENCH from counter attacks.
At 11.45 A.M. one Coy of the Dorsets arrived with bombs. This Coy took over the garrison of SERRE TRENCH.
At this time 200 of the enemy were seen working across the open towards SERRE TRENCH from the N.N.E. These retired when fired upon with Machine Guns and Lewis Guns.
At 3.30. P.M. a man of "C" Coy who went over the top with the Battalion managed to crawl back giving the following information:-
"The Battalion left the assembly trenches at the commencement of the barrage and proceeded to the enemys trench with very few casualties. The enemy trench was rushed, and the mopping up of the dugouts commenced. Soon after our men entered the trench they were fired upon by snipers and Machine guns from the flank. Simultaneously an hostile bombing party advanced from the other flank. A batch of prisoners was taken and sent over the top as we had no men to spare for escort. One large dugout was set on fire by our bombs and soon became a raging furnace. Due to no supply of bombs having come up the battalion had been compelled to go over the parapet with only 150. As a result of this they were unable to drive back the enemy bombing party, and were forced back fighting on to the burning dugout and the enemy snipers. One Lewis Gun which reached the enemy trench was got up on to the Parados and this gun managed to put the enemy Machine Gun out of action."
This informant stated that he was the last man standing in the trench when he managed to crawl out, and that he had to take cover in shell holes until he could reach our trench. During the night a patrol was sent out to investigate the trench taken and to listen

Novr 19th for signs of our men. This patrol reported no signs.
At 8 A.M. on the 19th. 26 hours after the attack a message was received stating where bombs could be drawn from.
At 2 P.M. a wounded K.O.Y.L.I. Officer reported at our H.Q. with the following information:-
"Both Battalions went over together at the commencement of the bombardment keeping good touch with one another. The first trench reached by his Company (on the K.O.Y.L.I. Left) was unoccupied and they passed over. From this point his company made an almost left form, and went across a valley to a small wood, where they charged a German trench, taking a number of Prisoners, who were sent back. From here Lt Davidson commanding our right Coy. ("D" Coy) could be seen advancing on, further on the left, and touch between the two was lost. The informant was wounded and managed to find his way back during the night.

Novr 20th.
At 4 A.M. on the 20th. the remains of the Battalion were relieved by the Dorsets and found their way back to MAILLY.
During the whole of the operations touch with the rear could only be maintained by runners who did most gallant work. It was found that messages took from 4 to 7 hours to get through and that the supply of messengers required on the work was exceedingly large. The wounded could not be evacuated either by day or night, and SERRE TRENCH itself contained some 60 cases some of whom had been there for over 6 days.

Novr 21st. On the 21st. the Battalion (6 Officers and 150 men) were moved back to the enemy original front line as a support.

Novr 23rd On the 23rd. The Brigade was relieved and moved back to MAILLY.

Nov 24th On the 24th. The Division moved back to the training area.

N. Luxmoore Lieut Colonel
Commanding 2nd. Bn. The Manchester Regiment.

2. MANCHESTER REGT

Lessons to be learnt from recent operations.

----

1. When the weather is bad and trenches almost impassable more time should be allowed for orders to reach Battalions. Then the objective can be thoroughly impressed on all ranks and more time is available for collecting bombs etc.

2. In bad weather the number of messengers must be increased. It was found that once a man was sent on a message he did not return for a considerable time. Messengers should not be expected to return at once after a long and dangerous journey across NO MANS LAND.

3. The pigeons were useless on account of getting their wings damp and covered in mud.

4. The difficulty of finding ones way across NO MANS LAND might be minimised by the first Battalion laying a tape across during the first night *after capture of enemy's trench.*

5. The trench (SERRE TRENCH) was handed over to me as LAGER ALLEY. It is as well to check trenches taken over after capture from the enemy by compass bearing.

6. Trenches are often so difficult to trace in an advance that it might be a help to impress on all ranks the distance to be traversed from the point of advance.

N. Luxmoore, Lieut Colonel,
Commanding 2nd. Bn. The Manchester Regiment.

14th Brigade.

32nd Division.

2nd BATTALION

THE MANCHESTER REGIMENT

DECEMBER 1 9 1 6

WAR DIARY or INTELLIGENCE SUMMARY

Army Form C. 2118

Vol 29
2nd MANCHESTER REGT

Place	Date 1916	Hour	Summary of Events and Information	Remarks and references to Appendices
HALLOY les PERNOIS	Sept 1		Battalion in billets HALLOY les PERNOIS. Training etc.	H.J.S.
do	2		-do-	H.J.S.
do	3		-do- Company Route Marches	H.J.S.
do	4		-do-	H.J.S.
do	5		-do- 3+ O.R. Reinforcements joined B℠	H.J.S.
do	6		-do-	H.J.S.
do	7		-do-	H.J.S.
do	8		-do-	H.J.S.
do	9		-do-	H.J.S.
do	10		-do-	H.J.S.
do	11		-do-	H.J.S.

Army Form C. 2118

WAR DIARY
or
INTELLIGENCE SUMMARY
(Erase heading not required.)

"D" 2nd MANCHESTER REGT.

Place	Date 1916	Hour	Summary of Events and Information	Remarks and references to Appendices
HALLOY les PERNOIS	Dec. 12		Bn. in Billets HALLOY-les-PERNOIS. Training etc.- 60 O.R.s reinforcements joined Bn. Battalion Route March	H.J.G.
	13		do	H.J.G.
	14		do	H.J.G.
	15		do 15 O.R.s reinforcements joined Bn. Attack practice	H.J.G.
	16		do 4 O.R. reinforcements joined Bn.	H.J.G.
	17		do	H.J.G.
	18		do	H.J.G.
	19		do Battalion Route March.	H.J.G.
	20		do	H.J.G.
	21		do Bn. Parade Tactical scheme.	H.J.G.
	22		do	H.J.G.

WAR DIARY or INTELLIGENCE SUMMARY

(Erase heading not required.)

2nd MANCHESTER REGT

Place	Date 1916	Hour	Summary of Events and Information	Remarks and references to Appendices
HALLOY les PERNOIS	Dec 23		Bn. in billets HALLOY-les-PERNOIS. Training etc. Brigade Route March.	H.H.
do	24		do	H.H.
do	25		do (CHRISTMAS DAY.)	H.H.
do	26		do	H.H.
do	27		do Tactical scheme in conjunction with Aeroplane.	H.H.
do	28		do Battalion Route March	H.H.
do	29		do	H.H.
do	30		do	H.H.
do	31		do	H.H.

H. J. Griffiths Capt.
Commanding 2nd Bn. The Manchester Regt.

Army Form C. 2118

WAR DIARY
or
INTELLIGENCE SUMMARY
(Erase heading not required.)

2 Manchester Regt
1 of 30

Instructions regarding War Diaries and Intelligence Summaries are contained in F.S. Regs., Part II. and the Staff Manual respectively. Title Pages will be prepared in manuscript.

Place	Date	Hour	Summary of Events and Information	Remarks and references to Appendices
Pernois les Hallon	May 1 1917		Bn in Billets PERNOIS-LES-HALLOY. Training etc. Practical scheme for the attack of PERNOIS in conjunction with aeroplane.	Nil
-"-	2		Bn in Billets PERNOIS-LES-HALLOY. Training etc.	N.T. Hd
-"-	3		do	N.T. Hd
-"-	4		do	N.T. Hd
-"-	5		do	N.T. Hd
Beauval	6		Bn marched to BEAUVAL in Bus. completed 1-15 P.M.	N.T. Hd
-"-	7		Bn in tents BEAUVAL.	N.T. Hd
Bertrancourt / Bks Courcelles	8		Bn proceeded by Bus to BERTRINCOURT marching to COURCELLES. Complete in billets 6-25 PM Relieved 15th HLI as Brigade Reserve.	N.T. Hd
Courcelles	9		Bn in Billets COURCELLES.	N.T. Hd
-"-	10		Bn in Billets COURCELLES. Working parties provided.	N.T. Hd

Army Form C. 2118

WAR DIARY
or
INTELLIGENCE SUMMARY
(Erase heading not required.)

Instructions regarding War Diaries and Intelligence Summaries are contained in F.S. Regs., Part II. and the Staff Manual respectively. Title Pages will be prepared in manuscript.

Place	Date 1917	Hour	Summary of Events and Information	Remarks and references to Appendices
Courcelles	Aug 11		Bn in Billets COURCELLES. Working parties provided	N.T. Ffd
Trenches	12		A & B Coys relieved 15th H.L.I. in C.2. Sect. A Coy in front line. B Coy in support - C & D Coys in reserve Billets COURCELLES. Working Parties provided. Relief complete 9.50 p.m.	N.T. Ffd. N.T. Ffd. N.T. Ffd
do	13		Bn two Coys bgn in trenches. B Coy moved to Attack in BUS. C Coy in Billets COURCELLES. Working parties provided.	N.T. Ffd N.T. Ffd
do	14		do	N.T. Ffd N.T. Ffd N.T. Ffd
Courcelles	15		A & B Coys relieved by 15th H.L.I. returning to Billets COURCELLES. Complete in Billets 2.30 P.M.	N.T. Ffd
do	16		Bn in Billets COURCELLES. Working parties provided.	N.T. Ffd
do	17		HQ Bn less A & B Coys returned the 15th H.L.I. in C.2. subsector. C Coy from SERRE ROAD to Junction of WICKER DELAUNEY trenches both inclusive. will posts at (1) CRATER on SERRE ROAD (2) TANK on SERRE ROAD. continued	N.T. Ffd

1875 W+. W593/826 1,000,000 4/15 J.B.C. & A. A.D.S.S./Forms/C. 2118.

Army Form C. 2118

WAR DIARY
or
INTELLIGENCE SUMMARY

(Erase heading not required.)

" 3 "

Place	Date	Hour	Summary of Events and Information	Remarks and references to Appendices
Courcelles & Tarnelles	Jany 17 (Cont)		D Coy from junction of WICKER & DELAUNAY trenches exclusive to BLENAU AVENUE inclusive, will Post at road of FLAG AVENUE. Supports at LYCEUM & LEGEND Trench & SACKVILLE STREET. BASIN WOOD & LA SIGNAY FARM in supports. A & B Coys in reserve in Bullets COURCELLES	N.E. front
-"-	18		Coys in trenches. A & B Coys in Bullets COURCELLES	N.E. front
-"-	19 20		A & B Coys in Bullets COURCELLES. C & D Coy in trenches. Relieved by 1/4 Northumberland Fus.	N.E. front N.E. front
BUS	21		Bt in Bullets Cour CELLES Bt marched to Bullets at BUS	N.E. front
Bullets Camp	22		Bt Marched to Huts BOLTON CAMP	N.E. front
Trenches	23		Bt marched to Trenches taking up right subsector BEAUMONT HAMEL. Relieved 2nd K.O.Y.L.I.	N.C. front
"	24/25/26		Bt in trenches BEAUMONT HAMEL	N.E. front
Bertrancourt	27		Bt relieved by 5/6 Royal Scots. Marched to Huts BERTRANCOURT.	N.E. front
-"-	28/29/30		Bt in Huts BERTRANCOURT. Working parties furnished	N.E. front
Trenches	31		Bt marched to trenches relieving 1st Gords in left subsection	N.E.

N. Luxmoore
Lt Colonel
Commanding 2nd Bn Manchester Regt

S E C R E T.

BATTALION DEFENCE SCHEME.

Reference Trench Map.

Jany 17/1917

General.
The Battalion holds the left sub-sector of PEPPER sector. The said sub-sector is known as C.2.

Boundaries.
The Battalion frontage is on a basis of a two Company frontage with outpost line, and boundaries are:-
RIGHT FRONT COY. SERRE ROAD to junction of WICKER and DELAUNEY trenches, both inclusive.
LEFT FRONT COY. Junction of WICKER and DELAUNEY trenches exclusive, to BLENEAU inclusive.

OUTPOSTS and POSTS.
Right front Coy.
    (1). Crater on South Side of SERRE ROAD at K25.a.2.3.
    (2) TANK on SERRE ROAD.
    (3) WOLF TRENCH K34.b.6.3.
Left front Coy.
    At junction of BLENEAU and old BRITISH FRONT LINE at K29.c.8.4.
Support Coy. will garrison SACKVILLE STREET and LEGEND TRENCH.
Reserve Coy.
    Two platoons LA SIGNY FARM. Two platoons BASIN WOOD.
Lewis Guns.
    Four guns are with the right front Coy.
    Three guns are with the left front Company.
    One gun is in an emplacement in SACKVILLE STREET.

S.A.A. and BOMBS.

Stores are situate as shewn in ske[tch] attached.

ENEMY ATTACK.

The outpost line will be held at all cost even if the flanks be turned and it must be distinctly understood by all ranks that on no account must any retirement take place from any line.

ATTACK OR THREATENED ATTACK.

In case of attack or threatened attack, front line Company Commanders will:-

(1) Communicate with artillery and ask for barrage.
(2) Get into touch with Battalion Head Quarters and report situation from time to time.
(3) Put C.S.M. in charge of S.A.A. and Bombs and detail a carrying party to act under his orders.

The post on WOLF will move up and reinforce WICKER.

On the order to STAND BY being given, the Support Coy. will move to the rig[ht] in SACKVILLE STREET and LEGEND making room for the RESERVE COY. who will form up in SACKVILLE.

On the order to **MOVE** being given the support and reserve coys. will move up across the open to the support of the left and right support Companies respectively, taking care to carry up with them supply of S.A.A. and Bombs.

ALL men engaged away from their Company and all working and ration parties will report to the nearest Officer.

Should he enemy succeed in capturing an outpost position or penetrating the front line, an immediate counter attack would be launched.

BLOCKS will be constructed in all C.T's leading to the front line as far forward as circumstances permit.

S.O.S. The S.O.S. will be sent by rocket and every other means available.

CODE. The B.A.B. Code as corrected will be used.

B.H.Q. will remain in LEGEND.

The Battalion Police will establish post of two men at the junction of C.T's with LEGEND.

WAR DIARY
or
INTELLIGENCE SUMMARY

Army Form C. 2118

2 Manchester Regt Vol 31

Place	Date 1917	Hour	Summary of Events and Information	Remarks and references to Appendices
TRENCHES	Feby 1		Battalion in Trenches Left Subsector. Headquarters WHITE CITY.	pps
do	" 2		do	pps
do	" 3		The Battalion was relieved by the 5/6th Royal Scots and marched to Billets (Huts) at BERTRANCOURT.	pps
BERTRANCOURT	" 4		Battalion in huts (Huts) BERTRANCOURT.	pps
do	" 5		do Working parties provided.	pps
Trenches	" 6		The Battalion relieved the 51st Royal Scots in the Left Subsector. Headquarters WHITE CITY.	pps
do	" 7		Battalion in trenches as above	pps
do	" 8		Battalion relieved by 5/6th Royal Scots in Left Subsector and marched to Billets (Huts) BERTRANCOURT.	pps
BERTRANCOURT	" 9		Battalion in Billets (Huts) BERTRANCOURT.	pps
do	" 10		do	pps
TRENCHES	" 11		Battalion relieved 51st Royal Scots in Left Subsector. Headquarters WHITE CITY.	pps

Philip Stephens
Major

Army Form C. 2118

WAR DIARY
or
INTELLIGENCE SUMMARY
(Erase heading not required.)

"2"

Instructions regarding War Diaries and Intelligence Summaries are contained in F. S. Regs., Part II. and the Staff Manual respectively. Title Pages will be prepared in manuscript.

Place	Date 1917	Hour	Summary of Events and Information	Remarks and references to Appendices
TRENCHES	12th		Battn in Trenches. Left subsector Headquarters WHITE CITY.	JD
MAILLY MAILLET	13		Bn relieved by 1/4th Duke of Wellingtons West Riding Regt. Marched to billets MAILLY MAILLET.	JD
do	14		Bn in billets MAILLY MAILLET	JD
LOUVENCOURT	15		Bn marched to billets LOUVENCOURT.	JD
CONTAY.	16		Bn marched to billets CONTAY.	JD
do	17		Bn in billets CONTAY.	JD
do	18		do	JD
do	19		do	JD
do	20		do	JD
VILLERS BOCAGE	21		Bn marched to billets VILLERS BOCAGE.	JD
RINERY	22		Bn marched to billets RIVERY.	JD

Major

Army Form C. 2118

WAR DIARY
or
INTELLIGENCE SUMMARY
(Erase heading not required.)

3

Place	Date 1917	Hour	Summary of Events and Information	Remarks and references to Appendices
THENNES	July 23		The Bn marched to Billets at THENNES.	
FRESNOY	24		Bn marched to billets FRESNOY.	
DUGOUTS BOUCHOIR	25		Battalion in dugouts BOUCHOIR as Brigade Reserve. The Brigade taking over the line from the French.	
do	26		Battalion in dugouts BOUCHOIR.	
do	27		do	
do	28		do	

Kluley Shrukula
Major,
Commander of 2nd Bn the Manchester Regt.

Army Form C. 2118

2 Manchester Regt
Vol 32

WAR DIARY or INTELLIGENCE SUMMARY

(Erase heading not required.)

Instructions regarding War Diaries and Intelligence Summaries are contained in F.S. Regs., Part II. and the Staff Manual respectively. Title Pages. will be prepared in manuscript.

Place	Date 1918	Hour	Summary of Events and Information	Remarks and references to Appendices
BOUCHOIR	Mar 1		Battalion in dugouts BOUCHOIR. Brigade Reserve. Working parties provided.	N.Z. Hdel
-"-	2		do	N.Z. Hdel
-"-	3		do	N.Z. Hdel
-"-	4		do	N.Z. Hdel
-"-	5		do	N.Z. Hdel
-"-	6		do	N.Z. Hdel
-"-	7		do	N.Z. Hdel
BEAUFORT	8		Battalion relieved by 1st Lancashire Fusiliers. Marched to Billets BEAUFORT.	N.Z. Hdel
-"-	9		Bn in billets BEAUFORT. Working parties provided. Training etc.	N.Z. Hdel
-"-	10		do	N.Z. Hdel
-"-	11		do	N.Z. Hdel
-"-	12		do	N.Z. Hdel
-"-	13		do	N.Z. Hdel
Trenches	14		Bn relieved 2nd Bn K.O.Y.L.I. in Left subsector (Marne Dugouts)	N.Z. Hdel
-"-	15		Bn in Trenches Left subsector (MARNE Dugouts)	N.Z. Hdel
-"-	16		do	N.Z. Hdel

Army Form C. 2118

WAR DIARY
or
INTELLIGENCE SUMMARY
(Erase heading not required.)

2.

Instructions regarding War Diaries and Intelligence Summaries are contained in F. S. Regs., Part II. and the Staff Manual respectively. Title Pages will be prepared in manuscript.

Place	Date 1917	Hour	Summary of Events and Information	Remarks and references to Appendices
Tencher	March 17		B⁺ in trenches Left subsector (Bois Dugnet) Ordered to attack at 11 a.m. (General immediate retirement) understood in morning. Pushed strong patrols. The B⁺ moved to LIANCOURT staying the night on the wood forward overlooking German line.	N.Z. Hd.d
LIANCOURT	18			N.Z. Hd.d
MESNIL St NICHAISE	19		Batt⁺ marched to Billets MESNIL ST NICHAISE via NESLE.	N.Z. Hd.d
do	20		Batt⁺ in Billets MESNIL ST NICHAISE	N.Z. Hd.d
VOYENNES	21		B⁺ marched to Billets VOYENNES. Working parties provided on Defence Line River SOMME.	N.Z. Hd.d
do	22		B⁺ in Billets VOYENNES. Working parties provided on Defence Line River SOMME	N.Z. Hd.d
do	23		do	N.Z. Hd.d
do	24		do	N.Z. Hd.d
do	25		do	N.Z. Hd.d
do	26		do — Less D Coy in billets BUNY	N.Z. Hd.d

Army Form C. 2118

WAR DIARY
or
INTELLIGENCE SUMMARY
(Erase heading not required.)

3

Place	Date 1917	Hour	Summary of Events and Information	Remarks and references to Appendices
LANCHY	Mar 27		Battn in Billets LANCHY	N.L. p. p. 66
BEAUVOIS	28		Bn in billets BEAUVOIS. B & D companies on outposts -	N.L. p. 66
			Working parties provided	
do	29		do (A & C in reserve) do	N.L. p. 66
do	30		do (do) do	N.L. p. 66
do	31		do (do) do	N.L. p. 66

N. Lunmore, Lt Colonel
2nd Manchester Regt.
1-4-17.

Addendum to 14th INFANTRY BRIGADE OPERATION ORDER No.120

Reference para. 4.

Battalions will meet their guides at WARVILLERS at the following times:-

15th H. L. I................5.45 p.m.
2nd MANCHESTER REGT.........6.30 p.m.
1st DORSET REGT.............7.15 p.m.
5/6th ROYAL SCOTS...........8.0 p.m.

All movement East of LE QUESNEL will be by Companies and after leaving WARVILLERS, by Platoons.

S E C R E T.   Office copy   Copy No. 1.

2nd BATTALION THE MANCHESTER REGIMENT OPERATION ORDER No. 1.

13-3-17.

1. The 14th Infantry Brigade will relieve the 97th Infantry Brigade on the 14th/15th March 1917.

2. The sector will be held as follows :-
    2nd Bn The Manchester Rgt............... Right Subsection.
    15th Bn H.L.I........................... Left Subsection.
    1st Bn The Dorset Rgt................... Support Battalion.
    5/6th Bn Royal Scots.................... Reserve Battalion.
    The 2nd Battalion The Manchester Regiment will relieve the 2nd Battalion K.O.Y.L.I.

3. The Companies will be distributed as follows :-
    "A" Company ... Right Front Company. "B" Company...Right Support.
    "C" Company ... Left Front Company. "D" Company...Left Support.

4. Guides, 1 per Platoon, 1 per Company H.Qrs, and 1 per Battalion Headquarters will be at Brigade Gum Boot Store WARVILLERS at 6.30 pm.

5. Order of March, "C","A","D","B" Companies, Headquarters.
    Interval 200 yds between Platoons.
    The leading Platoon of "C" Company will pass the Orderly Room at 5.55 pm.

6. Gum Boots will be drawn by Companies at Brigade Gum Boot Store at WARVILLERS and carried, special care being taken to get right sizes.

7. Bombing Sections will draw 5 bombs per man at Brigade Bomb Store WARVILLERS. These will be used to refill Grenade Stores in the line.

8. "B" and "D" Companies immediately on completion of relief will furnish carrying parties for the rations of "A" and "C" Companies respectively and themselves.
    The Transport Officer will have rations etc at Battalion Headquarters at 9 pm.

9. Water carts can be refilled at ROUVROY.
    Cooking will be done by Companies at Company Cookhouses, but no smoke must show.

10. Kit etc., will be handed in at the Quartermasters Stores as follows and in order named :-
    Blankets..... "A""B""C""D" ...... 10 am at 30 minutes interval.
    Officers Kits........................3 pm.
    Officers Trench Kits................5 pm.

11. The following will be sent to the Adjutant at times stated.
    Receipts for Trench Stores .... 10 am 15th inst.
    Map showing Dispositions of Company.... 4 pm.
    Plans in case of Attack................ 4 pm.

12. Battalion Headquarters will close at BEAUFORT at 6 pm., and re-open at Right Subsection at 6 pm.

(Continued)

(Continued) "2"

13. The following Code will be used to report relief :-
Relief Complete .... BRANDY.
No Unusual Shelling .... WHISKEY.
Unusual Shelling............... GIN.
"A" Company .... GALLERY.
"B" Company .... PIT.
"C" Company .... STALLS.
"D" Company .... BOX.

14. When in the Line, men will wear the Box Respirator in the "ALERT POSITION", in dugouts as well as outside.

15. Walking in the open near the front line in daylight is forbidden.

G. Rittson Thomas, Lieut A/Adjutant,
2nd Battalion The Manchester Regiment.

Army Form C. 2118

2 Manchester Regt
Vol 33

WAR DIARY or INTELLIGENCE SUMMARY
(Erase heading not required.)

Place	Date	Hour	Summary of Events and Information	Remarks and references to Appendices
	April 1st		The Battalion marched to billets in GERMAINE holding themselves in readiness to move forward at short notice.-	
			The 32nd Division continued the advance. The 97th Brigade attacked and took SAVY, and the 96th Brigade took BOIS DE SAVY but were unable to capture high ground Point 138. Several attempts were made but without success. The 14th Infantry Brigade were ordered to withdraw from their outpost line and moved to GERMAINE being relieved by 35th Division in (BEAUVOID After remaining in GERMAINE for a few hours the Brigade moved to CHATEAU DE POMERY and remained until 12 midnight.-	
	Apl 2		The Brigade then marched to BOIS DE SAVY being shelled on the way. 2nd 16th Manchester Regt having two casualties. On arriving at BOIS DE SAVY, the Point 138 had not been captured so that the plan was slightly altered.-	
		5 PM	At 5 PM the R's (on the right) and 1st Dorset Regt (on the left) led the attack, the objectives of the Battalion were FRANCILLY-SELENCY, and SELENCY, and that of the 1st Dorset Regt. HOLNON. The object of the manoeuvre was to envelope the BOIS DE HOLNON. to attack which it was about to fire one of the guns. Both villages were gained and consolidated. The enemy shelled both villages all day, cover being very slight.	
			The Battalion captured 1 Officer and 16 other ranks.-	
			Our casualties were:-	
			Killed 2 Officers I.W.O. 9 o.R's	
			Wounded 6 Officers - 52 oR's	
			continued.	

WAR DIARY or **INTELLIGENCE SUMMARY**

Army Form C. 2118

Place	Date	Hour	Summary of Events and Information	Remarks and references to Appendices
	April 2nd continued		A Company lost direction, and advanced to within about 1500 yards of ST QUENTIN and had to remain out until dusk.	
			During the night an attempt was made to get the captured guns away. The enemy allowed drag ropes to be put on by Lieut. and Adjt. G.R. Thomas, and a gunner officer, when fire from a battery 800 yards range was opened point blank. The ground was very heavy and the guns could not be withdrawn. The numbers of the guns are as under.	
			No. 59. 5960. 3381. 941. 2602. No. 4196 (Damaged) Ammunition wagons and ammunition were also captured.	
			During these operations Transport remained at GERMAINE.	
	April 3rd to 5th		A separate report of the Battalion's movement during this period is attached.	
	April 6th		The Battalion was relieved by the 14th H.L.I. on the night of this day marching to billets in BEAUVOIS.	
	April 7th		Battalion in billets BEAUVOIS. Working parties provided.	
	April 8th to April 10th		do do Training etc.	
	April 11th		do do do	
	April 30		A separate report of the Battalion's movement during this period is attached.	

E. Pitman Thomas
For Lieut. Col. Comdg. 2nd Glasgow etc. [illegible]

1875 Wt. W593/826 1,000,000 4/15 J.B.C. & A. A.D.S.S./Forms/C. 2118.

CAPTURE OF A GERMAN 77.MM.BATTERY.
FRANCILLY-SELENCY. APRIL.2nd.1917.

The record of the 2nd Bn The Manchester Regt during the Great War of 1914-1918 is so replete with deeds of heroism, devotion to duty as well as dogged perseverance and cheerfulness under all conditions that it is with great diffidence that I have consented to describe what I can remember of one of the leading incidents of their campaign.

At the end of May 1917 the Bn found itself after following up the Boche from the beginning of his rtirement the B 2nd Manchester Regt found itself enscensed in the cellars of BEAUVOIS which, until its arrival were filled with the homely mangel, and were hard at work at the seemingly unending task of filling up the enormous craters which had been made by the Boche at the various cross roads of this as well as other ruined villages.

On the morning of April 1st the Bn was ordered to move to a village about 5 miles distant on our right flank, called GKA GERMAINE. Billets were allotted and it was expected that we should stay there for at all events the night.

This was however not to be, for at about 1 o'clock an order came from the Bde to move at once and rendez-vous at a place called CHATEAU POMERY. The distance was only about 2 miles but owing to unavoidable delays the Bn did not start until 5.30 pm, soon after which hour it became dark. The place, although imposing enough on the map was in reality a few hedges and trees, marking no doubt a once magnificent chateau.

The Brigade halted here and made itself as comfortable as it could, resting and having some food in preparation for the work in the near future.

In the meanwhile the Commanding Officers reported at Bde headquarters for orders. At the conference we were informed that the 97th Infantry Brigade had captured the village of SAVY in the morning, whilst the in the afternoon SAVY WOOD was taken by the 96th Infantry Brigade. This latter Bde, however was unable to emerge out of the wood and capture the QUARRY which was situated about 500 yds up a glacis slope from the forward edge of the wood.

In 1918 this quarry was known as "The Manchester Redoubt" because another Bn held it during the Boche offensive.

It is rectangular in shape about 250yds long by 150yds broad with steep sides in which were dugouts.

It was known that the Boche was holding it strongly with Machine guns, which fired to the front and flanks.

Our orders were to move to SAVY WOOD that night and attack at 5am April 2nd.

The dispositions and objectives were as follows:-
Right. 15th Highland Light Infantry, to attack the The Quarry.
Centre. 2nd Manchester Regt. From FRANCILLY-SELENCY and SELENCY.
Left. 1st Dorset Regt. HOLNON.
The 5/6 Royal Scots were in reserve.

It was explained that the villages could be distinguished by the fact that one possesed a spire and the other a tower but as neither village was at that time more than about 8 ft high this information was not of much assistance in finding our objectives.

In order to allow for possible delays and for the men to have as long a rest as possible after the march, the Bde moved off at midnight the Bn following the Dorsets who were leading.

The only incidedt on the march was that as we neared SAVY a shell burst in the road and caused two casualties.

After passing through SAVY the column moved across open fields along the west edge of SAVY WOOD and halted behind the railway embankment.

Leaving the Bn to get some rest I went along the line to the right to find the Bn HQ of the Lancashire Fusiliers commanded by Capt (acting Lt-Col) H.G.Harrison. 2nd Manchester Regt. and to get information as to the situation.

The plan of attack had been slightly altered as the 15th H L I were not to advance on our right but to move in echelon.

(2).

This meant that our right flank would be exposed and 2 platoons of A Coy were detailed to watch this flank.
The coys were detailed as follows:- 1st Line.
Right .B Coy under 2/Lt R E Prouse.
Left   C "   "   Capt G M GLOVER.
2nd Line:-
Right. A Coy under 2/Lt A Heydon.
Left D "   "   2/Lt E H Briggs.
The railway ran through the SAVY WOOD but as the part north of the railway had been cut down it was very difficult to find the position of deployment which was along the northern face of the wood.
Beyond the railway the ground was open grass land which rises gently for about 1000 yds to FRANCILLY-SELENCY.
After this the ground slopes down into a shallow valley and again rises rather steeply to SELENCY which was the final objective, and which was connected by a road from S QUENTIN to HOLNON.
To the east of this valley there is a short and broad gorge on the top of which is the BOIS DES ROSES. This was about 900 yds from SELENCY and held by the Boche.
Punctually at zero hour, with the first streak of dawn, the line advanced to the attack and was immediately met by heavy rifle and machine gun fire.
This came principally from the Quarry and therefore A Coy suffered most. 2/Lt H Taylor who was in command of the two platoons of A Coy at once changed direction half right and attacked the Quarry on the flank which he captured, taking 4 machine guns and in addition 2 more machine guns in a trench adjoining the quarry.
This success materially assisted the H L I to advance.
These two platoons did not remain here but, in spite of losing touch with the coy on their left, pushed on until brought up short by a huge crater at the outskirts of S QUENTIN itself.
They took up a position in the crater, and under a very heavy fire remained there until darkness enabled them to withdraw.
A message was sent back to Bn H Q but no assistance could be sent by day.
The attack on FRANCILLY-SELENCY was successful but when the advance was continued C Coy and part of B Coy suddenly came up on a battery of 77 MM guns on the low ground north east of the village which was firing at point blank range.
Captain Glover by attacking both in front and on the flank captured the battery after a hand to hand fight with these gunners that remained.
An escort was left with the battery, and the advance was resumed and SELENCY was captured by 6.30 am 2½ hours after zero hour.
The line was reorganised by 2/Lt E H Briggs and the position consolidated.
Owing to the Boche still holding the BOIS DES ROSES our right flank went back to FRANCILLY-SELENCY forming a right angle, which with the few men available was very vulnerable and had he launched a counter attack instead of contenting himself with spasmodic shelling he might have made it very unpleasnt for us.
During the night efforts were made by the Adjutant, Lt G R Thomas to draw the guns out of their position with the aid of men and drag ropes but this proved to be impossible.
On the night of April 3rd the G O C 32nd Division ordered Major F W Lumsden DSO, the G S O 2 to the Division to withdraw them with the assistance of teams furnished by the Artillery and a covering party of the H L I who was now holding that portion of the line.
It appears that the Boche had selected this night to endeavour to recapture the guns for after some of the guns had been withdrawn he put down a very heavy barrage and attacked with a company of infantry. The H L I put up a stout resistance and although a few of the enemy were able to blow up the breech of the last gun he was driven off and all the guns were withdrawn.
The following night the limbers were withdrawn by the Bn assisted by teams from the Artillery, but there was not much shelling.

(3).

On the night of April 4th the Bn Transport Officer, Lt D C Pearse brought out the signalling limbered wagon, thus completing the withdrawal of the whole battery.

The Bn remained in this position until relieved on April 8th when withdrew to BEAUVOIS for a rest and ahere we met Lt-Colonel Vaughan DSO who was commanding a Bn of another Regt.

Our total trophies were 8 machine guns. 6, guns 77 mm. 6 ammunition wagons and 1 battery signalling limbered wagon complete with signalling stores.

The awards were as follows:-
Major F.W.Lumsden DSO the Victoria Cross.
Captain G M Glover, 2/Lt H Tayler, 2/Lt E H Briggs and R S M G.M Hastewell the Military Cross.

Pte C E Overton, signaller of A Coy, was recommended for the Victoria Cross for repeatedly repairing the telephone lines and carrying wounded back under a very heavy fire but was awarded the Distinguished Conduct Medal instead.

Capt Glover was wounded early in the fight but he refused to leave his company until after he had completed his task. On his way back to the Regimental Aid Post he encountered two Boche whom he captured with the aid of an empty revolver.

The guns were awarded as follows:-
2nd Manchesters, 2 guns.
15 H L I   1 gun.
161st Bde RFA   1 "
125th Heavy Batty 1 "
159th Bde R F A   1 "

Congratulatory wires were received from the higher command including one from F M Sir Douglas Haigh.

Our casualties were Officers Killed. 2.   Wounded 7.
                    Warrant Officer 1.
                    Other Ranks   9.   " 52.

The whole battle showed the spirit that animated all ranks for once it began it was not possible to issue orders and every one knowing what had to be done carried out their tasks with that courage and zeal for which the 2nd Bn Manchester Regt was alwys famous.

Note. My thanks are due to Capt H R C Green 1st Bn Manchester Regt for his notes which have been lent to me and without which I could have written little.

N. Luxmoore.
Commanding 2nd Manchesters
at the time.

NAMES OF OFFICERS & WARRANT OFFICERS who were in Action
April 2nd 1917.

T/Lt-Colonel N Luxmoore DSO	Commanding Bn.	Devonshire R
Lt G R Thomas	Adjutant.	Manchester
2/Lt H Wilkins. Wounded.	Intelligence Officer.	"
2/Lt A Heyden. Wounded.	Commanding A Coy	"
" C W M Smith. Wounded.		"
" H Taylor		"
" H Gaukroger. Killed		London
" R E Prouse	Commanding B Coy	"
" J C Tooley. Wounded.		London
" K W Eady. Wounded.		London
Capt G M Glover. Wounded.	Commanding C Coy	
2/Lt O Wild.		
" V A Hart.		
" H W Winch. Killed.		London
2/Lt E H Briggs	Commanding D Coy	Manchester
" T S Thomas		Welch
" R E Gooding		London.
" A T G L Nibbs. Wounded.		
Lt C G Skinner.	R A M C.	
Rev R Gillenders	C E.	

Warrant Officers:-
Regimental Sergeant Major G Hastewell   Manchester
Company Sgt Major T Mc Gudre. Wounded.   "
"   "   "   E Kent.   Killed.   "

Officers left out of Action as Reinforcements at the Transport Lines:-

Major J F Dempster.   2nd in Command.
"   G E Vickers.   Quartermaster.
Capt H R C Green. In action April 3rd.
Lt D C Pearse.   Transport Officer.   London
2/Lt A R Oldfield   Manchester
"   L Taylor.   In action later.   "
"   R C Essenhigh.   "   "   "   "
"   A C Kirby   West Surrey
"   T F Bayliss.   London
Capt S Serrell   In action later.   Manchester

Warrant Officers:-
Company Sgt Major J Lemon   "
"   "   "   Pearce.   "

Capt H J Gwyther MC rejoined the Bn from Divisional Headquarters and went into action later.

NOTE.   In the list names of C S M Mc Guire and Kent are shown with the Wounded and Killed bracketted, as it is presumed that the former died of wounds.

2nd Battalion The Manchester Regt.

Reference Sheet 62 B. S.W. 1/40,000

On the morning of the 2nd April 1917 the Battalion was ordered to take the villages of FRANCILLY-SELENCY and SELENCY, and to consolidate on the outside of the latter.

The attack was timed to commence at 5 A.M. with an artillery barrage. The Battalion advanced in three waves, "C" and "D" Companies in the first wave, followed by two platoons of "A" Company as the second wave, with "B" Company in rear as the third wave.

Two platoons of "A" Company were sent as a detached patrol to the right flank to stop any attack which might be made from that direction, and to deal with flanking Machine Gun fire.

Operations of each Company are given separately:

D Company.

This Company's position was the extreme left of the Battalion front and in "jumping off" encountered heavy Machine Gun fire. Despite this heavy fire and early losses of men, the Company advanced well to the attack, dispersing and driving back enemy gunners, who fled in disorder leaving two Machine Guns and equipment behind. They opened fire on the fugitives, and many of them fell.

The Company then made for its first objective FRANCILLY-SELENCY, which they captured, and on re-forming, proceeded to the second and final objective.

At this stage of the attack, the Company encountered heavy shelling, but kept on and reached the final objective SELENCY at 6.25 A.M.

Being the first Company to arrive at the village the the Company moved down the main road to point S.3.d.2.0 where work of consolidation was commenced.

C Company.

This Company on "jumping off" encountered heavy Machine Gun fire from the right flank, but pushing through this, saw the flash of guns immediately in front. On arriving at a point 50 yards in front of the Battery they executed

(Continued)

a flanking movement, which enabled them to capture the Battery.

Leaving a mopping-up party to clear the guns they pushed on to the village FRANCILLY-SELENCY.

Going across the open again they encountered Machine Gun fire from E of SELENCY, but pushed on and finally entered the village, where they started consolidating on the left of 'D' Company.

'A' Company.

Previous to "jumping off", this Company was warned about certain strong points on the right, including a quarry.
About 5.30 A.M. the right flank struck the quarry and were temporarily held up by heavy Machine Gun fire, but by a flanking movement the Quarry was rushed.

The enemy were seen on the opposite side of the Quarry evacuating it, and in doing so had pulled the Machine Guns from their positions and left them behind.

There were four German Machine Guns left in the Quarry and two in a trench leading from the right of the Quarry towards the road S.21.b. central.

The Guns were in good condition and had belts in them.

The Company then passed through the Quarry, and after reforming rushed the retreating enemy, but on reaching Crater at junction of road S.21.b.8.4. were held up by heavy Machine Gun fire, from front and right flank.

This Crater was consolidated, and runners sent out to try and get in touch with remainder of the Battalion. This they failed to do, but came across a Company of 15th H.L.I. who directed them to B.H.2.

This Company held the position until 7.30 P.M. when they were ordered to withdraw to SELENCY. This was done under cover of darkness, and the work of consolidation with the rest of the Battalion was carried on.

This Company effectively dealt with the Machine Guns on the flank of the Battalion, and eventually arrived nearly at the outskirts of ST QUENTIN. As the enemy were in force on this front and flanks, they were ordered to withdraw, which they did under cover of darkness

Continued

B Company

This Company was the third wave, and shortly after the advance started, ran into heavy Machine Gun fire, evidently the same Machine Guns that "C" Company encountered, as they passed over the same ground, and also helped to capture the battery.

Proceeding forward they obtained their objective and helped to consolidate the position. This position was held during very severe weather conditions, as it rained and snowed every day until the Battalion was relieved by the 17th H.L.I. on the 6th inst at about midnight.

April 2nd. – In the evening about 8 P.M an attempt was made by Lieut & Adjt G.R. Thomas, and Lieut Ward R.F.A. to get the Guns back without teams. A platoon of "D" Company acted as covering party and 24 men were employed to haul out the Guns. The enemy allowed these men to put drags on to the first gun, but directly they began to haul a battery of 77 mm opened fire at about 800 yards range. As it was impossible to get the Guns out without horses or long ropes, the party retired leaving a covering party out to guard the Guns until dawn. The Guns captured by the Battalion were covered by the 15th H.L.I. who had followed the Manchester Regiment into FRANCILLY-SELENCY and the guns could easily be judged from the trenches in daylight. & also from the trenches of the 16th Northumberland Fus: April 3rd at Point 138.

The Battalion remained on outpost and there was little shelling during the day. The 14th Infy Brigade made arrangements to evacuate the captured Guns at 8 P.M. under the direction of Major LUMSDEN D.S.O. S.S.O 2 32nd Division, Lt WARD 161 Bde and Lt LOMAX C 161 Battery assisted and did most heroic work with their teams.

The Guns were being removed when an intense barrage was placed round them, and on the village of FRANCILLY-SELENCY. In spite of this, work was carried on. The enemy attacked the covering party, consisting of one company 15th H.L.I. and surrounded them for a short while. The enemy were eventually driven off, suffering some

Continued

casualties, but they first managed to blow in the breech. of the sixth Gun which had not then been removed, but was taken out soon after. - The casualties were slight considering the fact that the work was done under the most intense Artillery fire. -

April 4th.

The weather was very bad and snow was falling heavily. It was expected the enemy would counter attack. Wiring was continued and trenches improved

In the evening, orders were received to furnish a covering party for the withdrawal of the ammunition wagons. - II Coy. was selected for this duty. The night was misty and the enemy only sent a few shells over. As the loop in the ammunition limbers was smaller than the limber hook, rifle slings were used to fasten the two together. They were brought away without any casualties. -

The total trophies taken from the enemy by the Battn: were 6 (six) 77 mm Guns with 6 (six) Ammunition wagons complete. & 1 signalling wagon & also 8 (eight) Machine Guns & some small arms & equipment

On the night of the fifth, the captured Battery Signalling limbered wagon with signalling stores on the wagon was man hauled into our lines under the supervision of Lieut and Adjutant G.R. Thomas and Lieut D.C. Pearse. Covering party and working party were taken from "B" Coy and although the wagon was very heavy, the wagon was brought into safety. Later Lieut Pearse the Transport Officer brought the wagon down from FRANCILLY - SELENCY. to 32nd Divisional Hd. Qrs. with a team. -

Only 17 prisoners were taken by the Battn: during this attack.

Movement of the Battalion during the period April 12th. to April 29th 1917
------oOo------

April 12th.
SAVY.

The Battalion moved to SAVY during the morning, and was accomodated in cellars and trenches round the village.
Due to the essential exposure which the troops had to undergo a certain number of Bivouac sheets were issued.
During the day instructions were received that the French intended to attack ST QUENTIN the following morning.
In the event of their attack being successful, the 14th. Brigade were to send two Battalions (2nd Manchesters and 15th. H.L.I.) to occupy the FAUBOURGE ST MARTIN, and protect the French left flank. A Third Battalion of the Brigade (1st. Dorsets) was to move patrols forward during the French advance to the spurs in S.23.a.5.6, S.17.c, S.16 Central, and BOIS DE ROSES, S.10.d.9.5 and S.10.d.5.9. thus keeping touch between the British and French flanks.
Orders were received later that the Battalion, together with the 15th. H.L.I. were to be assembled in the hollow ground S.W. of the Wood in S.26.b by Zero time.
In the event of the French attack being successful the 15th. H.L.I. were to move forward and occupy trenches in S.24., S.18., T.7 and T.8. forming a defensive flank to the North, the 2nd. Manchesters were to follow the H.L.I. and form up in reserve in T.24.b. Zero time was fixed for 5 A.M.
Orders were issued to Companies to be in their assembly positions by 2.30. A.M., and to commence digging in there.

April 13th.
SAVY

The Battalion was in position in S.26.a and c by 2.30. A.M. and commenced to dig themselves in, this was completed by 4.30. A.M. The French attack proved to be a failure, due to uncut wire, a heavy barrage and the strength with which the enemy trenches were held.
At 3 P.M. the Battalion received orders to move back to SAVY.
Instructions were received that the Battalion was to be prepared to move at 10 minutes notice, to deal with any counter-attack in the direction of FAYET.
A counter-attack from this direction was considered likely due to the precarious position of the Dorset outpost line which had gone forward with the French according to arrangement.
At 5 P.M. one Company (C Company under 2/Lt Prouse) was ordered forward to re-inforce the Dorset pickets at the BOIS DE ROSES. Instructions were received that the 97th. Brigade would attack FAYET and occupy the high ground beyond on the following morning, Zero hour being 4.30. A.M. In order to Co-operate with this attack and form a heavy barrage on the Eastern exits of FAYET 16 Machine Guns and Lewis Guns were massed in the BOIS DE ROSES.

April 14th.
SAVY.

The 97th. Brigade took FAYET and 350 prisoners without any difficulty, and moved forward to their second objective.
As things appeared to be progressing favourably, the 1st. Dorsets were ordered to send a company forward and occupy CEPY FARM. This was accomplished by the Dorsets, but the 97th. Brigade failed to reach their 2nd objective, being held up along the terraced road in M.36.c and S.6.a and b, and at the copse in M.28.d and 29c. The Company of the Dorsets was therefore isolated. At 8 A.M. the Battalion was ordered to move forward to SAVY WOOD. At 11 A.M. a telephone message was received warning the Battalion to be ready to move to S.11.b. and to be prepared to attack at 12.30.P.M. It was uncertain at this time whether the Dorsets occupied CEPY FARM or not. At 11.15. A.M. the Battalion was ordered to move. No instructions were received at this time as to what the Battalion was to attack, but the Colonel was sent for to go to Brigade, and receive instructions whilst the Battalion
continued

was moving into position.

In order to approach the assembly position in S.11.b. under cover, the Battalion moved along the low ground in S.20.D. and b, S.14.b., FRANCILLY, S.10.a. to the BOIS DE ROSES.
It was realised by the Battalion at the outset that it was impossible to cover the distance in Artillery formation with the loads and paraphanalia that the private soldier is called upon to carry in the attack, in the time given.
Upon arriving at the BOIS DE ROSES it was found that the remaining 1000 yards to be covered was in full view of ST QUENTIN, and that to cover this distance the whole Battalion would have to move in full view across the enemys front.
The Colonel rode back from Brigade at this moment (12.20. P.M.) and realizing the situation, in order to save the Battalion from being cut up, ordered them to approach the assembly position from ground under cover further North. The Colonel had then to ride forward to try and obtain news of the situation from the Dorsets at CEPY FARM. The Battalion moved back round SELENCY and FAYET to the valley in S.5.c. From here, whilst the troops were re-forming the assembly position was reconoitred and found to be the slope of a hill facing and in full view of ST QUENTIN. It was necessary to come over the top of this hill and move forward to a position more under cover from view, in full view of the enemy. On this account the Battalion went over in attack formation. Immediately the first wave passed over the crest of the hill the enemy placed a hurricane barrage on the ground to be crossed with 10.5 C.M. and 15 C.M. High explosive shells.
Though this barrage was straight in the middle of the Battalion they moved forward through it as steady as going on parade, each wave keeping its dressing and distance and every carrier retaining his load. By the Grace of God alone only 30 men were lost in this barrage.
The Colonel was met again at this point and informed us that the enemy were supposed to be still holding a trench running from S.6.b.5.0. and M.36 Central, and that we were to form up at CEPY FARM and attack this trench from the flank.
Zero time had been fixed for 1. O'clock, and a barrage placed on the trench at that time. It was now trwo o'clock.
Whilst the men were resting the Colonel went forward to CEPY FARM to see the best method of approach and place of assembly. It was found that to approach the farm it was necessary to go over a rise for 150 yards. This rise was swept with Machine Guns from ST QUENTIN which fired at anybody passing over. The neighbourhood of CEPY FARM was found to be quite impossible to assemble in, due to its exposure to view, and on account of Machine Guns and Artillery Fire.
The Trench to be taken was then reconnoitred. It was found to have no wire in front and could be easily approached under cover to within 50 yards. The Colonel therefore, decided to make a frontal attack. The actual trench was then approached and upon investigation proved to be empty. One Company was therefore sent up and occupied the trench. This trench was handed over to the 97th. Brigade at 8.30. P.M. and the Battalion less one Company at BOIS DE ROSES and one Company left as reserve to the Dorsets returned to SAVY.

April 15th. SAVY.	The Battalion took over the main line of defence in front of SAVY Wood with two Companies (B and D) from the 5th. Royal Scots. A and C Companies remained in reserve in SAVY WOOD.
Apl 16th. to Apl 21st. MAIN LINE	The Battalion remained in the MAIN LINE digging and connecting this line up, and making fire steps. The whole of the front (S.27.central to S.15.d.1.6.) was also wired. The Batalion was relieved on the night of the 21st. by a Battalion of the 182nd Brigade and moved to QUIVIERES, arriving in this village at 6.30. A.M. on the 22nd. inst where they were accomodated in cellars.

continued

April 22nd to April 30th. QUIVIERES.	The battalion remained at QUIVIERES training and preparing for inspections. See training programme attached.
April 27th.	The G.O.C. 14th. Infantry Brigade inspected the Brigade with its affiliated units (i.e. M.G. Coy., T.M. Battaery, R.E., Field Ambulance and A.S.C. Coy).
April 29th.	The G.O.C. 32nd Division inspected the Brigade with its affiliated Units, and in an address to the Brigade told the Troops how proud he and all the higher authorities were with the Brigade, for the excellent work that had been accomplished during the recent operations. (See attached congratulatiory telegrams from the C.in.C., G.O.C. 4th Army, and G.O.C. 5th. Army. After the inspection the Commanding Officer congratulated the undermentioned upon their being awarded their respective decorations for gallantry during the recent operations.-

Capt G.M. Glover.   )
2/Lt E.H.Briggs.   )
2/Lt H.Taylor   )   Military Cross.
No 5626 R.S.M. G Hastewell.)

No 1543 Sgt C. Coleman   )
No 8781 Pte C E Overton   )   Distinguished Conduct Medal

No 1028 L/Cpl R Gardner   )
No 16396 Pte R Best   )
No 1657 Sgt J W Young   )
No 15631 Pte G Halliwell   )
No 9025 "   W Glynn   )   Military Medal.
No 2393 "   M Glynn   )
No 9346 "   J Kelly   )
No 510   "   T Carter.   )

No 26777 L/Cpl J Roylance.   Bar to the Military Medal.

---oOo---

"A"

14th INFANTRY BRIGADE TRAINING PROGRAMME
(from 23rd to 25th APRIL inclusive)

REVEILLE   - 6.15.a.m.

BREAKFAST   - 7. a.m.

---

8 a.m. - 8.30 a.m.	Inspection on parade and Musketry drill, rapid loading.
8.30 a.m. - 9.30 a.m.	Organization of Company, proving of Company, Platoon &c. Platoon Drill, Dummy Grenade throwing.
9.45 a.m. - 10.45 a.m.	Company Drill. Standard Form of Attack.
11 a.m. - 11.30 a.m.	Physical Training and Bayonet Fighting.
11.30 a.m. - 12 noon	Extended order Drill by Platoons.
12 noon - 12.30 p.m.	Physical Training and Bayonet Fighting.

1.0 p.m. -	Dinner, which will be visited by Company Officers.
2.30 p.m. -	Sports and Games on well thought out lines. Programmes to be submitted to Brigade H.Q. by 9.0 a.m. the 24th inst.
5.0 p.m. -	Tea.
5.45 p.m. - 6.0 p.m. -	Musketry Drill.
6.15 p.m. -	Lectures by C.O. or 2nd in Command, and Officers to be followed by remarks on following day's work. Instruction in Map reading, Message writing &c.
8.0 p.m. -	Hot Meal.
9.0 p.m. -	Lights Out.

N.B. - All specialists except Signallers will attend with their Companies until 10.45 a.m.

"B"

14th INFANTRY BRIGADE TRAINING PROGRAMME
(from 26th to 28th April inclusive)

REVEILLE   -   6.15 a.m.

BREAKFAST   -   7.0 a.m.

8.0 a.m. - 8.30 a.m.	-	Inspection on Parade and Musketry Drill, rapid loading.
8.30 a.m. - 9.0 a.m.	-	Close Order Drill.
9.0 a.m. - 10.0 a.m.	-	Extended Order Drill by Companies and Standard Form of Attack.
10.15 a.m. - 10.45 a.m.	-	Physical Training and Bayonet Fighting.
11.0 a.m. - 12 noon	-	1 Company Musketry, ball practice. Rapid Loading. 1 Company Close Order Drill, Bayonet Fighting, and Physical Training.
12 noon - 1.0 p.m.	-	1 Company Close Order Drill, Bayonet Fighting and Physical Training. 1 Company Musketry, ball practice, Rapid loading.

1.0 p.m.	-	Dinner, which will be visited by Company Officers.
2.30 p.m.	-	Sports and Games on well thought out lines. Programmes to be submitted to Brigade H.Q. by 9.0 a.m. the 24th inst
5.0 p.m.	-	Tea.
5.45 p.m. - 6.0 p.m.	-	Musketry Drill.
6.15 p.m.	-	Lectures by C.O. or 2nd in Command and Officers to be followed by remarks on following day's work. Instruction in Map reading, Message writing &c.
8.0 p.m.	-	Hot Meal.
9.0 p.m.	-	Lights Out.

N.B. - All specialists except Signallers will attend with their Companies till 10.45 a.m.

14th INFANTRY BRIGADE
(Training of OBSERVERS from 23rd to 28th April).

8.15 a.m.   -   Inspection Parade.

8.30 a.m. - 12.30 p.m.   - Lecture and Practical Map reading.

=== ==============

1.0 p.m.   -   Dinner.

2.0 p.m. - 4.30 p.m.   -   Games.

5.0 p.m.   -   Tea.

6.0 p.m.   -   Lecture.

9.0 p.m.   -   Lights Out.

9.0 p.m. to 11.0 p.m. on 26th and 27th April, night marching by compass.

==

Noted, Seen, & Passed to Capt Griffin

J D Carpenter
Major

23/4/17

14th INFANTRY BRIGADE TRAINING PROGRAMME
for SUNDAY 29th April.

REVEILLE — 7.0 a.m.

BREAKFAST — 7.45 a.m.

CHURCH PARADE at times to be notified later.

11.30 a.m. — Lectures by M.O. Sanitation &c. or by Gas N.C.O's. on Gas appliances.

1.0 p.m. — Dinner.

2.30 p.m. — Sports and Games on well thought out lines.
Programmes to be submitted to Brigade H.Q. by 9.0 a.m. 24th inst.

5.0 p.m. — Tea.

14th INFANTRY BRIGADE
(Training of Reserve Specialists)

LEWIS GUNNERS — Under Battalion Lewis Gun Officer.

8.0 a.m. - 10.45 a.m.	Parade with their Companies.
11.0 a.m. - 12.45 p.m.	Under the Battalion Lewis Gun Officer, to carry out the Standard Course laid down. Battalions to submit detailed programme shewing hours, nature and place of training.

1.0 p.m.	Dinner, which will be visited by Company Officers.
2.30 p.m.	Sports and Games on well thought out lines. Programmes to be submitted to Brigade H.Q. by 9.0 a.m. 24th inst.
5.0 p.m.	Tea.
5.45 p.m. - 6.0 p.m.	Musketry Drill and Revolver practice.
6.15 p.m.	Lecture to Companies by C.O. or 2nd in Command and Officers to be followed by remark on the following day's work. Instruction in Map reading, message writing &c.
8.0 p.m.	Hot Meal.
9.0 p.m.	Lights Out.

14th INFANTRY BRIGADE
(Bombers and Rifle Grenadiers).

8.0 a.m. - 10.45 a.m.	-	Parade with their Companies.
11. a.m. - 12.45 p.m.	-	Under Battalion Bombing Officer, to carry out the Standard Course laid down. Battalions to submit detailed programme shewing hours, nature and place of training.

1.0 p.m.	-	Dinner, which will be visited by Company Officers.
2.30 p.m.	-	Sports and Games on well thought out lines. Programmes to be submitted to Brigade H.Q. by 9.0 a.m. 24th inst.
5.0 p.m.	-	Tea.
5.45 p.m. - 6.0 p.m.	-	Musketry Drill.
6.15 p.m.	-	Lecture to Companies by C.O. or 2nd in Command, to be followed by remarks on the following day's work. Map reading, message writing &c.
8.0 p.m.	-	Hot Meal.
9.0 p.m.	-	Lights Out.

14th INFANTRY BRIGADE
(Training of Signallers - ~~Runners~~).

8.15 a.m. - 12.45 p.m.   -   Under Battalion Signalling Sergeant.
To be supervised by Brigade Signal Officer.

A new class under instruction will be formed under Brigade Signal Officer.
This class consisting of 8 men per Battalion will report at Brigade Headquarters at 7.0 p.m. on the 23rd inst.

Brigade Signal Officer will submit a programme of Training

Army Form C. 2118

WAR DIARY
or
INTELLIGENCE SUMMARY   2 Manchester Regt
(Erase heading not required.)

Vol 3 4

Place	Date	Hour	Summary of Events and Information	Remarks and references to Appendices
QUIVIERES	May 1st		Battalion in billets QUIVIERES. Working parties provided. Training etc.	B
do	2nd		do	A & DS
do	3rd		Inspection by Corps Commander. He congratulated on its smartness.	
			Battalion in billets QUIVIERES. Working parties provided. (A & B Coys) Demonstration of a platoon attacking a strong point. C Coy attacking.	E
			"D" Company firing on range.	
do	4th		Battalion in billets QUIVIERES. Working parties provided. Training. Tactical scheme carried out.	F
do	5th/10th		Battalion in billets QUIVIERES. Working parties provided. Training etc. Tactical scheme carried out on 10th.	G
do	11th		do	
			A telephone message was received that the Bn would probably move and all training ceased at 12 noon. This was however cancelled and the Bn executed a scheme (trench to trench attack) by night leaving QUIVIERES at 11.30 P.M.	
do	12/14th		The Bn remained in billets QUIVIERES. Carrying on with training etc.	
VOYENNES	15th		Bn marched to billets VOYENNES.	III

J.H. Lloyd[?] Lt. Col.
Comdg 2 Manch. Regt

Army Form C. 2118

WAR DIARY
or
INTELLIGENCE SUMMARY
(Erase heading not required.)

Instructions regarding War Diaries and Intelligence Summaries are contained in F. S. Regs., Part II. and the Staff Manual respectively. Title Pages will be prepared in manuscript.

2.

Place	Date 1917	Hour	Summary of Events and Information	Remarks and references to Appendices
HATTENCOURT	May 16th		Battalion marched to Billets at HATTENCOURT.	JPD
LE. QUESNEL	17th		Battalion marched to LE QUESNEL Billets	JPD
do	18th-22nd		Battalion in Billets LE QUESNEL. Training etc.	JPD I
do	23rd		do Tactical exercises executed.	JPD
do	24th		do Training carried on	JPD
do	25th		do Tactical exercise carried out on Old Front Line Trenches.	JPD
do	26th		do do	JPD
do	27/28/29		do Training carried on.	JPD III
DEMUIN	30		Battalion marched to Billets DEMUIN	JPD
do	31		do Training etc.	JPD

During the period the Battalion has been in training special attention has been given to the attack in "Open Warfare".

J Philip Shepard Lt. Col.
Cmdg "9th Battn C.E.F"

Appendix A

2nd. Battalion The Manchester Regiment.

Demonstration of platoon attacking a strong point.

Map Reference:- ST. QUENTIN 18.

General Idea. The GERMANS hold the line DOUILLY-QUIVIERES-GUIZINCOURT. The BRITISH have occupied by 7 a.m. on the 3rd. inst. the line FORESTE-LANCHY-MONCHY-LAGACHE.

Special Idea. At 9 a.m. the aeroplanes report that the enemy are retiring towards the line TOULLE-MATIGNY-CROIX-MOLIGNAUX. At 10 a.m. the line is ordered to advance.

At 10-30 a.m. O.C."C" Company receives a report from his patrols that a strong point at D.6.a.39 is holding up his advance.

He orders No. platoon to take the post under cover of a section of Machine Guns.

[signature]

Major.

2-5-1917   Commanding 2nd Battalion The Manchester Regiment.

Appendix B

14th INFANTRY BRIGADE TRAINING PROGRAMME
(from 30th April to 5th May inclusive)

REVEILLE — 6.15 a.m.

BREAKFAST — 7.0 a.m.

---

8 a.m. – 8.30 a.m.	Inspection on parade and manual exercises.

One Company

8.30 a.m. – 12.45 p.m.	On range. Ball Practice, Musketry Drill (Rapid loading etc.).

Remaining Companies

8.30 a.m. – 9.0 a.m.	Close order drill.
9.0 a.m. – 10.0 a.m.	The attack in open warfare, or Standard Trench-to-Trench form of attack at discretion of O.C's Battalions.
10.0 a.m. – 10.45 a.m.	Physical Training Bayonet Fighting and Dummy Grenade Throwing.
11.0 a.m. – 12.15 p.m.	Formation and action of an advance guard. Taking up an outpost position. At discretion of O.C. Battalions. Conference on previous evening
12.15 p.m. – 12.45 p.m.	Extended order Drill by Platoons or Companies.

1.0 p.m.	Dinner, which will be visited by Company Officers.
2.0 p.m. – 3.0 p.m.	Specialists Training. Bombing Sections) Practice with Rifle Grenadiers Sections) live grenades. Lewis Gun Sections – Mechanism & Drill.
3.0 p.m. – 5.0 p.m.	Games according to programmes submitted.
5.0 p.m.	Tea.
6.0 p.m.	Lecture by C.O., 2nd in Command or Officer on Outposts, advance guards etc. Criticism of day's work and remarks on following day's work.
8.0 p.m.	Hot Meal.
9.0 p.m.	Lights Out.

Battalion Bombing Officer will instruct 8 recruits per Coy from 8.30 a.m. to 12.45 p.m. on Bombing and Rifle Grenade Work. These recruits will rejoin their Company as soon as the necessary standard of efficiency is obtained.

Lewis Gun Officer will instruct 8 recruits per Coy from 8.45 a.m. to 12.45 p.m. in the Lewis Gun in addition to supervising the work of the Lewis Gun Sections on the range. These recruits will rejoin their Coys. as soon as they are efficient.

Appendix C

2nd Bn The Manchester Regiment.

SKETCH OF PLAN OF A PLATOON ATTACKING A STRONG POINT.

2nd Bn The Manchester Regt Instructions No. 1.

1. A demonstration of a platoon attacking a strong point will be held at 10 am on the 3rd inst in accordance with the General and Special Idea issued on the 2nd inst.

2. "C" Company (less 1 platoon and 1 section M.G.Coy) will furnish the Main Guard of the 14th Infantry Brigade. One platoon of "C" Company will furnish the tactical Vanguard of the Advanced Guard.

3. At 10.30 am the Vanguard will find themselves hung up by an enemy strong point. Information will be immediately sent back and a section of the M.G.Company ordered forward to provide covering fire for the advance of the tactical Vanguard.

4. Under cover of the M.G.fire the Lewis Gun Section will move forward to a position from which it can develope a heavy fire on the strong point.

5. Under cover of the Lewis Gun fire the rifle section will advance and attempt to envelope one or other of the flanks.

6. Under cover of a rifle grenade barrage produced by the rifle bomb section the bombing section will advance as near as possible to the enemy position.

7. When the riflemen and bombers have advanced under cover of their respective barrage near enough to charge the enemy, the strong point will be assaulted by the riflemen and bombers.

8. The Machine Gun and Lewis Gun barrages will be represented by drums.

9. The rifle grenadiers will fire dummy grenades

Major,

2-5-17.   Commanding 2nd Bn.The Manchester Regiment.

Appendix D

2-3-17.

2nd Battalion The Manchester Regiment. Major,
Commanding 2nd Bn The Manchester Regiment.
DEMONSTRATION ON PLATOON ATTACKING A STRONG POINT.

Map Reference :- ST.QUENTIN 18. 1/40.000.

General Idea. Information has been received from a reliable source that the enemy who are holding a line TOULLE - MATIGNY - CROIX MOLIGNAUX contemplate retiring from this position. The British hold a line OFFOY - BUNY - Y.

Special Idea. At 7 am our aeroplanes report that the enemy are retiring towards the line ETREILLERS - BEAUVOIS - VILLEVEQUE. At 8 am the British line is ordered to advance.
The advance guard of the 14th Infantry Brigade which will march in the direction MATIGNY - LANCHY will be found by the 2nd Bn The Manchester Regiment.
O.C., Advance guard is to be warned that the enemy in his retirement is likely to leave behind strong points with Machine Guns to hinder the advance of our troops.
At 10-30 am O.C., Vanguard reports that he is held up by an enemy strong point.

[signature]

Major,

2-3-17.   Commanding 2nd Bn The Manchester Regiment.

Scheme forwarded yesterday
is cancelled.

[signature]

Appendix E

14th INFANTRY BRIGADE
(Training of Signallers.)

8.15 a.m. - 12.45 p.m. — Class "B" - Men with no pervious Training in Signalling under Battalion Signalling N.C.O's.

Class "A" Battalion Signallers under instruction at Brigade Headquarters.

Both the above classes are under the supervision of the Brigade Signalling Officer.

14th INFANTRY BRIGADE
(Training of OBSERVERS from 3rd May to 9th May inclusive.)

8.15.a.m.	Inspection parade.
8.30.a.m. - 12.30.p.m.	Lecture and Practical Map-reading.
1.0.p.m.	Dinner.
2.0.p.m. - 4.30.p.m.	Games.
5.0.p.m.	Tea.
6.0.p.m.	Lecture.
9.0.p.m.	Lights Out.

9.0.p.m. to 11.0.p.m. on 3rd and 5th April, night marching by compass.

Appendix F

2nd Battalion The Manchester Regiment.

POINTS ON THE DEMONSTRATION OF A TACTICAL PLATOON.

1. The screen of scouts should not go forward with the attacking force but should form a screen in front, immediately the strong point has been captured.

2. A long delay exists in sending back a message from the scouts to the Main Guard. Messengers should run. Signallers with shutters should be with the scouts, the Vanguard and Main Guard.

3. Lewis Gun Sections must realize our own M.G. fire and not run into it. They should rush forward during the pause in the bursts. They must realize that they cannot go forward until our Machine Guns are in action.

4. Riflemen and Bombers must realize that they cannot go forward until the enemy fire has been got under hand. This is done by our Lewis Guns. If however it is found that the enemy is not firing, riflemen and bombers should push forward at once.

5. Riflemen must realize that they have to push round the enemy flank and fire at him from behind. This should be accomplished if possible before the bombers attack.

6. Bombers must realize that they are working with the rifle bombers and must take advantage of their barrage. Bombers must be realistic when bombing the enemy trench. Those not bombing should be pushing through the wire.

7. The Tactical Platoon must realise,

   (a) That everything should be done in phases and that the attack is a system which should become automatic.
   (b) That when the strong point has been captured the scouts will go forward again, the Platoon will reform and the advance of the Advance Guard continue.

Major,

4-5-17. Commanding 2nd Battalion The Manchester Regiment.

Appendix G

Operation Orders by Major J.F.Dempster

Commanding 2nd Battalion The Manchester Regiment.

19-5-17.

Map Reference 66D & 62C 1/40000.

1. **Information.** The enemy is holding a system of trenches consisting of 3 lines from D.6.d.20 to D.6.b.36. Frontage of 400 yards.

2. **Intention.** The 2nd Bn The Manchester Regiment will attack those trenches at dawn on the 12th inst.

3. **Position of Assembly.** (a) The position of assembly will be E.1.d.7.6. and can be recognised by a line of telegraph poles running from N.S to S.E.
    (b) The Battalion will form up in Mass with ranks closed up on the Position of Assembly.
    (c) An Outpost Line will be pushed forward by the advance guard when the Battalion reaches the Position of Assembly.
    (d) The Battalion will depart from the position of assembly at 3-30 am., on the 12th inst.

4. **Order of March.** The Battalion will march from Billets at 9 pm. on the 11th inst in the following order:- "A" "B" "C" & "D" Coys. Distances between Companies will be closed up. "D" Company will furnish the Advanced Guard of two platoons under 2/Lieut. J.J.Kirby. O.C. "D" Company will detail an officer to march in rear of the Battalion. The pace on the road will be at the rate of 3 miles per hour.
    Dress. Fighting Order without jerkins. Greatcoats will be worn.
    The Battalion will march, on leaving the Position of Assembly in the following order, proceeded by a line of scouts at 50 yards distant and 3 yards interval.
    1st line. "A" and "B" Companies, in close column of platoons at 5 yards interval between Companies.
    2nd line. "C" Company, in column of platoons in fours in line at 5 yards interval and 15 yards behind the 1st line.
    3rd line. "D" Company, in column of platoons in fours in line at 5 yards interval and 15 yards behind the 2nd line.
    The Outpost will close and join their Company as soon as the third line has past their line.

5. **Compass Bearing.** The centre of the Battalion will march from the position of assembly on a compass bearing of 350 degrees.

6. **Drill.** On leaving the position of assembly the Battalion will halt every 100 yards to correct the formation. Troops will not move faster than 1 mile per hour in preparatory formation. C.O. will march 3 paces from the right of the leading platoon of "A" Company.

7. **Position of Deployment.** Position of deployment will be regulated by the centre of the Battalion. The centre of the Battalion will deploy at D.4b.d. 300 yards from point of attack.
    At the position of deployment 1st and 2nd lines ("A" & "B" Coys) will form up in column of half companies. "A" Company will extend to 5 paces to the right, "B" Company will extend to 5 paces to the left. 2nd line will be 20 yards behind the 1st line.
    3rd Line. "C" Company will be 60 yards behind the 2nd line in line of sections in file.
    4th Line. "D" Company will be 60 yards behind the 3rd Line in line of sections in file.

(Continued)

8. **Re forming up.** One section from each platoon of "D" Company will be
   detached and will form up immediately in rear of platoons
   of "A" and "B" Companies forming 1st line and will be used as
   a cover up. One section from each platoon of "C" Company
   will be detached and will form up in rear of platoons of "A"
   and "B" Companies forming 2nd line.

9. **Direction.** Captain H.J.Gwyther who will march with the centre of
   the Battalion from the position of assembly, will be
   responsible for the direction of the Battalion.

10. **Action in case enemy opens fire.** Troops will at once lie down.
    Hostile patrols will be rushed in silence with the bayonet.

11. **Special Instructions.** (a) No one to load without distinct order.
                              (b) Until daylight, bayonets are not to be fixed.
                              (c) Absolute silence.
                              (d) No smoking and no matches to be struck.

12. **Distinctive marks.** C.O. and Adjutant will wear white sleeves.
    Company Officers will have white diamond on their backs.

13. **Watches.** Officers will synchronise their watches with the Adjutants
    at 7 pm on the 11th inst and 5 am on the 12th inst.

14. **Zero.** Zero will be 6 am on the 12th inst.

15. Acknowledge.

                                                        Capt for Adjt.
                                        1st Battalion The Manchester Regiment.

Issued to ....

        No 1 and 2 Copies   War Diary.
        No 3   ...   ...   Commanding Officer.
        No 4   ...   ...   Office Copy.
        No 5   ...   ...   "A" Company.
        No 6   ...   ...   "B" Company.
        No 7   ...   ...   "C" Company.
        No 8   ...   ...   "D" Company.
        No 9   ...   ...   Quarter Master & Transport Officer.
        No 10   ...   ...   11th Infantry Brigade.
        No 11   ...   ...   Battalion in Support.

Appendix I.

Fourth Army No. G.S.702.

32nd Division.

As the Division will shortly be leaving the Fourth Army I desire to express to all ranks my warm thanks for the excellent services they have performed whilst under my Command. The gallantry and dash displayed by the Division during the advance in March and April, especially in the actions resulting in the capture of SAVY, BOIS de SAVY, FRANCILLY, HOLNON, SELENCY, FAYET and CEPY FARM, reflect the highest credit on all concerned.

The skilful leadership of all ranks, coupled with the close co-operation between Artillery, Infantry and Aircraft, was a feature in these operations deserving the highest praise, and I heartily congratulate the Division on the successes they have achieved.

I much regret that the Division is now leaving the Fourth Army, but I shall hope that at some future date I may again have the good fortune to find them under my Command.

H.Q., Fourth Army,
22nd May, 1917.

H. Rawlinson
General,
Commanding Fourth Army.

On His Majesty's Service.

D.A.Q.M.G.
Q.M.G.
2nd Echelon

SECRET

Original
War Diary
D.H.S. Second Army
JUNE 1917

2 Manchester R.
No 35

Army Form C. 2118

WAR DIARY
or
INTELLIGENCE SUMMARY
(Erase heading not required.)

Instructions regarding War Diaries and Intelligence Summaries are contained in F.S. Regs., Part II. and the Staff Manual respectively. Title Pages will be prepared in manuscript.

Place	Date 1917	Hour	Summary of Events and Information	Remarks and references to Appendices
DEMUIN	June 1		Battalion in Billets in DEMUIN. Training carried out - Instructions having been received D Company marched to MARCELCAVE railhead entraining for BAILLEUL, leaving DEMUIN at 7.45 AM entraining about 10.30 AM. The Battalion (less D Coy) left DEMUIN at 3.55 PM marching to MARCELCAVE and entraining at 6 PM.	
BAILLEUL	" 2		The Battalion detrained at BAILLEUR about 9.30 AM and marched to billets in this area. The Commanding Officer and Adjutant visited the trenches in Messines Area.	See appendix No 1 & 2
do	" 3		Battalion in billets at BAILLEUL billeting area. Training carried on under Coy arrangements	See appendix No 3 & 4
do	" 4		do The Commanding Officer, Adjutant, Company Commanders and Transport Officer visited trenches in Messines Area	
do	" 5		do The Commanding Officer, Adjutant and as many Officers and NCOs as could be spared visited the trenches and approaches to the line.	See appendix No 5
do	" 6		do As many Officers and NCOs as could be spared visited trenches. The Bn. "Stood by." Battalion "Stood by" 2 hours notice to move.	See appendix No 6 & 8
do	" 7		Training carried on. ZERO day for MESSINES offensive. Bn scored by	See appendix No 9

WAR DIARY or INTELLIGENCE SUMMARY

Army Form C. 2118

Place	Date 1917.	Hour	Summary of Events and Information	Remarks and references to Appendices
BAILLEUL	June 8		Battn in billets BAILLEUL billeting area. "Stand by" cancelled 12 noon. Training carried on under Coy Arrangements. BAILLEUL LA BLANCHE	See Appendix nº 9
do	9		do	
do	10		The Divisional Commander presented the V.C. ribbon to 14# Infy/Bde Commander in the Battalion parade ground.	See appendix no 10 + 11.
do	11		Bn in billet BAILLEUL LA BLANCHE. Training carried on.	
do	12		do	
TERGEDHEM	13		Battn marched to the EECKE billeting area and took at TERGEDHEM.	
do	14		Battn in billets and tents TERGEDHEM. Transport of the Battn left at 9.55 AM marching independently to the new billeting area.	
TETERGHEM	15		The Battalion less Transport embussed for the COUDEKERKE billeting area starting from TERGEDHEM at 6.30AM, arriving at TETERGHEM and being complete in billets at 11.40 AM. Transport arrived and were complete in billet at 4.30 pm.	
do	16		Battn in billets TETERGHEM.	

WARRY DIARY or INTELLIGENCE SUMMARY

Army Form C. 2118

Place	Date	Hour	Summary of Events and Information	Remarks and references to Appendices
NIEUPORT	June 19		The Battn entrained and embarqued to trenches in NIEUPORT C & D Coys A & B Coys in the trenches	See appendix No. 13 & 19.20
do	1920-21		do	See appendix No. 14
do	22		C & D Coys in trenches A & B Coy in support, trench NIEUPORT	Appendix 21
do	23		C & D Coy in trenches do	See appendix No 15 & 22 & 76
do	24/25		do do	
do	27		A & C Coy in trenches B & D Coy in support trench NIEUPORT	See Appendix No. 17
do	28		do do	See appendix 14 + 18
do	29		do do	
do	30		do do	See appendix No 25 & 26

Signed Major
Comg 3rd Canadian Battn

APPENDIX No 1

2ND BATTALION THE MANCHESTER REGIMENT.   SECRET.

CONCENTRATION ORDERS   No 2.

JD 3/6/17

1...... The 14th. Infantry Brigade has been ordered to be ready to concentrate at very short notice, and to be prepared to pass one of two starting points at an hour and date to be notified later.

2...... The 2 starting points referred to above are as follows:-
(a) Road junction at S.27. Central, in which case the column will march along the route, point S.27.Central--road junction B.1.Central--NEUVEGLISE. This route will be known as NEW ROUTE.
(b) Road junction A.17.d.0.5. in which case the column will march along the route, point A.17.d.0.K5--road junction B.8.a.7.7. --road junction B.4.a.5.0.

3...... The Battalion will be prepared to fall in, in "fighting order", ready to move off, within half hours notice.

4...... The assembly point upon which the Battalion will rally will be the Battalion parade ground at B Company's billet.

5...... Starting point for the Battalion will be the junction of B Companies billet with the main road.

6...... Upon receipt of orders from Brigade for the Battalion to concentrate the "Rally" will be blown on the bugle at Bn. H.Qrs. This call is to be picked up by Company buglers.
This order to "Rally" will also be confirmed by cyclist orderly, and by telephone.

7...... Upon the order to "Rally", packs and blankets will be left in the billet and will be collected together by men left out of action, ander arrangements to be made by the Quartermaster.

8...... Each platoon will carry ten Haversacks, each containing 3 Lewis Gun drums. In case of Companies with webbing equipment, these haversacks will be worn on the left side in place of the ordinary haversack. In case of Companies with leather equipment the ordinary haversack will be worn on the left hand side, the haversack containing Lewis Gun drums will be worn on the shoulders as a knapsack.

9...... The fighting portion of the transport as detailed in Concentration orders No 1 of the 3rd. inst. will rally with the Battalion.

10..... Upon the order to "Rally" all grooms will bring Officers chargers to their respective officers billets.

11..... All fighting men left behind from the executive side of the Battn. will fall in upon the "rally" in loose order in rear of the Battalion.

12..... (a) Upon the order to "rally" 4 snipers (one per Company) detailed to be attached to Battalion H.Qrs. will draw at once telescopic rifles (one per man) from the Q'master Stores.
(b) Four spare Lewis Gun barrels and four extra Lewis Gun cylinders (one each per company) and barn stroud (as already detailed) will be sent at once to Battalion H.Qrs and handed over to the N.C.O i/c Pioneers

continued.

2.

13.......Any additional orderlies which may be called for later will
         fall in with Head Quarters on the ASSEMBLY GROUND.

14.......Battle parade states will be handed in to the Adjutant on the
         ASSEMBLY GROUND.

15.......Signalling Officer will ensure that signallers on duty collect
         all telephones in use before falling in on the ASSEMBLY GROUND.

16.......No 8904 Cpl Boyd W. and No 2698 Cpl Donneley J. who are witnesses
         on a delayed Court Marshall will remain out of action, and will
         given [not be considered] as re-inforcements.

17.......Arrangements for the collecting of Battle stores will be
         notified later.

18.......Petrol tins will be carried full on water carts. Steps are to be
         taken at once to strengthen the super-structure to take the
         extra weight

                                                                             Capt & A/Adjt.,
                              2nd. Bn. The Manchester Regiment.

Issued at...10.30pm
Issued to.-
No 1 to 14th Inf Brigade.
No 2 to Commanding Officer
No 3 to O.C."A" Coy
No 3 to O.C."B" Coy
No 4 to O.C."C" Coy
No 5 to O.C."D" Coy
No 6 to Q'Master & Transport Officer
No 7 to R.S.M.
No 8 File.

APPENDIX No 2

2ND. BATTALION THE MANCHESTER REGIMENT.   SECRET.

C O N C E N T R A T I O N - O R D E R.   3.6.17.

Map Reference sheet 28 and sheet 36 1/40,000.

1...... The 14th. Infantry Brigade will march to a position of assembly West of SWAYNE'S FARM O.23.b.3.0.

2...... Brigade starting point will be the road junction S.27.a.9.1. The Battalion will pass this point at 5.35 A.M.

3...... The Battalion will march by the following route. Starting point cross roads A.2.c.9.0.--A.3.a.1.3--S.27.a.9.1.

4...... Head of the Battalion will pass "B" Company's billet at 5.10½ A.M. tomorrow 4th. inst.

5...... Dress. ~~March~~ Fighting Order.

6...... The following Transport will accompany the Battalion. S.A.A. Lewis Gun, Grenade, and Tool limbers, Water carts with tins full, Maltese cart, Lewis Gun handcarts, and pack animals.

7...... Great care must be taken to keep the roads clear and to avoid any congestion.

8...... Watches will be synchronised with the Adjutant at 4.30. A.M.

9...... Signalling Officer will arrange to obtain Brigade time from Brigade at 4 A.M.

10..... O.C. "D" Company will arrange to join the column before the column passes B Company's billet.

11..... Order of March. H.Qrs, A.B.C.D. Companies.

12..... Acknowledge.

                              Capt & A/Adjt.,
                              2nd. Bn. The Manchester Regiment.

Issued at... 3 p.m.
Issued to.
No 1 to Commanding Officer.
   2 " Adjutant.
   3 " O.C.A Company.
   4 " O.C.B Company.
   5 " O.C.C Company.
   6 " O.C.D Company.
   7 " 14th Infantry Brigade.
   8   File.

Later.

13... Breakfasts will be arranged for on the march. O.C. Companies

   will however, arrange for their men to have tea and biscuits

   before starting. Breakfast arrangements will be made by the
   Quartermaster. Lewis gunners will carry their Lewis gun drums in
   the haversacks provided for that purpose.

2ND. BATTALION THE MANCHESTER REGIMENT.

After Order.

1......Concentration Orders of to-night are cancelled.

2......Training will be carried on to-morrow in accordance with Battalion Orders on tonight, ~~and~~ G.H.Q Standard Trench to Trench attack will not be practised.
32nd. Divisional Trench to Trench attack is not cancelled

3......32nd Divisional Trench to Trench attack will be practiced in place of G.H.Q Standard Trench to Trench attack ~~as stated in orders~~.

4......All parades to-morrow will be under Company arrangements.

H.J.Gwyther   Capt & A/Adjt.,
2nd. Bn. The Manchester Regiment.

2ND. BATTALION THE MANCHESTER REGIMENT.
                                           Alfer Orger.

1........Concentration Orders to-night are cancelled.

2........Firing will be netted to-morrow in accordance with
         Brigade Orders as follows. 2nd. B.H.Q Strength Trench to Trench
         attack will not be practiced.
         2nd. Divisional Trench to Trench attack is not cancelled.

3........Bns Divisional Trench to Trench attack will be practiced
         as nearly as possible to Trench attack B.H.Q of place in
         Orders.

4........All parades to-morrow will be under Company arrangements.

                                    Capt & A/Adjt.
                                    2nd. Bn. The Manchester Regiment.

                        C.O. + Hd Officer

2nd Battalion The Manchester Regiment.

Appendix no 3
4/6/17

The following is an extract from 14th Infantry Brigade letter S.G.136 dated 4/6/17.

1. Reference 1/20,000 Map (Secret).

2. All Company Commanders should be able to locate the probable points to which units of the Brigade may be brought up, and where they would reform for a further advance.
   The most probable points are :-

   (a) The Valley running from O.31.d. Central to O.32 Central.
   (b) The Steenebeek Valley about U.2.a.2.2.
   (c) The Valley in U.2.c and d, lying between the Stinking Farm - Messines Road and the Hyde Park Corner - Messines Road.

   All Company Commanders should be able to lead their Companies to any of the above points, and should study the ground and approaches, with this possibility in view.

3. The South Bank of the R.DOUVE is a useful line of approach for the point mentioned in para 2 (c), and should be reconnoitred.
   The South Bank of this river can be followed, under-cover from view of the enemy, as far as STINKING FARM.

6. Transport Officers of Units must reconnoitre the roads and overland approaches.

Capt & A/Adjutant
2nd Battalion The Manchester Regiment.

4 / 6 /17.

Appendix No 4

AFTER ORDERS BY LIEUT. COLONEL J.F. DEMPSTER
COMMANDING 2ND. BATTALION THE MANCHESTER REGIMENT.

4-6-17

1. Reference Concentration Order No. 1 and Concentration Order No. 2 of the 4th inst. the Battalion will be prepared to concentrate in accordance with "NEW ROUTE" tomorrow morning at a time to be notified later.

2. Reference Battalion Orders of tonight, para 4 will be complied with at a later hour than stated, under mutual company arrangements. O.C. Companies will mutually arrange with Transport Officer for the Transport required.

    Para 7 is cancelled.

Capt. & A/Adjt,.
2nd. Battalion The Manchester Regiment.

2.

Scouts and Snipers 16.			Lewis Gunners. 32.			
No 41729 Pte King H.	)		No 9282	Pte	Egan J.	)
No 39769 " Tindall J.	) B Coy		No 89775	"	Williams E	)
No 203214 " Guiton J.	)		No 34908	"	Buckley J.	) A Coy.
No 26695 " Clark J.	)		No 29857	"	Fletcher J.	)
			No 1189	"	Wolstencroft W	)
No 24305 " Charlson T	)		No 22637	"	Horton A	)
No 303055 " O'Reilly J.	) C Coy		No 23436	"	Fox T	)
No 2801 " Cox J	)		No 2062	"	Lewis C	)
No 1603 " Woodley J.	)					
No 2437 " Delany	)		No 20231	"	Horrox F	)
No 7473 " Ford G	) D Coy		No 41346	"	Allen A	)
No 301712 " Martin E	)		No 31902	"	Atkinson J	)
No 1601 " Cooper T	)		No 32947	"	Warhurst R	)
			No 29404	"	Jones E.	) B Coy.
		HQ	No 47128	"	Ashton W	)
			No 24	"	Kenworthy A	)
			No 29665	"	MacMahon J	)
			No 31203	"	Lambert J.	)
			No 2109	L/c	McGarry M	)
			No 2007	Pte	Wilson W.	)
			No 41403	"	Coup W	)
			No 47373	"	Harrison H.	) C Coy.
			No 19662	"	Hickling J	)
			No 41581	"	Winterbottom W.	)
			No 5003	"	Tiplady W	)
			No 25161	"	Hopkins W.	)
			No 23189	"	Hyde J.A.	)
			No 35224	"	Hackett J.	)
			No 29470	"	Lowden A	) D Coy.
			No 34661	"	Chapman J.	)
			No 19439	"	Linney E	)
Total Re-inforcements			No 29621	"	Shaw E	)
108.			No 36259	"	Dixon G.H.	)

These names of re-inforcements are subject to variation at the discretion of the Company Commanders.

Men leaving the Battalion will be replaced, and names may be changed to include sick men, but any alteration MUST be reported AT ONCE to Battalion H.Qrs.

O's C. Companies will arrange to alter their Battle parade states in accordance with the above.

Appendix No 5
5-6-17

2ND BATTALION THE MANCHESTER REGIMENT.

INSTRUCTIONS M.No 2.

1. When proceeding into action the following Officers, W.O's, N.C.O's and Men will be left behind as reinforcements.
   In addition to those detailed below Nos 2698 Cpl Donnelly and 8904 Cpl Boyd W. witnesses on a delayed F.G.C.M. will be left behind but will not be considered as reinforcements.

OFFICERS. 4.

Captain	A.R.	Oldfield	"C" Company.
Lieut	E	Tanner	"A" "
2/Lieut	J.W.	Culley	B.H.Q.
2/Lieut	H.M.	Gooding	B.H.Q.

Warrant Officers. 2.

| No 6608 | C.S.M. | Pearce A.E. | C Coy |
| " 9226 | " | Winterbottom A. | "E" |

N.C.O's and Men.
Signallers. 10

No 2063	L/C	King E.	"D" Coy.
" 18593	Pte	Green J.	"A" "
" 25131	"	Platt F.	"A" "
" 27025	"	Preston W.	"B" "
" 41460	"	Holmes S.	"B" "
" 35845	"	Sutcliffe	"B" "
" 46659	"	Clayton H.	"A" "
" 23705	"	Bostock A.	"E" "
" 36524	"	Slater A.	"C" "
" 41394	"	Crabbe J	"D" "

Drums. 16.

Bombing Instructor 1.

No 2027 L/C Bailey J. R. "B"

Gas Instructor 1.

No 46640 Sergt Gregory W. B Coy

Lewis Gun Instructors.

No 2104 Sergt Hamilton F. D Coy
No 7538 L/Cpl Edwards A Coy.

Sergeants.

No 2281	Sergt	Bates W.	(A)
" 7885	"	Cook J.	(B)
" 896	"	Brownsill	(C)
" 89	"		

Corporals. 4.

No 2720	Cpl	Burkmar J.	A. Coy.
" 9025	"	Glynn W.	B. "
" 41389	"	Carr J.C.	"
" 1459	"	Chadwick H.D.	"

Lance Corporals. 4.

No 1028	L/C	Gardner R.	A. Coy.
" 2593	"	Glynn M.	B. "
" 33021	"	Gill H.	C. "
" 2036	"	Wilkinson J D.	"

Rifle Bombers. 16

No 39574	Pte	Hartshorne G.	)
" 27610	"	Dutton J.	) A.
" 27840	"	Birchall J.	)
" 16435	"	Leah H.	)
" 303133	"	Allen J.	)
" 26076	"	Hart	) B.
" 252540	"	Holmes S.	)
" 35795	"	Kenworthy J.	)
" 39901	"	Smith R.	)
" 34149	"	Smith S.	) C.
" 36211	"	Heaton E.	)
" 29821	"	Matthews F.	)
" 377168	"	Smith J.	)
" 203255	"	Mc Laughlin C.	) D.
" 1036	"	Buckley D.	)
" 25163	"	Matthews F.C.	)

Snipers and Observers. 16.

No 1784	Pte	Bradshaw	A Coy
" 2057	"	Condron W.	A Coy
			A Coy
" 7490	"	Shaw R.	A Coy

Part 2.

The executive portion of Battalion H.Qrs. will be composed of the following:-

OFFICERS.

Commanding Officer	1.
2nd. in Command	1
Adjutant.	1
Intelligence Officer	1
Signalling Officer	1

Other Ranks.

Sergeant Major	1
Orderly Room Clerks	4
Gas N.C.O's	2
Signallers	17
Snipers	4
Runners	14
Pioneers	11
Cooks	2
Batmen	6
Mess	3
	Total 69. 65. and 5 O.R.

The administrative portion of the Battalion when in action will be composed as under:-

OFFICERS.

Quaetermaster	1
Transport Officer	1

Other Ranks.

Q.M.Sergeant & Storeman	3
C.Q.M.S & Storemen	8
Transport Establishment & Grooms & Cook.	45
Shoemakers	5
Tailors	3
Butchers	2
Postman	1
Cooks	8
Batmen	3
Master Cook	1
Sanitary Squad	2
	Total 80

Capt & A/Adjt.,
2nd. Bn. The Manchester Regiment.

5.6117.

AFTER ORDERS BY LIEUT COLONEL J.F.DEMPSTER,　　　　S E C R E T.
COMMANDING 2ND BATTALION THE MANCHESTER REGIMENT.

Appendix 6

6.6.17.

1...... **Zero Day.** Zero day will be tomorrow.

2...... **Move.** The Battalion will from now on be prepared to move at half an hours notice.

3...... **Breakfasts.** O.C.Companies will arrange for breakfasts to be ready for issue at 3 A.M.. Breakfasts will however, not be issued until 7.30. A.M. unless the "Rally" is blown previous to this time. This paragraph cancels verbal instructions issued to Company Commanders tonight.

4...... **Re-inforcements.** Re-inforcements will after the Battalion has moved off, and after they have collected from companies and taken packs and kits to the Quartermasters store, move into the billet vacated by B Company. Captain A.R.Oldfield will be in command of re-inforcements.

5...... **Lewis Guns.** All the ammunition will be loaded on the Lewis Gun Limbers tonight. Lewis Gun haversacks will be carried empty.

6...... **Lewis Gun Officer and Bombing Officer.** Lewis Gun Officer, and Bombing Officer will each personally check the loading of the Lewis Gun and Bombing establishment on their respective limbers tonight. These Officers will accompany the Battalion to Brigade assembly ground, and will when Lewis Guns and Ammunition are issued from limbers, supervise the correct allottment according to establishment. These Officers will report "establishment complete" to the Adjutant when issued.

7...... **Wire Cutters.** O.C's C and D Companies will arrange to hand over all their wire cutters to O.C's A.and B Companies respectively tonight. No 5 wirecutter will be carried slung under the shoulder straps by a piece of string, *and tucked in the belt*

8...... **Battle parade states.** Battle parade states will be rendered to Orderly room tonight. A further state will again be handed to the Adjutant on the parade tomorrow.

9...... **No 1. Prisoners.** O.C's Companies will arrange to transfer No 1. prisoners belonging to their Companies from the main Guard Room to their Company Guard Room tonight.

10..... **Officers Mess Kits.** O.C.Companies will arrange that their Company Mess kit is packed up tonight.

11..... **Tools.** When moving off for the assault C and D Companies only will carry picks and shovels.

continued.

2.   6.6.17.

12......<u>Carrying Parties.</u>O.C. Companies will estimate tonight the
        amount of Ammunition, flares, Rockets that they require
        and will have parties detailed for drawing these at a moments
        notice. O.C C and D Companies will have parties ready to
        collect tools. The number to be carried will be notified later.

                                        H.J.Lowther. Capt & A/Adjt.,
                                        2nd. Bn. The Manchester Regiment.

<u>6.6.17.</u>

Issued at..9 pm

Issued to.
No 1 Copy to 14th Inf Bde.
No 2   "   Commanding Officer.
No 3   "   O.C.A Company
No 4   "   O.C.B Company
No 5   "   O.C.C Company
No 6   "   O.C.D Company
No 7   to   Quartermaster
No 8   "   Transport Officer
No 9   "   R.S.M.
No 10 "   File.

SECRET.   appendix 7

        2nd. Battalion The manchester Regiment.   6.6.17.

This document is to be considered SECRET, and is never to be out of
         the hands of an Officer.

PRELIMINARY OPERATION ORDERS No. 1.

Reference Maps. Sheet 28 S.W. 1/20,000 Sheet 28 and Sheet 36 1/40,000
      and HAZEBROUCK Sheet 1/100,000.

---

1. GENERAL IDEA. An attack on a large scale is shortly to take place along the whole of the Second Army Front.
    The 2nd. Anzacs will take the enemy system of trenches in front of, and North and South of MESSINES.
    The 2nd. Anzacs consists of 4 Divisions, Three Divisions will be in the front line. 3rd Australian Division, New Zealand Division, and 25th. Division (from right)
    The remaining Divisions will be in support.
This Division consists of 4 Brigades.

2. SPECIAL IDEA. (a) The 2nd Anzacs will capture the first System of enemy trenches up to a line running roughly from U.4.Central through O.28 Central to O.22.Central.
    The 32nd Division ~~will be in support~~ has been attached to the 2nd. Anzacs as a Reserve Division.

    (b). The probable role of the 32nd Divisions if employed will be
(2) To repel a possible counter attack on the left and centre of the Corps.
(1) To repel a possible counter attack from WARNETON
    Of these (1) appears more probable.

3. INFORMATION. The MESSINES Ridge on our right from the left to PETIT DOUVE FARM presents the following features:-
    (a) A Spur running West from 4 HUNS FARM,
    (b) then a valley
    (c) A spur running East from MOULIN de L'HOSPICE.
    (d) A valley running up to the AU BON FERMIER CABARET.
    (e) A valley running down towards LA PETIT DOUVE FARM
    These features are repeated on the Eastern Side in a more pronounced form.

    The approaches to these positions on our side are:-

                              continued.

"2"

    (a) WULVERGHEM - MESSINES Road.
    (b) WULVERGHEM-STINKING FARM-MESSINES Road.
    (c) HYDE PARK CORNER-PETIT DOUVE-MESSINES ROAD.

Routes and distances to WULVERGHEM or HYDE PARK CORNER are as follow
    (a) From VIEUX BERQUIN- Via NOOTE BOOM- LE LEUTHE-
CROSS ROADS 1 mile East of STEENWERCK- NEUVE EGLISE
or PETITE PONT. 12 miles.
    (b) From DOULIEU Via LE VERRIER and STEENWERCK STATION
10 Miles.
    (c) From NEUF BERQUIN by the same routes as in (b)
12 miles.

It would be possible to bring troops up for an advance and reform at the following points:-
    (a) West of SWAYNE'S FARM. This would be concealed from observation from the direction of WARNETON.
    (b) Valley from BIG BULL COTTAGE to the AU BON FERMIER CABARET.
    (c) Any advance on the right will have to be over the open and would be exposed to view from the direction of WARNETON after leaving the wood south of Hill 63.

4. INTENTION.
    (a) At Zero hour all troops in the Corps will be prepared to move forward.
    The 14th. Infantry Brigade has been ordered to be prepared to move forward at half an hours notice to some assembly position vacated by the Division in Support.
    This will probably be in Squares T.26 and T 27. or Squares S.17.and S.18
    This move will take place in accordance with 2nd Bn The Manchester Regiment Concentration order No 2 of the 4th. inst., already issued.

    (b) <u>Approaches</u>. Approaches from this area forward will probably be by way of the routes; RED, BLUE, GREEN, BROWN, W, X, Y, Z, or BLUE and RED dotted routes.
These routes have already been shown on the Map to Company Commanders, and have been copied by them.

5. RECONNOITRING. All Company Commanders will reconnoitre tracks and approaches to the line as instructed in this office "Extract from Brigade Letter S.G.136 dated 4.6.17." (issued 4.6.17.) and this office "Extract from 14th Brigade S.G.136 dated 6.6.17." (issued 6.6.17)

6. ATTACK. Formation for the attack will be detailed in Operation Orders to be issued later.

7. BATTLE STORES. Battle stores will be drawn later from some forward Dump.

                                                  continued.

6.6.17.

8 HAVERSACKS. Haversacks have been provided for carrying Lewis Gun Drums and for carrying Rifle Grenades. These haversacks will be worn on the left hand side, and O.C. Companies who possess men with leather equipment will arrange to have this equipment adjusted to carry the haversack in this manner.

9 S.A.A Etc. AMMUNITION

When moving forward for the attack the following ammunition will be carried by the men:-

S.A.A.
- Riflemen — 170 rounds per man.
- Bombers — 120 rounds per man (in addition to bombs)
- Rifle Bombers — 120 rounds per man (in addition to bombs)
- Lewis Gunners — 70 rounds per man in pouches and 50 rounds in bandolier inside the haversack carrying the Lewis Gun drums. This is for refilling the drums.
- Scouts and Observers) 120 rounds per man.
- Signallers — 50 rounds per man.
- Runners — 50 rounds per man.

BOMBS.

Each man will carry two bombs.
Bombers will carry 6 bombs and two P bombs.
Rifle Bombers will carry 6 Rifle Bombs.

10. Wire Cutters. All wire cutters in the Battalion will be distributed between the two Companies forming the assaulting waves. Company Commanders of the assaulting companies will arrange to draw the wire cutters of the 3rd and 4th Companies prior to the attack.

11. FLARES. Each Rifleman will carry two flares.

12. SIGNAL ROCKETS. Each Company Headquarters will carry two Signal Rockets for communication with the artillery.

13 RATIONS. Each man will carry his Iron Ration, one days preserved ration, and the unconsumed portion of the current days ration

14 WATER. All water bottles will be full.
Petrol Tins will be carried full on the water carts.

All ranks are warned that this water is to be husbanded. as it is possible a further supply of water may not be available.

continued.

4.   6.6.17.

15.
SUPPLY OF AMMUNITION.

Each Company will detail four men (with Yellow Armlets) to report to the R.S.M., when the Battalion concentrates. These men will establish a dump at Headquarters from the Mobile reserve as soon as possible. Notification will be made of further dumps, giving location of these, when known. Each Company, after consolidation is under weigh, will have parties ready to send for ammunition and stores.

16. **PREVIOUS ORDERS.**

Attention is drawn to Concentration Orders No 1 & 2 and instructions No M.L. which must be studied carefully. Further instructions for the coming attack will be issued.

17.
CIRCULATION.

The General Idea and possible function of the Battalion must be made known to all ranks, who must be warned to keep these matters strictly SECRET.

(Sd) H.J. Gwyther, Capt & A/Adjt.,
2nd Bn. The Manchester Regiment.

6.6.17.

Issued at 8.30.P.M.
Issued to:-
No 1 to 14th. Infantry Brigade.
" 2 " Commanding Officer.
" 3 " Adjutant.
" 4 " Quartermaster.
" 5 " Transport Officer
" 6 " O.C. "A" Company
" 7 " O.C. "B" Company
" 8 " O.C "C" Company
" 9 " O.C "D" Company.
" 10 " R.S.M.
" 11 " War Diary.
" 12 " File.

JD   *Appendix 8*

2ND BATTALION THE MANCHESTER REGIMENT.

6.6.17.

Extract from "Instructions regarding routes in the event of a Forward Move of the 14th. Infantry Brigade.

-o-o-o-o-o-o-o-o-o-o-o-o-o-o-o-o-o-o-o-o-o-o-o-o-o-o-o-o-o-o-o-o-o-o-o-o-

In addition to the routes already reconnoitred Company Commanders will see that the following roads are known to them.

(a) The STEENWERK - TROIS ARBRES - PONT D'ACHELLES ROAD leading up through LAMPERNISSE to squares T.26 and T.27. which might form the billeting area of the Brigade.

(b) A variation of the RAMORIN - HYDE PARK CORNER route, namely via PLOEGSTEERT VILLAGE.

                               Capt & A/Adjt.,
                          2nd. Bn. The Manchester Regiment.

Appendix No 9

2ND BATTALION THE MANCHESTER REGIMENT.

AMENDMENT TO PROGRAMME OF TRAINING FROM JUNE 7TH to 10TH. INCLUSIVE.

8 A.M. to 5 P.M.   One company will fire on Range. Ball practice.
Lectures will be given to men not firing on
(1) Theory of the Rifle and its practical
application. (2) Care of Arms. (3) Aiming Instructions
M.R. Chapter III Section 25. Tripods will be used.
(4) Rapid loading with dummies. (5) Fire orders
Chapter 17 Secs. 55 to 60 (6) Practice Standard
Tests in Musketry.

[signature]

Lieut Colonel,
Commanding 2nd. Bn. The Manchester Regiment.

7.6.17.

2nd Battalion The Manchester Regiment. Appendix 10

INSTRUCTIONS M.3.

1. With reference to Instructions No M.2., personnel composing reinforcements for "Snipers and Observers 16 etc" read "Snipers and Observers 16.

30465	Pte	Marler A.	"A"	Company.
7479	"	Shaw E.	"A"	"
203214	"	Guiton J.	"B"	"
26695	"	Clark J.	"B"	"
2801	"	Cox J.	"C"	"
1603	"	Woodley J.	"C"	"
301712	"	Martin E.	"D"	"
1601	"	Cooper T.	"D"	"

Eight (8) Pioneers Headquarters.

2. Company Battle Headquarters will in future consist of thirteen (13).

3. Platoon Battle Headquarters will in future consist of two (2) i.e., Platoon Sergeant and Batman.

4. Company Commanders will arrange to alter their Battle Parade States in accordance with these amendments.

Capt & A/Adjt.,
10-6-17.   2nd Battalion The Manchester Regiment.

Appendix No 11

EXTRACT FROM 32ND. DIVISIONAL ROUTINE ORDERS.

10th June 1917.

AWARDS.

The Divisional Commander has much pleasure in announcing that the VICTORIA CROSS has been bestowed on the undermentioned Officer.-

        Major (now Brig.Gen.) FREDERICK WILLIAM LUMSDEN D.S.O.
                             ROYAL MARINE ARTILLERY.

The circumstances were as follows:-

Major FREDERICK WILLIAM LUMSDEN D.S.O., R.M.A.

"For most conspicuous bravery, determination, and devotion to duty.

Six enemy Field Guns having been captured, it was necessary to leave them in dug-in positions, 300 yards in advance of the position held by our troops. The enemy kept the captured guns under heavy fire.

Major LUMSDEN undertook the duty of bringing the guns into our lines.

In order to effect this he personally led four artillery teams and a party of Infantry through the hostile Barrage. As one of these teams sustained casualties he left the remaining teams in a covered position, and, through very rifle, machine gun and shrapnel fire, led the Infantry to the guns. By force of example and inspiring energy he succeeded in sending back two teams with guns,, going through the barrage with the teams of the third gun. He then returned to the guns to await further teams, and these he succeeded in attaching to two of the three remaining guns, despite rifle fire, which had become intense at short range, and removed the guns to safety.

By this time the enemy, in considerable strength, had driven th through the infantry covering points and blown up the breach of the remaining gun.

Major LUMSDEN then returned, drove off the enemy, attached the gun to a team and got it away."

The six Guns mentioned above were captured by this Battalion during the attack (and capture) of FRANCILLY and FRANCILLY-SELENCY on April 2nd.1917.

This is to be read out to all ranks on parade.

                                                  Capt., & A/Adjt.,
                               2nd. Bn. The Manchester Regiment.

2ND BATTALION THE MANCHESTER REGIMENT.

Appendix 22-6-17
No 12

14th. Infantry Brigade.

Headquarters.

Preliminary prospects for a raid to be undertaken by the 2nd. Bn. Manchester Regiment in D Subsector, NIEUPORT.

1. The Raid will take place against the enemy trench in the proximity of the point N.19.c.3.1.

2. This point has been chosen because:-

   (a) The left flank is protected from hostile Machine Gun Fire.

   (b) Any Machine Gun fire likely to be brought to bear on the raiding party from the right can be silenced by massed Machine Guns, and Lewis Guns in ROODE POORT FARM.

   (c) The position is such that a Machine Gun might very likely be situated there, in which case it would be captured.

   (d) A light Railway leads up to this point; this suggests a dump, and possible Company H.Qrs. In this case several enemy officers would be killed.

   (e) The ground west of the embanked road is not swampy to appearance, and should lend itself to the assembly of Troops.

   (f) This point should be an unlikely spot for the enemy to expect a raid.

3. A barrage of Stokes Guns can be obtained, if necessary on the enemy front line or the immediate support line, running from N.19.c.6.6. to M.24.d.9.2.

   This latter barrage would cut off all reinforcements coming up.

4. A barrage at points N.19.c.6.6., N.19.c.3.5., and M.24.d.9.2. would cut off all main communication trenches from the area to be raided.

5. The ground in front of this point is being reconnoitred.

22.6.17.

Lieut Colonel.,
Commanding 2nd. Battalion The Manchester

Appendix No 13.

SECRET.   2nd. Battalion The Manchester Regiment.

NIEUPORT RAID INSTRUCTIONS No 1.

21.6.17.

To O.C. "A" Company.

1....... It is the intention of the Battalion to carry out a Raid in the near future, on the enemy trench in the proximity of point N.19.c.3.0.

2....... Please arrange for patrols to be sent out to-night to investigate the ground thoroughly between this point and our trench from N.25.a.2.5. to M.30.b.7.6.

3....... Information required is as follows:-

(a) General Condition of NO MAN'S LAND.
(b) Paths across NO MAN'S LAND, and round swamps, if any.
(c) Positions in NO MAN&S LAND that would give cover for troops to form up.
(d) Positions for assembly of the raiding party immediately prior to the attack.
(e) The extent, type, and condition of the enemy's wire. This should give:-
   (1) Type of wire, whether barbed, concertina or plain.
   (2) The Depth of the outer belt of wire.
   (3) Distance of outer edge of outer belt from enemy trench.
   (4) Distance of outer edge of inner belt from the inner edge of the outer belt.
   (5) The depth of the inner belt of wire.
   (6) The distance of the outer edge of the inner belt from the enemy trench. ~~THIS IS MOST IMPORTANT.~~
THIS IS MOST IMPORTANT.
(f) The condition of the enemy trench, how manned, position of possible saps, and position of possible Machine Guns.

4....... It is realised that this information cannot be obtained in one night. Patrols are to be sent out for the next few nights to amass this information.

5....... It is absolutely essential that all information brought in is strictly correct. Negative information is of great importance. The lives of many men may depend the accuracy of this information. upon

6....... Results of these patrols are to be sent SECRET, as soon as received to Battalion Hd. Qrs.

Capt & A/Adjt.,
2nd. Bn. The Manchester Regiment.

2nd BATTALION THE MANCHESTER REGIMENT.

22-6-17

Appendix No 14

127th. Infantry Brigade.

Headquarters.

Preliminary proposals for a raid to be undertaken by the 2nd. Bn. Manchester Regiment in R.Inchester. NIEUPORT.

1.   The raid will take place against the enemy trench in the proximity of the point N.12.c.8.4.

2.   This point has been chosen because:-

   (a) The left flank is protected from hostile machine gun fire.

   (b) Any Machine Gun fire likely to be brought to bear on the raiding party from the right can be silenced by personal Machine Guns, and Lewis Guns in NORDE WEST BEND.

   (c) The position is such that a Machine Gun might very likely be situated there, in which case it would be captured.

   (d) A light Railway leads up to this point; this suggests a dump, and possible Company H.Qrs. In this case several enemy officers would be killed.

   (e) The ground west of the embanked road is not easy to appear men, and should lend itself to the assembly of troops.

   (f) This point should be an unlikely spot for the enemy to expect a raid.

3.   A barrage of Stokes Guns can be obtained, if necessary on the enemy front line or the immediate support line, running from N.12.c.8.4. to N.12.d.3.2.

   This latter barrage would cut off all reinforcements coming up.

4.   A barrage at points N.12.c.6.6., N.12.d.5.4., and N.12.d.4.3. would cut off all main communication trenches from the area to be raided.

5.   The ground in front of this point is being reconnoitred.

H.Col.

Lieut Colonel..
Commanding 2nd. Battalion. The Manchester

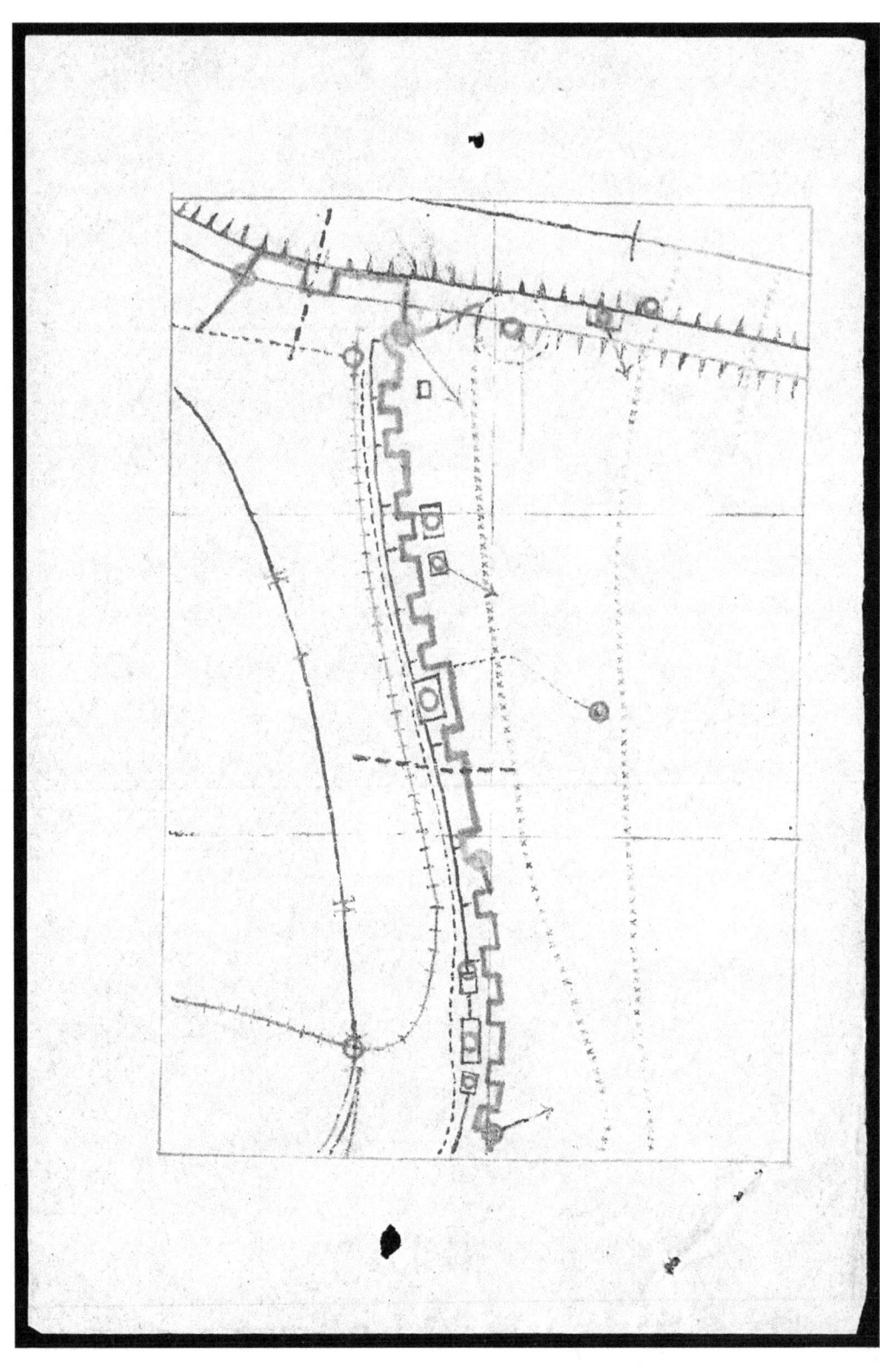

Appendix 15

RAID AGAINST THE HANOVERIAN REGIMENT.
21.6.17.

Reference Map 1/10,000 and sketch map attached.

SCHEME OF PROPOSED RAID ON THE ENEMY TRENCHES BETWEEN POINTS

N.19.c.55.15. and N.19.c.15.65.

1. **INTENTION.** It is our intention to raid the enemy's trenches between points N.19.c.55.15. and N.19.c.15.65. "frontage" of 100 yards" at an early date.

2. **INFORMATION.** Aeroplane photographs, and large scale Trench maps show the following points with regard to this area.

   TRENCHES.
   (a) 4 dugouts.
   (b) 8 Machine Gun emplacements (5 of which are probable alternative emplacements.
   (c) A light railway running behind the trench and ending without the area to be raided.
   (d) A listening post in the enemy wire.

   These points seem to suggest that a number of troops are accommodated in this area, and that it is a place of importance.

   It is therefore considered a place at which considerable damage could be done to the enemy by a successful raid.

   WIRE.
   The enemy wire consists of 2 belts which are 3 to 4 yards deep, and about 20 yards apart. A gateway runs through the inner belt of wire at about point N.19.c.31.41.
   The wire is thick and consists of knife rests intermingled with loose barbed wire. There is a certain amount of loose wire in front of the outer belt of wire.

3. **ARTILLERY.** It is proposed to protect the flanks of the raiding party from M.G. fire in the following manner:-

   (a) Vickers M.Guns and Lewis Guns in QUEBEC CITY line. These guns are to battle all machine gun fire which may come from the N or N.E.

   (b) Vickers Machine Gun and Lewis Gun fire at about points N.19.b.89.70. These guns are to battle any hostile M.G. fire which may come from the North i.e. German strong point on the Canal.

continued.

2.

(c) Any Machine Gun fire from the direction of point N.9.d.4.1. is to be halted by Machine Gun fire from or about point N.31.b.5.0.

4. **METHOD OF CUTTING ENEMY WIRE.**

It is proposed to cut the outer belt of wire by a Bangalore Torpedo.
The following methods are under consideration for the inner belt of wire.

(a) By the same Bangalore Torpedo that cuts the outer belt if sufficient length of torpedo can be obtained.

(b) By asking for Divisional artillery to register along the whole of our front, and for it to be so arranged, that, during this registration a certain number of rounds to fall short at various places along our front, one of which places would be point N.19.c.25.12. (at which pathway already exists in the wire)

(c) By using the existing pathway be referred to about N.19.c.25.12.

In case it is not possible for the Bangalore torpedo party to lay the Torpedo on account of hostile M.G. fire it is proposed to silence this M.G. fire with an 18 pdr battery enfilading the enemy front line trench. Under cover of this barrage the Bangalore would be laid and blown. The signal for the assistance of this Battery will be arranged.

5. **METHOD OF ATTACK.** (a) It is proposed to divide the assaulting parties of the raiding party into 4 groups. These groups will rush forward on the blowing of the Bangalore Torpedo. The first group will establish a block in the enemy trench at point N.19.c.15.05. The 2nd group will rush any Machine Guns in the front line and mop up dugouts in the front line. 3rd. group will establish a block at N.19.c.35.15. 4th. group will work up the enemy's sap, and mop up any M.Guns or any of the enemy that may be found there.

(b) It is proposed to blow a 2nd Bangalore torpedo at point N.19.c.99 in order to connect up to a gap for group 4 to move out of the sap.

(c) The blowing of the Bangalore Torpedo will be the signal for the Commencement of Stokes Mortar and Machine Gun barrage.

1. The Stokes mortar barrage will be established at points N.19.d.1.9. N.19.c.49 and continued.

2.

and R.19.c.4.5.7. This barrage will prevent any re-inforcements of the enemy moving up from the trenches.

3. The Machine Gun barrage will be established as a direct enfilade of the enemy trenches running from R.25.a.0.9.1. R.19.c.6.2. and a direct enfilade of the enemy trenches running from R.19.c.6.4.6. to R.19.c.4.5.5. This barrage will prevent any re-inforcements of the enemy moving across the open.
These barrages will be kept on for half an hour.

6. TIME IN TRENCH.

The probable duration of time the raiding party will spend in the enemy trench will be from 15 to 30 minutes.

7. SIGNAL FOR RETIREMENT

The signal for the party to move back will be:-

(a) "Lights out" blown on the bugle from H.Qrs. O.C. Bn.

(b) In case there is any trouble and the raiding party have to move back quickly they will be covered by:-
   (1) An Artillery barrage enfilading the enemy trenches from R.19.c.6.2. to R.19.c.6.5.
   (2) By a covering party established with a Lewis Gun at a suitable point in NO MAN'S LAND.

8. COMPOSITION OF RAIDING PARTY.

The following will be the composition of the assaulting party:-
  1st Group............1 N C O and 6 men
  2nd. group..........1 officer 16 O.R's.
  3rd " ....1 N C O and 6 men
  4th " ....1 officer and 15 O.R's.

It is estimated that including sappers party, covering parties and parties to receive back, the total number composing the raiding party will be 3 officers and 60 O.R's

9. ENTRY INTO ENEMY TRENCH

The suggested point of entry into the enemy trench will be R.19.c.4.5.5.

10. SIGNALS.

A Signal will be arranged with the artillery for the co-operation of the guns with the raid.

11. INTER-COMMUNICATION.

Forward Battalion report centre will be established at or about R.25.a.4.5. at which liason will be established
continued.

4.

with the Artillery M.Gun, Trench Mortars Raid I.O. and Battalion H.Qrs.

12. Further information with regard to the organisation of the raiding party and the administrative details required will be forwarded later.

Capt & A/Adjt.,
For O.C. 2nd Bn. The Manchester Regiment.

Appendix No. 16

S E C R E T   2ND. BATTALION THE MANCHESTER REGIMENT.   26.6.17

Reference Map LOMBARTZYDE Ed. 1 A. 1/20,000 and

Trench Map CANAL DE PLASSCHENDAELE 1/1000.

Scheme B of the proposed raid on the enemy trenches between points N.19.c.35.15. and N.24.d.08.15.

1. **MODIFICATION.**

    This scheme is a modification of the scheme submitted on the 24th. inst. for a proposed raid between points N.19.c.35.15. and N.19.c.15.02.
    This latter scheme will, in future, be known as scheme "A".

2. **OBJECT.**

    The object of the raid is:-
    (1) To impress upon the enemy that we are sitting opposite him in an offensive spirit, and to make him clearly understand that we are masters of the situation.
    (11) To take as many prisoners, as possible.

3. **COMBINED RAID.**

    It has been decided to make a combined raid on the enemy trench. The extent of trench to be raided by a raiding party is from N.19.c.35.15. to N.19.c.15.02.
    The extent of of enemy trench to be raided by "B" raiding party is from N.19.c. 15-02 to N.24.d.08.15.

4. **INFORMATION. GENERAL.**

    In continuation of information given in scheme "A", the portion of trench to be raided by "B" raiding party contains 5 dugouts and two Machine Gun emplacements.

    A WIRE.

    The wire in front of the trenches to be raided by "A" raiding party has been thoroughly examined, and is found to consist of two belts of wire 25 yards apart, and each 5 yards deep, the inner edge of the outer belt is 30 yards from the enemy parapet.
    A gap 5 yards wide which is closed by single knife rests exists in the outer belt at point N.19.c.25.02. An open gap exists in the second belt behind this point. A gap 1½ yards wide exists at about point N.19.c.20.05.
    There is also a pathway along the ZRUIS DYKE by the western edge of the enemy gap.

    B   The wire in front of the trenches to be entered by raiding party "B" consists of two belts of wire about 5 yards apart and each 5 yards deep. No gap has, as yet been located in this wire but it is thought (from study of aeroplane photographs) that a gap exists at N.19.c.00.15.

26.6.17.

5. METHOD OF CUTTING ENEMY WIRE.

A. Raid A. It is proposed to cut the outer belt of wire by a Bangalore Torpedo.

The following methods are under consideration for the inner belt of wire.

(a) By the same Bangalore Torpedo that cuts the outer belt if sufficient length of Torpedo can be obtained.

(b) By asking for Divisional Artillery to register along the whole of our front, and for it to be arranged, that, during this registration a certain number of rounds to fall short at various places along our front, one of which places would be point N.19.c.25.01. (at which, pathway already exists in the wire).

(c) By using the the existing pathway as referred to above i.e. N.19.c.25.01.

B. In case it is not possible for the Bangalore torpedo party to lay the Torpedo on account of hostile M.G. fire it is proposed to silence this M.G. fire with an 18 pdr battery enfilading the enemy front line trench. Under cover of this barrage the Bangalore would be laid and blown.
The signal for the assistance of this battery would be arranged.

Raid B. The gap in the wire in front of trench to be entered by raiding party B will be blown by Bangalore Torpedo.

6 METHOD OF ASSAULT.

(A) Raid A will consist of 6 parties and will be distributed as follows:-

Party A (1). will enter the enemy trenches in front of the gap, and will work Westward i.e. to the left, mopping up the existing dugouts, commencing on the left of the point of entry. This party is not to move beyond this last dugout (shown on attached sketch) until the overland parties have obtained touch.

Party A (2). will enter the enemy's trench opposite the gap, following party A (1), and will work East i.e. to the right mopping up the enemy's dugouts, and clearing the trench as far as its junction with sap.

Party A (3). will move through the gap following party A (2), and thence over the open to the junction of the enemy's sap with their front line.

continued.

2.   6.6.17.

It will then move up the front line running North, and
establish a block about 20 yards beyond the corner
formed by the junction of the Bay with the main line.
This party will drop a party of 6 O.R's into the enemy
trench about 20 yards Eastwards i.e. to the right, and
will protect the rear of the main blocking party.

Party A (4)   Will move through the gap and advance across the top
                of the trench eastwards i.e. to the right, to the base
                of the enemys sap. They will then enter and mop up
                the enemy sap.
                This party when it has mopped up the enemys sap, will
                return with such prisoners and booty as it may possess,
                to our front line, reporting on the way to O.C. "A" raid.

Party A (5)   Will move through the gap and thence Eastwards i.e. to the
                right, along the top of the enemys trench to the sap.
                This party is for, and is responsible for dealing with
                any of the enemy, counter-attacking over the open, and
                for warning parties in the trenches, of any unforeseen
                action on the part of the enemy which they can observe,
                and which cannot be seen by the men in the trenches,
                and generally to assist those mopping up in the
                trenches.

Party A (6)   Will move through the gap and thence work westwards
                i.e. to the left, along the top of the enemys trench until
                they obtain touch with party B (4) of B raid. The
                duties of this party are as laid down for party A (5).

B   Raid B will assault the enemy's trenches in the following manner,
     and will be distributed as follows:-

Party B (1)   Will move through the gap and advance westwards i.e.
                to the left, across the open and establish a block
                at point H.24.d.90.15, about 20 yards beyond the enemys
                dugout. When this block is established, two men will be
                left in the trenches, and the remainder of the blocking
                party will lie out on the top of the enemys parapet.

Party B (2)   Will enter the enemy trench opposite the gap, and work
                from there Westward i.e. to the left, mopping up the
                enemy dugouts.

Party B (3)   Will enter the enemy trench opposite the gap, working
                from there Eastwards i.e. to the right, mopping up two
                enemy dugouts. This party is not to go beyond the last
                dugout until touch has been obtained between parties
                B (4) and A (6).

Party B (4)   Will move through the gap, and thence along the top of
                the enemy trench eastwards i.e. to the right, till they
                obtain touch with party A (6). The duties of this
                party are as laid down for parties A (5) and A (6)
                                continued.

4.   26.6.17.

The position of operations of the above parties are shown diagrammatically on the attached sketch.

(C) SUPPORT.

Each raiding party will have in support a party composed of 1 Lewis Gun Section, as shown in diagram attached.

(D) BARRAGE.

The blowing of the Bangalore Torpedo will be the signal for the commencement of Stokes Mortar, and Machine Gun Barrage.

(1) The Stokes Mortar Barrage will be established at points N.24.d.90.15., N.19.c.40. and N.19.c.42.30.
This barrage will prevent any re-inforcements of the enemy moving up from the trenches.

(2) The Machine Gun Barrage will be established as a direct enfilade of the enemy trenches running from N.24.d.9.2. N.19.c.6.5. and a direct enfilade of the enemy trenches running from N.19.c.4.4. to N.19.c.1.8. This barrage will prevent any re-inforcements of the enemy moving across the open.

These barrages will be kept on for half an hour.

7. TIME IN THE TRENCHES.

The probable duration of time in the trenches raiding parties will spend in the enemy trenches will be 15 to 30 minutes.

8. SIGNAL FOR RETIREMENT.

The signal for the party to move back will be "Lights Out" blown on a Bugle, from the combined raid H.Qrs and repeated at "A" and "B" Raid H.Qrs.

(a) In case there is any trouble, and the raiding parties have to move back quickly they will be covered:-

(1) By Artillery Barrage enfilading the enemys trench from N.24.d.9.2. to N.19.c.6.5.

(2) By the covering parties provided in support of each raid.

(b) The raiding parties will move back in the following order. -

(1) First.- Moppers up. 2.-Blockers. 3.- Overland parties 4.- Support parties.
Each Party will cover the retirement of the party preceeding it.

(c) In case of B Raid failing, when falling back they will form a protective flank for "A" raid.

5.
23.6.17.

In case of a raid failing, when falling back they will form a protective flank for B raid.

9. COMPOSITION OF RAIDING PARTY.

The following will be the composition of the assaulting parties:-

Party A	(1)	1 Off.	1 N.C.O.	10 O.R's.	}
A	(2)	1 Off.	1 N.C.O.	10 O.R's.	}
A	(3)	1 Off.	1 N.C.O.	10 O.R's.	} "A"
A	(4)	1 Off.	1 N.C.O.	10 O.R's.	} Raid.
A	(5)		1 N.C.O.	10 O.R's.	}
A	(6)		1 N.C.O.	10 O.R's.	}
Party B	(1)		1 N.C.O.	6 O.R's	}
B	(2)	1 Off.	1 N.C.O.	10 O.R's.	} "B"
B	(3)	1 Off.	1 N.C.O.	10 O.R's.	} Raid.
B	(4)		1 N.C.O.	10 O.R's.	}

It is estimated that, including Bangalore parties, Covering parties, connecting files, and parties to collect booty and to deal with any prisoners:-

A Raid will be 5 Officers and 80 O.R's
B Raid will be 3 Officers and 60 O.R's
Total will be 8 Officers and 140 O.R's.

10. ENTRY INTO ENEMY TRENCHES.

The proposed points of entry into the enemy's trench are:-

A raid.....points N.19.c.30.02.

B raid.....Point N.19.c.00.15.

11. Signals for co-operation of the Artillery with the raid are being arranged with the raid, and will be detailed in Operation Orders.

12. LIAISON COMMUNICATION.

Telephone and Runner communications will be maintained between headquarters and O.C. A and B raids, and H.Q of the combined raid.

continued.

6.

Liaison will be established at H.Qrs combined raid between Artillery, Machine Guns, Trench Mortars, and Battalion H.Qrs. by means of telephone and Runners.

The location of the different H.Qrs. will be detailed in operation orders.

Points of Exit.

Points of exit from our front trenches will be at about E.25.a.2.5. for "A" raid, and
E.30.b.8.6. for "B" raid.

13. **LINES OF DIRECTION.**

The lines of direction for each raid will be marked by tapes with connecting files posted at each 20 yards along the tapes.

14. Operation Orders detailing positions of ammunition, situation of Bangalore Torpedoes, and connecting files, dress carried by assaulting parties, and administrative orders will be issued later.

2 Sketch Maps attached.

Major,
Commanding 2nd. Bn. The Manchester Regt.

Issued at....
Issued to

No 1 Lieut Thomas.
   2 Capt Mayhew
   3 14th. Inf Bde.
   4   do
   5 Commanding Officer
   6 Adjutant
   7 168th Bde R.F.A.
   8 206th Coy R.E.
   9 219th M G Coy
10 14th. T.M. Bty.
11)
12) War Diary
13
14
15
16

appendix 17.

2ND BATTALION THE MANCHESTER REGIMENT.

<u>S E C R E T.</u> --- 29.6.17.

Reference Map LOMBARTZYDE Ed. 1 A. 1/20,000 and

French Map CANAL DE PLASSCHENDAELE 1/1000.

Scheme C, a modification of Scheme B, of proposed raid on
enemy trenches between points N.19. c.2.0. & M.24.d.98.15

1. <u>MODIFICATION.</u>

Reference Scheme B and sketches attached submitted on the 27th.
inst. It has been found that the enemy has closed the gap in
his belt of wire at N.19.c.25.02.
Since the whole of Scheme B hinged upon this gap in the wire
it has been decided to modify the raid.
The portion of the raid known as Raid "B" alone will be carried
out.

2. <u>OBJECT.</u>

The object of the raid is:-

(1) To impress upon the enemy that we are sitting opposite him
in an offensive spirit, and to make him clearly understand
that we are masters of the situation.

(11) To take as many prisoners as possible.

3. <u>INFORMATION.</u>

A <u>GENERAL.</u>

The portion of trench to be raided contains three dugouts
and two Machine gun emplacements.

B <u>WIRE.</u>

The wire in front of the trenches to be entered consists
of two belts of wire about 50 yards apart, and each, 3 yards
deep, the outer belt being 25 yards from the enemy trench.

4. <u>METHOD OF CUTTING WIRE.</u>

Gaps in the wire in front of trench to be entered by raiding
party will be blown by Bangalore Torpedos. These will be
fixed mechanically by the R.E's
R.E. will place and fire two Bangalores 5 yards apart,
simultaneously, mechanically.
The raiding party, with Bangalore party (R.E.), will be
formed up in NO MAN'S LAND at Zero hour- notified later-
at 40 paces from the wire.
As soon as formed up, the two R.E. Bangalore parties will
crawl forward and place the torpedos, and fire them
simultaneously as soon as both are in position.

                                                                              continued.

The firing of the Bangalores will be the signal for the raiding party to rush forward.

5. METHOD OF ASSAULT.

(A) Raid will assault the enemy trenches in the following manner, and will be distributed as follows:-

PARTY (1) will move through the gap and advance westwards i.e. to the left across the open and establish a block at point M.24.d.98.15., about 20 yards beyond the enemy's dugout. When this block is established, two men will be left in the trenches, and the remainder of the blocking party will lie out on the top of the enemy's parapet.

PARTY (2) will enter the enemy trench opposite the gap, and work from the westward i.e. to the left, mopping up the enemy dugout. 5 men of this party will be in the trench, the remainder will follow along the top of the trench and keep touch with those in the trench.

PARTY (3) will enter the enemy trench opposite the gap, and work from there Eastwards i.e. to the right, mopping up two enemy dugouts. This party is not to go beyond the last named dugout. 5 men of this party will be in the trench, the remainder will follow along the top of the trench, and keep touch with those in the trench.

PARTY (4) will move through the gap, and then split into two parties, one party working to the left along the top of the trench and the second party to the right along the top of the trench. These parties will move through the gap and thence Eastwards i.e. to the right, along the top of the enemys trench to the sap. These parties are for, and are responsible for dealing with any of the enemy, counter attacking over the open, and for warning parties in the trenches of any unforseen action on the part of the enemy which they can observe, and which cannot be seen by the men in the trenches, and generally to assist those mopping up in the trenches.

Party 5 will move through the gap and then across the open and establish a block 20 yds beyond the scared dugout to this right.

The order of entry of these parties is at the discretion of O C Raid

(B) SUPPORT.

Each raiding party will have in support a party composed of one Lewis Gun Section, as shown in diagram attached.

(C) BARRAGE.

Blowing up of the Bangalore torpedo will be the signal for the commencement of an Artillery, Stokes Mortar, and Machine Gun barrage. and rifle grenade barrage

(1) The Artillery barrage will be established on,-

continued.

2. Stokes Guns will barrage the enemy sap at N.19.c.35.00 and thence along the enemy front line to N.19.c.25.02. (3 guns) and from M.24.d.95.15. to M.24.d.9.3. 3 guns.

(a) The enemy's lines of trenches running from N.19.c.4.0. to N.19.c.6.5.

(b) The enemy's line of trenches running from M.24.d.9.2. to N.19.c.6.6.

(c) The enemy strong point at M.24.d.5.3.

(d) The enemy Machine Gun position at about M.24.d.7.4.

(2) The stokes mortar barrage will be established at points M.24.d.90.15., N.19.c.4.4., and N.19.c.42.30. This barrage will prevent any re-inforcements of the enemy moving up from the trenches.

(3) The Machine Gun Barrage will be established as a direct enfilade of the enemy trenches running from M.24.d.9.2. N.19.c.6.5., and a direct enfilade on enemy trenches running from N.19.c.4.4. to N.19.c.1.8. This barrage will prevent any re-inforcements of the enemy moving across the open.

These barrages will be kept on for half an hour.

6. **TIME IN THE TRENCHES.**

The probable duration of time the raiding parties will spend in the enemy trenches will be 10 to 30 minutes.

7. **SIGNAL FOR RETIREMENT.**

The signal for the party to move back will be "LIGHTS OUT" blown on a bugle from the rear raid Hd. Qrs. and repeated at Forward raid Hd.Qrs.

(A) In case there is any trouble, and the raiding party has to move back quickly, they will be covered:-

(1) By Artillery Barrage enfilading the enemy's trench from M.24.d.9.2. to N.19.c.6.5. (see signals with Artillery.

(2) By the covering party provided in support of the raid.

(B) The raiding party will move back in the following order:-

(1) 1.st. - Moppers up, 2nd. - Blockers, 3rd.- Overland parties, 4th.- Support Parties.
Each party will cover the retirement of the party preceeding it.

continued.

8. COMPOSITION OF RAIDING PARTIES.

The following will be the composition of the assaulting parties:-

                Party (1)   1 N.C.O. 6 O.R's
                     (2)   1 Off.   1 N.CO   10 O.R's
                     (3)   1 Off   1 N.C.O. 10 O.R's
                     (4)   1 N.C.O 10 O.R's
                     (5)   1 NCO   6 ORs

It is estimated that, including Bangalore parties, covering parties, connecting files, and parties to collect booty and deal with any prisoners, the raid will be composed of

3 Officers 60 O.R's.

9. ENTRY INTO ENEMY TRENCHES.

The point at which party will enter enemy trench will be at N.19.c.00.15.
N.19.c.05.00

10. SIGNALS WITH ARTILLERY.

The following code words will be arranged between Infantry and Artillery:-

Code word for "ALL READY"............ GUARD.
Code word for "BANGALORES HAVE GONE OFF"................... COSSACK.
Code word for "CALLING FOR COVERING FIRE ~~WHEN RAIDING PARTIES ARE RETIRING~~". BANG.

This will be duplicated by a rocket bursting into a gold and silver rain.
A direct visual station will also be established to the Artillery O.P.

11. LIASON AND COMMUNICATION.

Liason and Communication will be established at the rear raid H.Qrs. between the Artillery, Infantry, Machine Guns and Trench Mortars.
Direct telephonic communication will be maintained at rear raid H.Qrs., between forward raid H.Qrs., Artillery, and Bn. H.Qrs.
Communication by runners will be maintained at rear raid H.Qrs. between forward H.Qrs. Bn. H.Qrs., Machine Guns, and Stokes Mortars.

Visual Communication will be maintained between Battalion Hd. Qrs., and Brigade report centre, and between rear raid Hd. Qrs. and Battalion Hd. Qrs.

Visual from Raid Hd. Qrs. to Battalion Hd. Qrs. will be able to be picked up by Brigade report centre.

continued.

12 POINT OF EXIT.

The point of exit from our front line will be at about N.30.b.8.6.

13 LINE OF DIRECTION.

The line of direction of the raid will be marked by tape with connecting files posted to each 20 yards along the tape.

14 ARMS.

Arms carried by raid will be as per attached table appendix A

15 DISTINGUISHING MARKS.

The raiding party will be distinguished by wearing split sandbags over the chets and shoulders.

Faces and hands will be blackened.

16 BADGES.

All badges will be taken off, identity discs will ~~be~~ not ~~taken-off~~ be worn. All papers will be taken from the pockets of the raiding parties.

17 HOT FOOD.

(a) Raiding parties will be provided with a hot meal ~~bef~~ before ~~proceeding~~ leaving their Camp.

18 ROUTES.

The raid will move to and from the front line via Support trench, NICE ALLEY, the dotted track, and thence by the communication trench by the side of the CRIQUE de NIEUWENDAMME marked B route on the attached map.

In case the communication trenches are blown in or blocked, the parties will move along the open paralell to their route.

19 TIME OF ARRIVAL.

O.C. Raid will arrange to be ready to move out of the front line at 11 P.M.

20 RAID Hd. Qrs.

Forward RAID Hd Qrs will be at about point M.30.b.9.8. Rear raid Hd.Qrs. will be at point M.30.b.7.6. the present dugout occupied by officers of the Company in NICE TRENCH.

21. DUMPS.

The supply of S.A.A. and bombs will be established at the point of exit under a reliable N.C.O. to be detailed by O.C. Raid.

22. MEDICAL ARRANGEMENTS.

Regimental Aid post will be established at the BRIQUETTERIE.

The evacuation of killed and wounded in advance of our front line, will be carried out by

continued.

the raiding party.
The evacuation of the wounded from the front line to the BRIQUETTERIE will be done by the Battalion Stretcher bearers. The evacuations from the BRIQUETTERIE to the Dressing Station will be done by the R.A.M.C.

10 Stretcher Bearers will be established in the bay immediately West (i.e. left) of the exit point of the raid for the purpose of evacuating the wounded of the raid.

10 extra Bearers will report to the Medical Officer at the BRIQUETTERIE at 9 P.M. for this purpose.

The Medical Officer will be responsible that these Stretcher Bearers are in position by 11 P.M.

23. EVACUATION TRENCHES.
The wounded of the raid will be evacuated down NICE TRENCH thence along B route to its junction with the road leading to the BRIQUETTERIE. This route is marked D route on the attached sketch.

24 EVACUATION OF PRISONERS AND BOOTY.
Prisoners and booty will be brought to the rear raid Hd Qrs. for the evacuation of the wounded above.
These will be evacuated via D route to Bn Hd. Qrs. at the BRIQUETTERIE. This party will carry back any booty that may be obtained.

25 CHECK POINT.
A post will be established at the junction of B route with the River YSER marked E on the attached sketch, for taking the names of the raiding party when they return.

26. CONTROL POST.
Control Post composed of the Regimental police will be established at the present Bn Hd. Qrs. M.34.b.7.8. for the purpose of controlling the traffic, and raiding parties moving forward, and collecting the raiding parties moving back.

27. DISTRIBUTION OF TROOPS.
The garrison of the Trenches will be distributed on the night of 30/June- 1st July 1917 as follows:-

(a) NICE TRENCH......3 platoons C Coy.
ROODE POORT FME..1 platoon C Coy.
NICE SUPPORT ....2 platoons D Coy. 15th. H.L.I.
NICE WALK........D Coy 15th. H.L.I. (less 2 platoons)

(b) NUN TRENCH.......2 platoons A Coy.
NUN WALK......... 2 platoons D Coy.
BRIQUETTERIE.... B Company.

In case of a bombardment supports will act in the same manner as
continued.

detailed in Operation Orders No 112.

28. CODE CALLS.

The following Code Calls will be used from forward raid Hd. Qrs. to rear raid Hd. Qrs. and from Rear Raid Hd. Qrs to Battalion Hd. Qrs.

```
Bangalore in Position..................One.
All ready.............................Two.
Bangalore has gone off................Three.
Bangalore has not gone off............Four.
Raiders have entered trench...........Five.
Prisoners taken (number in figures)...Six.
Raid held up..........................Seven.
Raiders clear of Trench...............Eight.
Raiders returned .....................Nine.
```

29. ZERO HOUR.

Zero hour and the pass word will be issued later.

30. SYNCHRONISING.

Watches will be synchronised with the Adjutant at 8 pm.

31. ACKNOWLEDGE.

Capt. & A/Adjt,.
2nd. Battalion The Manchester Regiment.

Issued at........

Issued to
No 1 14th Inf. Bde
   2 14th Inf. Bde.
   3 ~~Lieut G.R.Thomas~~
   4 Capt. L.Taylor
   5 168th Bde R.F.A.
   6 ~~219th~~ M.G.Coy 14th M.G.Coy.
   7 14th T.M.Batty
   8 Commanding Officer

No 9 Adjutant
10 File
11 File
12 File
13 206th Field Co R.E.
14 M.O.
15
16

Appendix A to Scheme C dated 29.6.17.

TABLE OF ARMS TO BE CARRIED BY THE RAIDING PARTY.

Party	Number composing Party	Rifles	Bayonets	Revolvers	Bludgeons	Bombs	Rifle Gr.	Torches	Ladders
1	1 N.C.O. / 6 O.R's	2	7	-	2	40	25	-	-
2	1 Off / 1 N.C.O. / 10 O.R.	10	10	3	5	40	-	2	1
3	1 Off / 1 N.C.O / 10 O.R.	10	10	3	5	40	-	1	1
4	1 Off / 1 N.C.O. / 10 O.R.	11	11	-	2	20	-	1	1
5	1 N.C.O / 6 O.R.	2	7	-	2	40	25	-	1
Bangalore		Rifle per man	Bayonet per man	-	-	-	-	-	-
Connecting file	12	12	12	-	-	-	-	-	-
Support	L.G section	6	6	2	-	-	-	-	-

2ND. BATTALION THE MANCHESTER REGIMENT.

Appendix 18

O.C. "A" Company
O.C. "B" Company
O.C. "C" Company
O.C. "D" Company

29.6.17

The 1st. Battalion DORSET Regiment will take over the line of trenches at present held by the 2nd. Battalion Manchester Regiment ~~tomorrow~~ the day after tomorrow.

I wish particular attention paid to the following points by companies in the line.

(a) That log books are written up to date and give all necessary information.

(b) That communication trenches are open and clean.

(c) That wire where broken is effectively re-wired - this must be considered as a point of honour.

(d) That the trenches be repaired and rebiult as far as possi[ble]

(e) That the interior of the trenches be left clean and tidy, latrines, refuse pits etc. filled up and marked. All stores, ammunition etc. collected at dumps.

(f) Fire steps firm and secure.

(g) All officers must be prepared to give the fullest information of the particular portion of the trenches for which they are responsible. By this is meant not only the position of his platoon or company, but also the complete intelligence of the line and tender spots. 32nd. Divn. Trench Standing Orders, Sec. 2 and 3 must be carefully studied by all officers.

scrupulously
Companies in Support billets must hand these over scrup

olson, and that sketches show dumps and routes to the support line are handed over.

                                                                Major.

29.6.17   Commanding 2nd. Battalion The Manchester Regiment.

COPY.

appendix 19

2nd. Bn. The Manchester Regiment.
OPERATION ORDERS No 107.

1...The Ammunition and Trench Stores of C and D Coys is to be in the Support line and not in the Billets.

2...C and D Coys will arrange to have 1 platoon each in the support line by night.
C Coy will have in addition, a Lewis Gun section of a second platoon

3...No Staff Officer or Foreign Officer who is unknown, or who possesses no pas is to be allowed to move about in the front of Support line.

4...At "Stand To" in the morning, and at "Stand Down" at night, all ranks will practice putting on Gas Respirators. Gas respirators will be inspected at "Stand to" and "Stand down"

5...At "Stand to and "Stand down" ammunition will be inspected and every man made up to 120 rounds. Only one box of S.A.A. per platoon to be open at the same time.

(Sd) H.J.Gwyther Capt & A/Adjt.,
2nd. Bn. The Manchester Regiment.

18.6.17.

Appendix No 30

2nd. Battalion The Manchester Regiment.   SECRET.

OPERATION ORDERS No. 108.   20.6.17.

1...... The following modifications in the method of holding the Sector at present occupied by the Battalion will take place at once.
   (a) B Company (Left Sub-section) will have two platoons in the front line and one platoon along the Southern bank of the NIEUPORT Canal. One platoon in the Support trench running S.E. of their present Comp Company H.Qrs.
   FORTIN St BERNARD Sap will not be held, but will be denied to the enemy and periodically and systematically patrolled.
   (b) C Companies dispositions (Right Support) will be as follows:-
   1.. By night, 2 platoons in the support trench running through the present A Company H.Qrs. to the CRIQUE de NIEWENDAMME. 2 platoons and Company H.Qrs in the present existing support trench.
   2.. By day the Company will be in billets in the area contained between the present support trench and the RUE DE CINQ PONT.
   3.. Tomorrow morning C Company will move back into their present billets in NIEUPORT. In the morning O.C. C Company will reconnoitre for billets in the area detailed above and move his Company into these billets as soon as possible.
   (c) D Companies dispositions (left support) will be as follows:-
   1.. By day, 2 platoons in the BRIQUETTERIE. These platoons will, in case of a bombardment, take up a position in the unfinished support trench running S.E from the NIEUPORT Canal to the CRIQUE de NIEUWENDAMME.
   2 platoons and Company H.Qrs. in the present existing support trench.
   2.. By day, D Company will withdraw to billets in the area contained by their present support trench and the RUE DE CINQ PONT
   3.. Tomorrow morning D Company will move back into their present billets in NIEUPORT. In the morning O.C. D Company will reconnoitre for billets in the area detailed above and move his Company into these billets as soon as possible.
   4.. Two Lewis Guns at present attached to Bn. H.Qrs. will return at once to command of O.C. D Company.
   These instructions are in confirmation of verbal instructions already issued to Company Commanders.

2...... The position of a forward Battalion H.Qrs will be notified later.

3...... O.C B Company (Left sub-section) is to call for R.E. assistance for the re-construction of the FORTIN St BERNARD Sap.
   Covering parties are to put out by O.C. B Company during this reconstruction.

4...... O.C. B Company will ensure that Bombers and Rifle Bombers are in readiness to take on an attack on the FORTIN St BERNARD Sap-head at any moment.

5...... Stokes Guns are being put in position in the unfinished support trench, and will be ready to come into action in support of B Company tomorrow. O.C. B Company will obtain direct touch with these Stokes Guns.

6...... While carrying out the extensive work which is required in the sector, it is to be impressed on all ranks that absolute silence must be maintained in order to reduce the otherwise certain shelling on the part of the enemy.

7...... Tasks are to be allotted and are to be carried out under the supervision of an officer.

Lieut Colonel,
Commanding 2nd. Bn. The Manchester Regiment.

SECRET.

2ND. BATTALION THE MANCHESTER REGIMENT.

OPERATION ORDERS NO. 110.

Appendix H

1. The raiding party of 60 O.R. detailed from "D" Company will withdraw from the line tonight, and will be billeted provisionally in NIEUPORT.

2. The reinforcements which arrived today from the Transport Lines are attached, temporarily irrespective of their companies to the command of O.C. "D" Company.

3. O.C. "D" Company will arrange to send a billeting party of 2 N.C.O's to Bn. H.Q. at once to take over billets allotted. These N.C.O's will be picked up as guides at Bn. H.Q. when the party moves back from the line.

4. The raiding party will not withdraw from the line until relieved by the reinforcements.

5. Lieut. C.H.Thoms will be billeted with "B" Company officers.

6. Lieut. C.H.Thoms will arrange for patrols composed of his raiding party to go out tonight to investigate the ground on which the raid is to take place, and to examine and obtain details of the enemy wire.

7. 2/Lieut. A.C.Kirby will arrange to report to Lieut. Thoms to act as a guide for patrols going out tonight.

8. A report of the patrols is to be sent at once to Bn. H.Q.

9. O.C.Raid will report his party complete in billets to Bn. H.Q.

10. Acknowledge.

26-6-1917

Capt. & A/Adjt.
2nd. Battalion The Manchester Regiment.

Issued at 5.15p.
Issued to:-
No.1 Copy to Commanding Officer
" 2 " " O.C. "A" Company.
" 3 " " O.C. "B" Company.
" 4 " " O.C. "C" Company.
" 5 " " O.C. "D" Company.
" 6 " " File.

2ND BATTALION THE MANCHESTER REGIMENT.   Appendix No 22

OPERATION ORDER   No. 111.   26.5.17.

1. **RELIEF.**

    After completion of work tonight A Company will relieve D Company in the left subsection. This relief will not take place before 2 A.M.

    All trench maps, stores and work in hand are to be handed over.

    A.C. "A" Company will be responsible for sending in, the morning and intelligence reports.

    A list of stores handed over is to be submitted to Battalion Hd. Qrs. by 12 noon tomorrow.

    O.C. D Company will send down 2 N.C.O's as a billetting party to report to Bn H.Qrs. as soon as possible, to take over billets etc. vacated by A Company.

2. **WORKING PARTIES.**

    A Company will work on the parapet and parados of MUN TRENCH (left subsection front line) tonight. O.C. D Company will detail the work required to be done, to this Company. B Company will furnish all carrying parties tonight. B Company (less carrying parties) and those on special duty, will report to O.C. C Company for work on the parapet of NICE TRENCH.

    Battalion Snipers and H.Qrs. Units will work on the Communication trench allotted to them.

3. **WORK DONE.**

    The work at present being done on the front line is below the normal. All ranks are again reminded that the work now, is so pressing that it has to be above the normal.

Appendix No 23

SECRET. 2ND BATTALION THE MANCHESTER REGIMENT.

29.6.17

OPERATION ORDER NO 115.

The special operations as detailed for tonight are postponed until tomorrow night 30th June -1st. July.

A modified scheme will be circulated.

Capt & A/Adjt.,
2nd Bn. The Manchester Regt.

Issued at... 2p

Issued to
168th Bde R.F.A.
219th M.G. Coy
14th T.M. Batty
O.C. A Coy
O.C. B Coy
O.C. C Coy.
OC D Coy
206th Coy R.E.
O.C A raid
O.C. B raid.
Commanding Officer
Adjutant.
File.

SECRET.

Copy

Appendix No 24
28.6.17.

2ND BATTALION THE MANCHESTER REGIMENT

Reference attached Sketch.

OPERATION ORDERS No 114.

1. **DATE OF RAID.** The raid to be carried out by the Battalion as detailed in scheme B (sent to all concerned) will be carried out on the night of the 29/30th June 1917.

2. **COMMANDERS.** The Commanders of the raid will be as follows:-

   Combined raid. - Capt H.J.Gwyther M.C.

   Raid A. - Lieut G R Thomas.

   Raid B. - Capt L Taylor.

3. **ARMS.** The arms carried by the raiding parties will be as appendix A.

4. **DISTINGUISHING MARKS.**
   The raiding party will be distinguished by wearing split sandbags over the chest and shoulders.

   Faces and hands will be blackened.

5. **BADGES.** All badges will be taken off, identity discs will not be worn. All papers will be taken from the pockets of the raiding parties.

6. **HOT FOOD.**
   (a) Raiding parties will be provided with a hot meal before leaving the Camp.

   (b) Hot coffee will be provided at the present Battalion H.Qrs. for the raiding parties before proceeding to the raid, and after returning from the raid.

7. **ROUTES.** The raiding parties will march to and from the front line by the following routes:-

   "A" raid will move by road to NICE ALLEY, and NICE AVENUE marked A raid on the attached map.

continued.

2.

B raid will move to and from the front line via SUPPORT TRENCH?, NICE ALLEY, the dotted track, and advance by the communication trench by the side of the CRIQUE de NIEUWENDAMME marked B route on the attached map.

In case the communication trenches are blown in or blocked, the parties will move along the open parralel to the route.

8. TIMES OF ARRIVAL.

O.C A raid will arrange for his troops to be ready to move out of the front line by 11 P.M.

O.C B raid will arrange to be ready to move out of the front line at 11 P.M.

Bangalore parties of both raids will be prepared to move out of the front line trench by 10.30. P.M.

Sappers for blowing the Bangalore torpedo will be attached to these parties.

9. RAID HEADQUARTERS.

A   Headquarters of A raid will be about point N.25.a.2.7 marked A on attached map.

Headquarters of B raid will be at about point M.30.b.9.8. marked B on attached map.

Headquarters of combined raid will at point M.30.b.7.6. the present dugout occupied by officers of the Company in NICE TRENCH. (marked C on attached map).

B   O.C's A and B raids are at liberty to move forward from their raid headquarters for the purpose of controlling threi raid, but they must leave a reliable Officer behind at their raid headquarters.

10. DUMPS.

The supply of S.A.A. and bombs will be established at each of the points of exit under a reliable N.C.O. to be detailed by each Company respectively.

11. COMMUNICATION AND LIASON.

Communication and liason will be established at the combined raid H Qrs between the Artillery, Infantry,

continued.

Machine Guns and Trench mortars. Direct telephonic communication will be maintained at combined H.Qrs. between raid H.Qrs. Artillery, Battn H.QRS. A raid H.Qrs., and B raid H.Qrs.

Communication by runners will be maintained at combined raid H.Qrs between raid H.Qrs. Bn. H Qrs. Machine Guns, Stokes Mortars, A and B raid H.Qrs.

Visual communication will be maintained between Bn. H.Qrs. and Brigade report centre, and between combined raid H.Qrs and Bn. H.Qrs.

Visual from raid H.Qrs to Bn. H.Qrs will be able to be picked up by Brigade report centre.

12. LIASON WITH ARTILLERY.

The following code words will be used between Combined raid Hd. Qrs. and the Artillery.

Code word for "All Ready"	"GUARD"
Code word for "Bangalores have gone off"	"COSSACK"
Code word for "calling for covering fire when raiding parties are retiring	"BANG"

This will be duplicated by a rocket bursting into silver rain.

13. MEDICAL ARRANGEMENTS.

Regimental Aid post will be established at the BRIQUETTERIE.

The evacuation of killed and wounded in advance of our front line, will be carried out by the raiding party.

The evacuation of wounded from the front line to the BRIQUETTERIE will be done by the Battalion Stretcher Bearers. The evacuations from the BRIQUETTERIE to the Dressing station will be done by the R.A.M.C.

10 Stetcher bearers will be established in the bay immediately adjoining "NICE POST", for the purpose of evacuating the wounded of A raid.

10 Stretcher bearers will be established in the bay immediately West (i.e. left) of the exit point of B raid for the purpose of evacuating the wounded of B raid.

10 extra bearers will report to the Medical Officer at the BRIQUETTERIE at 9 P.M. for this purpose.

The Medical Officer will be responsible that these Stretcher bearers are in position by 11 P.M.

continued.

4.

14 EVACUATION TRENCHES. The wounded of A raid will be evacuated down NICE AVENUE, thence along NICE WALK and thence along track to the BRIQUETTERIE, marked C route on attached sketch.

The wounded of B raid will be evacuated down NICE TRENCH thence along B route to its junction with the road leading to the BRIQUETTERIE. This route is marked D route on the attached sketch

15. EVACUATION OF PRISONERS AND BOOTY. Prisoners and booty will be brought down by both routes to the combined raid Hd Qrs. for the evacuation of the above.

These will be evacuated via D route to Bn Hd Qrs at the BRIQUETTERIE. This party will carry back any booty that may be obtained.

16. WITHDRAWAL OF TAPE.
O.C Raids will arrange that their connecting files will move marking out tapes before the withdrawal.

17 CHECK POINTS.
Posts will be established at the junction of B route with the River YSER, marked E and F respectively on the attached sketch, for taking the names of the raiding parties when they return.

18. CONTROL POSTS.
A control post composed of the Regimental police will be established at the present Bn. H Qrs. M.34.b.7.8. for the purpose of controlling traffic and raiding parties moving forward and collecting the raiding parties moving back.

19 GARRISON OF THE LINE.
The Companies in the line are to be on the alert throughout the night.

20 DISTRIBUTION OF TROOPS.
The garrison of the trenches will be distributed on the night 29/30th June 1917. as follows:-

    (a) NICE TRENCH   3 Platoons C Coy
        ROODE POORT FME   1 Platoon C Coy
        NICE SUPPORT   2 Platoons D Coy 15th. H.L.I.
        NICE WALK   D Coy 15th H.L.I. less Two platoons

    (b) NUN TRENCH   2 platoons A Coy.
        NUN WALK   2 platoons D Coy.
        BRIQUETTERIE   B Coy.

Continued.

5.

In case of a bombardment supports will act in the same manner as detailed in Operation Orders No 112.

21. BATTALION Hd Qrs. will be established at the BRIQUETTERIE.

22. **WITHDRAWAL**.

When the raid has been completed both raiding parties will move back independently to their present Camp.

23. **CODE CALLS**.

The following Code Calls will be used from Raid H Qrs. to combined raid H Qrs. and from combined raid Hd Qrs. to Bn. Hd Qrs.

Bangalore in position	One
All ready	Two
Bangalore has gone off	Three
Bangalore has not gone off	Four
Raiders have entered trench	Five
Prisoners taken (number in figures)	Six
Raid held up	Seven
Raiders clear of trench	Eight
Raiders returned	Nine.

"A" raid messages will be preceeded by AAA
"B" raid messages will be preceeded by BBB

24. **ZERO HOUR**.

Zero hour and the pass word will be issued later

25. **SYNCHRONISING**.

Watches will be synchronised with the Adjutant at 8 P.M.

26. **ACKNOWLEDGE**.

Capt & A/Adjt.,
2nd. Bn. The Manchester Regiment.

Issued at 10 A.M.
Issued to
- No 1 14th. Inf Bde
- 2 14th Inf Bde
- 3 Lieut Thomas
- 4 Capt Taylor
- 5 168th Bde R.F.A.
- 6 14th. M.G. Coy
- 7 14th T.M. Batty
- 8. Commanding Officer
- 9 Adjutant
- 10 File
- 11 File
- 12 File
- 13 206th Field Coy R.E.
- 14 M.O.
- 15
- 16.

Appendix No 25

SECRET.

2ND BATTALION THE MANCHESTER REGIMENT. 30.6.17.

OPERATION ORDERS   No 116.

The following modifications are made in Scheme C for raid to be undertaken by the above Unit.

Para 5. Method of Assault.

(a) The order of the parties will be as follows:-

  Party 2.
  Party 3.
  Party 1.
  Party 5.
  Party 4.

(B) For each raiding party read "THE" raiding party.

Para 7. (A) (1) The Artillery barrage will be changed to the enemy front line, as this is the place where trouble would come from, if the raiding party has to move back quickly.

Para 8. The composition of Parties.
Nos (1) and (5) should be each 1 N.C.O. and at least 8 O.R.

Para 10. For "This will be duplicated" read "This last code word BANG will be duplicated"

Para 11. Brigade Signal Officer has gone to your Headquarters to arrange this.

Para 12. For M.30.b.8.6. read M.30.b.8.6.

Para 27 Distribution of Troops will be as follows:-

NICE TRENCH	-	2 Platoons
ROUDE PORT EME	-	1 platoon
NICE SUPPORT	-	Nil
NICE WALK	-	2 platoons
NUN TRENCH	-	1 Platoon
NUN SUPPORT	-	1 platoon
NUN WALK	-	2 platoons
BRIQUETTERIE	-	1 Company.

In para 5. Party No 4 Omit lines 4 and 5 from "These" to "Sap".
Omit- The order of entry of these parties is at the discretion of O.C. Raid.

Capt & A/Adjt.,

2nd. Bn. The Manchester Regiment.

Appendix No 6.

SECRET.

2ND BATTALION THE MIDDLESEX REGIMENT.   30.6.17.

OPERATION ORDER No 117.

1. INTRODUCTION.
   A minor operation will be carried out tonight from C Company
   sector. This will be done by a raiding party under
   Capt L. Taylor.

   Zero hour will be 12 midnight, but this is variable.

2. DISPOSITIONS.
   (a) The dispositions of the Battalion for tonight will be as
       follows:-

       NICE TRENCH   2 platoons C Coy.
       MOORE MOUNT FARM   1 platoon C Coy.
       NICE SUPPORT   Nil
       NICE WALK   2 platoons (1 platoon C Coy
                                              1 platoon B Coy)

       NUN TRENCH   1 platoon A Coy.
       NUN SUPPORT   1 platoon A Coy.
       NUN WALK   2 platoons A Coy.
       BATTALION HDQRS   D Company.

   (b) The remainder of B Coy will be in their billets.
       D Coy 18th. R.W.F. will remain in their billets.

   (c) A COMPANY. Only essential work is to be carried out tonight.
       (1) ~~A party is to be in NO MAN'S LAND~~. The covering, wiring
           parties and patrol of A Coy. will withdraw at 12.15. AM,
           1st July. Both these parties are to be taken from a
           platoon in NUN WALK.

       (2) 1 platoon will withdraw from NUN TRENCH to NUN SUPPORT
           at 12 midnight.

       C COMPANY.
       (1) 1 platoon will be withdrawn from NICE TRENCH to NICE
           WALK at 10.30. P.M. via NICE AVENUE.
       (2) Knife rests are to be ready to close the gap in our
           wire used by the raiders as soon as they have withdrawn.
       (3) The platoon in NICE WALK is to stop all traffic
           up or down (except runners and carrying parties between
           10 P.M. and 12 midnight) in NICE AVENUE.

   (d) Only essential work is to be carried out tonight and this
       is to cease at 12 midnight.

   (e) D Coy will carry to A Coy tonight and then withdraw to the
       BATTALION HDQRS.
       B Coy will carry to C Coy tonight and then withdraw to
       NICE WALK.

                               continued.

2.   31.6.17.

3. ORDERS.
   A (1)   D Coy. 15th. M.L.I. (attached 22nd Manchesters) will move
           back to CHURCH AVENUE POST tomorrow morning commencing at
           8 A.M.
           This party will move by the Southern road and will not be in
           parties bigger than sections.

                                                        (D Coy)
      (2) B Coy. will move into the billets vacated by 15th M.L.I.
           ~~Rifles~~ tomorrow morning at 9 A.M.
                      and remainder of B Coy.
      (3) The party of B Coy. at present at CHURCH AVENUE POST will
           rejoin their companies tomorrow morning commencing at 8 A.M.
           This party will move by the southern road and will not go in
           parties greater than a section.

      (4) The raiding party of A company will withdraw to the Transport
           lines at 12 noon tomorrow.

   B (1) The Battalion will be relieved by the 1st. Dorset Regt.
           tomorrow.

      (2) Dorset advance parties are now attached to Companies.

      (3) B and D Companies will arrange for guides to take their
           particular officers round their right positions in
           accordance with instructions given in this office M.S. 104 o
           of today.

4. Acknowledge.

                                                        Capt & A./Adjt.
                                                  2nd Bn The Manchester Regiment.

Issued at.........
Issued to   Commanding Officers.
             O.C A Coy
             O.C B Coy.
             O.C D Coy.
             O.C C Coy.
             D Coy 15th. M.L.I.
             Special Coy.
             Bear M. GB.

WAR DIARY
or
INTELLIGENCE SUMMARY

Army-Form C. 2118.

WO 36

Place	Date 1917	Hour	Summary of Events and Information	Remarks and references to Appendices
NIEUPORT	July 1		A & C Companies held the front line trenches & D. & B. in Support. A and B Companies remaining in support in NIEUPORT. The Raid as planned to take place at midnight 30 June/1st July was successfully carried out although the Bangalore torpedo was not exploded until 2.15 A.M. Owing to an element of enemy working party being in the front. It was proposed to blow the wire. Several of the enemy were killed, but none were captured, owing to identification secured. Some of the raiding party were wounded but got back to our front line trenches. The raiding party withdrew to the Special training ground at GROOTE LABEUR FARM. In the morning of the 1st, the Battalion were relieved by the 1/5th Glo'ster Regt. Wounds as appendix No 1 attached. The relief was carried out without a casualty to the Bn.	Appendix No 1 JAS
CAMP RABILLET	July 2		After relief the Battalion marched into CAMP RABILLET, being complete in hut 8 A.M. Something after having arrived the day, the duty for work on the trenches. The rest of the Battalion spent the remainder of the day on a general clean up.	JAS
do	July 3		After the Bn had been relieved, Lt. T.E. Boughey (Adjutant) M.C. and 26 O.R.s went out on patrol to prevent the enemy mending the wire blown by the raiding party and to obtain identification if possible. In this however they were not successful. On the enemy offering resistance Lt. Boughey was wounded in the leg by a piece of French Mortar Shell. 5 O.Rs Ranks were also wounded. The Battalion remained in CAMP RABILLET and training was carried out under Company arrangements.	JAS
GHYVELDE	July 4		The Battalion marched to the GHYVELDE Training area, being accommodated in huts GHYVELDE Camp. Complete in Camp 6 P.M.	30346

Army Form C. 2118.

WAR DIARY
or
INTELLIGENCE SUMMARY.
(Erase heading not required.)

Place	Date 1917	Hour	Summary of Events and Information	Remarks and references to Appendices
GHYVELDE	July 5		Battalion in CAMP, GHYVELDE. The Bn was engaged in digging practice trenches.	Appendix No 2
do	" 6		Training carried out as per programme	
do	" 7		-do-	
do	" 8		to Church Parades.	
do	" 9		do	
do	" 10		Battalion took part in Brigade training scheme. Trench to trench attack.	
			The enemy opened a heavy bombardment in front and rear areas. Infantry attack expected. The Bn warned to be ready to move at half an hours notice.— Orders were received to move off at once and the Bn left GHYVELDE en Motor Lorry at 10 P.M arriving in JEAN BART Camp 3 A.M. 11th inst	
JEAN BART CAMP	" 11		Battalion in JEAN BART Camp. Warned to be prepared to move immediately. This order came through at 4 P.M. Relieved 16th Bn H.L.I in C Subsector Bn heavily shelled during relief. Relief complete 4 AM 12th inst	

J.A.Stephen
Lt Col

Place	Date 1917	Hour	Summary of Events and Information	Remarks and references to Appendices
NIEUPORT	July 12		The Battalion in Trenches "C" Subsector. Gas shells were freely used by the enemy.	AMS
do	" 13		The Battalion in Trenches "C" Subsector. A heavy bombardment commenced 9 P.M. Gas shells were used on front line and communication trenches. Bombardment finished 11.45 P.M.	AMS
do	" 14		Battalion in Trenches "C" Subsector.	AMS
do	" 15		do Inter-Company relief carried out without interruption B by ranks enemy trenches. Enemy shelled 1st and 2nd lines. 3rd line shelled very heavily.	AMS

Brewster Lt Col

Army Form C. 2118.

WAR DIARY
or
INTELLIGENCE SUMMARY.
(Erase heading not required.)

Instructions regarding War Diaries and Intelligence Summaries are contained in F. S. Regs., Part II. and the Staff Manual respectively. Title pages will be prepared in manuscript.

Place	Date 1917	Hour	Summary of Events and Information	Remarks and references to Appendices
NIEUPORT	July 16		Battalion in trenches "C" Subsector. Heavy hostile Bombardment in front and support lines lasting about 45 minutes.	
do	" 17		Battalion in trenches "C" subsector. Relieved by 15th Lancashire Fusiliers in trenches, taking over defences of the REDAN.	
do	" 18		The Battalion was relieved by 5th York and Lancs. Regt. in the REDAN, marching to JEAN BART Camp arriving there at 5 PM for ZUYDCOOTE. Battalion complete in billets at 8.30 P.M. Took over Coast defences Nos 6, 7, and 8 Posts.	
ZUYDCOOTE	" 19		Bn in Billets ZUYDCOOTE. General Clean up.	
do	" 20		do	Training carried out
do	" 21		do	—

J.F. Shepherd
Lt Col

Army Form C. 2118.

WAR DIARY
or
INTELLIGENCE SUMMARY.
(Erase heading not required.)

5

Instructions regarding War Diaries and Intelligence Summaries are contained in F. S. Regs., Part II. and the Staff Manual respectively. Title pages will be prepared in manuscript.

Place	Date 1917	Hour	Summary of Events and Information	Remarks and references to Appendices
ZUYDCOOTE	July 22		Battalion in fields ZUYDCOOTE Training carried out -	
do	" 23		do -"-	
do	" 24		do -"-	
do	" 25		do -"- Night operation Manning of Posts.	
do	" 26		do Training carried out -	
do	" 27		do -"-	
do	" 28		do Battalion scheme Trench to Trench Attack	
do	" 29		do Church Parade.	
do	" 30		do Training carried out.	
do	" 31		do Battalion took part in Brigade scheme Trench to Trench Attack	

J.S.Humberston Lt Col

APPENDIX 20 / Appendix No 29

2ND BATTALION THE MANCHESTER REGIMENT.

1 July 1917.

Operation Orders No 118.

1. The Battalion will be relieved by the 1st Dorset Regt. on the night of the 1st/2nd July 1917.

2. B Coy 1st Dorset Regt will relieve A Coy 2nd Manchesters in left sector
   C " do do B " " in support.
   D " do do C " " in right sect
   A " do do D " " in support.

3. Relief will take place with Companies in their day positions. i.e.

   A Coy with 2 platoons in NUN TRENCH.
             1 " NUN AVENUE.
             1 " BRIQUETTERIE.
   B Coy in Billets in NIEUPORT.
   C Coy with 3 platoons in NICE TRENCH
             1 L.G. section in ROODE POORT FARM.
             remains of platoon in Coy support.
   D Coy with Company in billets in NIEUPORT.

4. Companies will ensure that the advance parties of the Dorsets are thoroughly cogniscent of their right positions.

5. O.C. Companies and 4 runners per Company will remain behind until the 1st. Dorset Regt. are in their night positions, and their opposite numbers are satisfied that the position and tactical situation is correct. Certificates will be obtained that the tactical situation has been taken over satisfactorily.

6. O.C Companies will ensure that all dumps and stores as laid down in 32nd Div Trench Standing Orders are handed over correct.

7. Regimental trench stores are to be brought out of the trenches correct vide list (appendix A).

8. All trenches are to be left clean and sanitary and the full details and intelligence of the line is to be handed over to the relieving Unit.

9. Platoon Commanders will not leave their positions until they are certain that all their men are accounted for, and that all their trench stores as detailed in A.R.O. 1098 are correct.

10. Relief complete will be reported to Bn.Hd.Qrs, Correct in billets will be reported to the Adjutant.

continued.

2.   1.7.17.

11   The Battalion will move from the front line to Camp RIBAILLET tonight via the NIEUPORT-NIEUPORT BAINS road to point M.21.c.3.8. and thence S.E. along the (NIEUPORT-NIEUPORT BAINS)-OOST DUNKERQUE Road.

12   The march to Camp will be made by Companies at, at least 200 yards interval.

13   Lewis Gun Limbers and Signalling Limbers will be at point M.27.b.5.7 at the point where the railway crosses the NIEUPORT-NIEUPORT BAINS road at 11.30. P.M.
Companies will carry out their Lewis Guns and ammunition to this point where they will be placed on the limbers.
The Lewis Gun Officer will supervise the loading of the limbers.
Signallers will carry their apparatus to this point and load them on the limbers.

14   Limber for trench Kit Orderly room kit and mess stores will be at the old Bn H.Qrs SARDINERIE at 10.30. P.M.

15   Limber to collect tools will be at the Battalion dump at 9.30.P.M.

16   Captain H.R.C.Green will arrange the biletting at RIBAILLET CAMP and will arrange to have 4 guides per Company and 2 guides for Hd. Qrs. at 11.30.P.M. on the road of entry

17   Platoon Commanders will see that their platoons are correct, and have their correct number of stores and L.G. Buckets and magazines at the end of the communication trenches.
Any material left behind is to be sent back for at once.

18   Upon arrival in billets platoon commanders will again call the roll, check their stores, see to the food of their men, and report their platoon correct in billets to their Company Commander.   Company Commanders will report their Companies correct in billets to the Adjutant.

19   All ranks are to have it thoroughly impressed upon them that the discipline of a Battalion is shown by the manner in which they come out of the trenches. Any straggling or lounging along the road is to be checked at once, men are to keep in step, cover off, and obey all the laws of march discipline.
Officers servants and Company or Bn H.Qr. oddments are not allowed to move back independently in twos and threes, they are to march back with their Unit.

20   Upon arrival in camp the reinforcements of other Companies at present attached to D Company to form a composite Company, will rejoin and be billetted with their proper Companies.
The Draft at present at the Transport Lines will be distributed equally between the Companies, and billetted accordingly.
Captain H.R.C. Green will make arrangements for this accordingly when billetting.

                                        continued.

3.   1.7.17.

21 Upon arrival in billets the Battalion will be in Divisional reserve and will be prepared to move at ½ hours notice. Other Ranks are not allowed beyond ¼ mile of the Camp withour a pass.

22 The Commanding Officer will see the new drafts at 12 noon tomorrow in Marching Order.

23 Reveille will be at 7 A.M. tomorrow.
    Tomorrow will be spent in cleaning up, and Company inspections.

24 Working parties tomorrow will be found by B and D Companies

25 Acknowledge.

                                        Capt & A/Adjt.,
                          2nd. Bn. The Manchester Regiment.

Issued at... 3.40 p
Issued to
Commanding Officer and H Q Officers
Quartermaster & Transport Officer
O.C A Coy
O.C B Coy
O.C C Coy
O.C.D Coy
R.S.M.
File.

Appendix 2

2nd Battalion The Manchester Regiment.
PROGRAMME OF TRAINING FROM 7TH TO 14TH JULY 1916/1917.
2.7.17.

July 7th	8 to 9 AM	Physical Drill. (Sections).
	9 to 10 AM	Section Drill. (With Arms, bringing in Guard Drill).
	10 to 11 AM	Bayonet Fighting, Judging distance. (Platoons)
	11 noon to 12.45	Fire Control (Sections).
	11 to 12 noon	Extended order drill (Sections).
July 8th	8 to 9 AM	Physical Drill. (Sections).
	9 to 10 AM	Platoon Drill (Bringing in substitution drill)
	10 to 11 AM	Bayonet Fighting, Judging distance (Platoons)
	11 to 12 noon	Extended order drill (Platoons).
	12 to 12.45 PM	Gas Helmet Drill & passing messages. (Platoons)
July 9th	8 to 9 AM	Physical Drill. (Platoons).
	9 to 10 AM	Company Drill (Bringing in substitution drill)
	10 to 11 AM	Company inter-communication, passing of messages.
	11 to 12.45 PM	Platoon attack on strong point. (With detailed orders)
July 10th	8 to 12.45 PM	Brigade Training.
July 11th	8 to 9 AM	Physical Drill (Platoons)
	9 to 10 AM	Company Drill.
	10 to 12.45 PM	Company Attack. (22nd Div scheme with detailed orders).
July 12th	8 to 12.45 PM	Battalion scheme. (Scheme and orders to follow later.)
July 13th	8 to 12.45 PM	Battalion Scheme. (Scheme and orders to follow later).
July 14th	8 to 12.45 PM	Brigade Training.

Notes:- (1) Afternoon work daily.
2 to 3.30 PM. 2 Companies, Musketry Drill (Camp)
2 to 3.45 PM. 1 Company. Range.
Evening lectures on days work.
(2) In the event of dates of Brigade training days being altered, programme will be amended accordingly. It is assumed that there will be two Brigade days, although the dates of these days may be altered.
(3) Specialist officers will be put at the disposal of Company Commanders at hours detailed daily in Bn orders. During these hours specialists sections may, at the discretion of O.C. Companies, be trained in live bomb throwing, firing rifle Grenades, or Lewis Gun, instead of Physical training etc. Regards to be paid in this training to the fact, that the section is the Unit. Sections will be taken independently for this, and bombers etc. of the Company will not be grouped in one party.

Major,
Commanding 2nd Bn. The Manchester Regt.

PROGRAMME OF TRAINING FROM 7TH TO 14TH JULY INCLUSIVE.

6.7.17.

July 7th	8 to 9 AM.	Physical Drill. (Sections).
	9 to 10 AM.	Section Drill. (with Arms, bringing in Guard Drill).
	10 to 11 AM.	Bayonet Fighting, Judging distance. (Platoons)
	12 noon to 12.45	Fire Control (Sections).
	11 to 12 noon	Extended order drill (Sections).
July 8th	8 to 9 AM.	Physical Drill. (Sections).
	9 to 10 AM	Platoon Drill (Bringing in Substitution Drill)
	10 to 11 AM.	Bayonet Fighting, Judging distance (Platoons)
	11 to 12 noon	Extended order Drill (Platoons).
	12 to 12.45 PM.	Gas Helmet Drill & passing messages.(Platoons)
July 9th.	8 to 9 AM.	Physical Drill. (Platoons).
	9 to 10 AM.	Company Drill (Bringing in Substitution drill)
	10 to 11 AM.	Company inter-communication, passing of messages.
	11 to 12.45 P.M	Platoon attack on strong point.(with detailed orders.)
July 10th	8 to 12.45 PM.	Brigade Training.
July 11th	8 to 9 AM.	Physical Drill (Platoons)
	9 to 10 AM.	Company Drill.
	10 to 12.45 PM.	Company Attack. (32nd Div scheme with detailed orders).
July 12th	8 to 12.45 PM.	Battalion scheme. (Scheme and orders to follow later.)
July 13th.	8 to 12.45 PM.	Battalion Scheme. (Scheme and orders to follow later).
July 14th.	8 to 12.45 PM.	Brigade Training.

Notes:- (1) Afternoon work daily.
2 to 3.30 P.M. 3 Companies, Musketry Drill (Camp)
2 to 3.45 PM. 1 Company. Range.
Evening Lectures on days work.
(2) In the event of dates of Brigade training days being altered, programme will be amended accordingly. It is assumed that there will be two Brigade days, and although the dates of these days may be altered.
(3) Specialist officers will be put at the disposal of Company Commanders at hours detailed daily in Bn orders. During these hours specialists sections may, at the discretion of O.C Companies, be trained in live Bomb throwing,-firing Rifle Grenades, or Lewis Gun, instead of Physical Training etc. Emphasis to be paid in this training to the fact, that the section is the Unit. Sections will be taken independently for this, and bombers etc. of the Company will not be grouped in one party.

J Inglis
Major,
Commanding Bn. Manchester Regt.

Appendix 3

2ND BATTALION THE MANCHESTER REGIMENT.

```
5.45 A.M.     Reveille
5.45 A.M.     Hot Tea.
7 A.M.        Breakfast
7.30 A.M.     Sick Parade.
1 P.M.        Dinner.
5 P.M.        Tea
8 P.M.        Hot Tea or Soup.
9.15 P.M.     Lights Out.
```

Battalion	Time	Nature of Training	Locality.
2nd Bn The Manchester Regiment	Friday July 27th 6.15 to 6.45 daily	Gas Drill and Bayonet Fighting	G.7.a.8.8.
	8 to 8.45 daily	Section Drill	D.1.c.Central.
	9. to 9.30 daily.	Battalion parade as strong as possible	D.1.c.Central
	9.45 to 12.45	Platoon and Company Training. During training there will be breaks of 10 minutes every hour.	D.7.a.
	2 P.M to 4 PM. daily	One Company on range Specialists Training under L.G. Bombing Officer, Intelligence Officer and Signalling Officer	D.7.a.5.4. D.7.a.3.3.

2pm Daily Lectures to Officers
6 pm " Lectures to NCO's

Lieut Colonel,
Commanding 2nd Bn. The Manchester Regiment.

27.7.17.

2ND BATTALION THE MANCHESTER REGIMENT.

Battalion	Time	Nature of Training	Locality.
2nd Bn The Manchester Regiment.	July 28th Saturday 8.45 to 12.45	Battle Practice by Companies	D.7.a.
		Brigade day?	
	9 P.M.	Outpost Scheme	D.7.a.6.5.

[signature]

Lieut Colonel,
Commanding 2nd Bn The Manchester Regiment

27.7.17.

2ND BATTALION THE MANCHESTER REGIMENT.

Battalion	Time	Nature of Training	Locality.
2nd Bn The Manchester Regiment	July 30th. Monday 9.45 to 11.45 ~~12.45 PM.~~ 12 6 1	Platoon Training Sections to work in Co-operation under Platoon Commanders. (S.S.143) Battalion Training	D.7.a.
	11 P.M.	Night operations. Attack at dawn	D.16.b.Central

Lieut Colonel,
Commanding 2nd Bn The Manchester Regiment

27.7.17.

2ND BATTALION THE MANCHESTER REGIMENT.

Battalion	Time	Nature of Training	Locality
2nd Bn The Manchester Regiment	31 July Tuesday 8.45 to 12.45 P.M.	Battle practice by Battalion (Trench to Trench attack) 2 Sections 14th M.G.Coy and 2 Stokes Guns will be attached to the Battalion for the purpose of Co-operating in this exercise	C.16.b.Central.

[signature]

Lieut Colonel,
Commanding 2nd. Bn. The Manchester Regiment.

27.7.17.

2ND BATTALION THE MANCHESTER REGIMENT.

Battalion	Time	Nature of Training	Locality.
2nd Bn The Manchester Regiment	Aug 1st Wednesday	Battle Practice by Battalion Trench to Trench attack 1 Section 14th. M.G.Coy and 2 Stokes Mortars will be attached for Co-operating in this practice.	C.15.b Central

Lieut Colonel,
Commanding 2nd Bn The Manchester Regiment.

27.7.17.

2ND BATTALION THE MANCHESTER REGIMENT.

Battalion	Time	Nature of Training	Locality.
2nd Bn The Manchester Regiment	Aug 2nd Thursday 9.45 to 12.45 P.M. 11-45 P.M 12-1	Platoon Training, Sections to work in Co-operation under Platoon Commanders (S.S.143.) Battalion Training	D.7.a.

J. B. Dempster

Lieut Colonel,
Commanding 2nd Bn The Manchester Regiment.

27.7.17.

Army Form C. 2118.

WAR DIARY
or
INTELLIGENCE SUMMARY.
(Erase heading not required.)

2 November 1917

Vol 37

Place	Date 1917	Hour	Summary of Events and Information	Remarks and references to Appendices
ZUYDCOOTE	Aug 1		Battalion in huts ZUYDCOOTE. Training carried on.	
OOST-DUNKERQUE	2		Bn moved to huts OOST DUNKERQUE. Complete in huts 5.30 P.M.	
—do—	3		Battalion in huts OOST-DUNKERQUE. On a/c of the weather outdoor training could not be carried on. The men being lectured in their huts.	
LA PANNE	4		The Bn moved to huts in LA PANNE. Training carried on under Company arrangements.	
—do—	5		Church parades.	Appendix
—do—	6		Battalion in huts LA PANNE. Training carried out as per programme.	
—do—	7		—do—	
—do—	8		—do—	
—do—	9		—do—	

A. Shepherd Lt Col.
Comdg 2 Monmouth Regt

Army Form C. 2118.

WAR DIARY
or
INTELLIGENCE SUMMARY.
(Erase heading not required.)

2

Place	Date 1917	Hour	Summary of Events and Information	Remarks and references to Appendices
LA PANNE	10 Aug		Battalion in Huts LA PANNE. - Training carried on as per programme. -	MS MS
do	11 "		- do -	MS
do	12 "		Church Parade.	MS
do	13 "		Battalion in Huts LA PANNE. Training carried on. The Battalion was inspected by the Queen of the Belgians in front of the 15th Inf. Bde.	MS
do	14 "		Bn in Huts LA PANNE The Duke of Athlone arrived & met the Officers & men -	MS
do	15 "		- do - Training carried on.	MS
do	16 "		- do - Training carried on. The Bn. took over the trench defences & set manning the Yprenau -	Appendix D Bs.

M. Stanbah Lt Col Comdg 2 hour Regt

Army Form C. 2118.

WAR DIARY
or
INTELLIGENCE SUMMARY.
(Erase heading not required.)

3

Place	Date 1917	Hour	Summary of Events and Information	Remarks and references to Appendices
LA PANNE	Aug 14		Battalion (less A Coy) on coast defence. B Coy & part of C Coy on working at Cox/DE in trenches LA PANNE. Night operations.	AP
do	18		A Coy (less B Coy) and part of C at Cox/DE in trenches	AP
do	22		A Coy relieved on coast defence on 19th Aug.	AP
do	27/28		Bn in billets LA PANNE. Training in Box respirators	AP Gunnery
do	29		The Bn marched to AUSTRALIA CAMP. Left CAMP 8.15 PM relieving 2nd Royal at 11.35 P.M in NIEUPORT DEFENCES. Relief complete at 1.35 AM on the 30th inst. Brigade Reserve.	AP
			Bn in reserve NIEUPORT DEFENCES.	AP
NIEUPORT	30		Working and carrying. Parties found for 15 hrs in the line.	AP
do	31		NIEUPORT DEFENCES Company's: Swimming, Newel Trench M.011½-2, Canal Bank Trench, Howitzer pit, Bryants New Parade (Bn HQrs) M.31.d.1.0 PRESQUILE DEFENCES	AP MD

Cannot L. March Reg

Army Form C. 2118.

WAR DIARY
or
INTELLIGENCE SUMMARY.

(Erase heading not required.)

2 /1 Mnchester & Nr 38

Vol 38

Place	Date	Hour	Summary of Events and Information	Remarks and references to Appendices
	September 1st.		Battalion moved from the Prescuire Defences and New Parade and relieved the 5/6th Bn Royal Scots in the Right (Sub- sector LOMBARTZYDE SECTOR. Relief was completed by 11-30 p.m.	APS
Right Subsector LOMBARTZYDE SECTOR	2nd		Battalion in Trenches.	APS
" "	3rd		— do —	APS
" "	4th		— do —	APS
" "	5th		— do — Casualties 2/Lt E.T.B. Horley and 1 Other Rank Killed by Shell fire.	APS
" "	6th		Battalion was relieved by the 5/6th Bn Royal Scots relief being completed 12 midnight. Battalion took over the NIEUPORT DEFENCES and the PRESCUIRE DEFENCES.	APS
	7th		Battalion in NIEUPORT and PRESCUIRE DEFENCES. Working parties furnished for the consolidation of the 1st, 2nd and 3rd lines.	APS
	8th		— do —	APS
	9th		— do —	APS
	10th		— do —	APS
	11th		— do —	APS

N.B. Blenkinsop
Lieut Colonel
Comdg 2nd Bn The Manchester Regiment

WAR DIARY or INTELLIGENCE SUMMARY.

Army Form C. 2118.

Place	Date	Hour	Summary of Events and Information	Remarks and references to Appendices
	Apl 12th		Battalion in NIEUPORT and PRESCUIRE DEFENCES. Battalion was relieved by the 2nd Bn Inniskilling Fusiliers, relief being completed at 12 noon. Marched to CANADA CAMP, COXYDE and took over huts vacated by the 2nd Bn Inniskilling Fusiliers.	MS
COXYDE	13d		Battalion in huts at CANADA CAMP, COXYDE. Inspections and General cleaning up. Took over Anti aircraft Defence of the COXYDE AREA.	MS
"	14d		Battalion in huts, CANADA CAMP. Lectures to the men by Company and Platoon Officers on 32nd Decl French Standing Orders. Painting and Repair Working parties furnished.	MS
"	15d		Battalion in huts CANADA CAMP. General clean up of equipment and clothing. Working parties furnished.	MS
"	16th		Battalion in huts CANADA CAMP. Working parties furnished.	MS
"	17d		do	MS
"	18th		do	MS
"			Demonstration with "NJ Grenade" and British Flame Projector at 2-30 pm. All Officers and N.C.O's not on duty attended. Working parties furnished.	MS
"	19d		Battalion in huts CANADA CAMP. Working parties furnished. One Officer and 4 N.C.O's left the Battalion at 5 pm to reconnoitre the various routes to the Front Line and get as much information as possible regarding the ST.GEORGES SECTOR. Major General G.D. (Auth. 32nd Divisional Commander inspected Transport.	MS

[signature] Lieut Colonel
Comdg 2nd Bn The Manchester Regiment

WAR DIARY
or
INTELLIGENCE SUMMARY.

(Erase heading not required.)

Army Form C. 2118.

Place	Date	Hour	Summary of Events and Information	Remarks and references to Appendices
COXYDE	Sept 20th		Battalion in huts CANADA CAMP, COXYDE. The G.O.C. 32nd Division, after his inspection of the Brigade Transports of the Brigade, were the best in the Division.	AA
			Battalion moved from CANADA CAMP at 10.30 p.m. and relieved the 16th Bn H.L.I. in the Left Subsector ST GEORGES SECTOR, relief being completed by 3-15 a.m. 21st inst., Battalion Headquarters at the SARDINERIE, NIEUPORT.	AA
	21st		Battalion in trenches, Left subsector, ST GEORGES SECTOR. Casualties :- Capt R. Gillenders, Chaplain of the Battalion wounded. 3 O.R's Killed and 4 O.R's Wounded.	AA
	22nd		Battalion in trenches, Left subsector, ST GEORGES SECTOR.	AA
	23rd		— do —	AA
	24th		— do —	AA
			Cloud Gas reported by O.C. "B" Company about 8 p.m. but it was not diffused. A sample was started and despatched to Brigade Headquarters. Battalion relieved by the 5/6th Bn Royal Scots, and marched to OOST-DUNKERKE. Bn Headquarters, "A" and "C" Companies in Billets, "B" Company in dugouts and "D" Company in WELLINGTON CAMP.	AA

[signature]
Lieut Colonel
Comdg 2nd Bn The Manchester Regiment.

Army Form C. 2118.

WAR DIARY
or
INTELLIGENCE SUMMARY.
(Erase heading not required.)

Instructions regarding War Diaries and Intelligence Summaries are contained in F. S. Regs., Part II. and the Staff Manual respectively. Title pages will be prepared in manuscript.

Place	Date	Hour	Summary of Events and Information	Remarks and references to Appendices
OOST-DUNKERKE	Sept 25th		"A" "B" and "C" Companies employed on making concertina barbed wire coils which are delivered each night to TRICAR DUMP. "D" Company furnishing daily working parties.	M
" "	26th		Test S.O.S barrage by artillery, zero hour 4 pm and ending at 4.11 pm. ——do——	M
" "	27th		At 6.15 am the enemy commenced a heavy bombardment of our trenches S. of LOMBARTZYDE, the Left Divisional Front also being shelled. The S.O.S was sent up, and our batteries opened fire. Battalion was ordered to "Stand To", until the hostile bombardment died down about 6.35 am, when news was received to "Stand Down".	M
" "	28th		"A" "B" and "C" Companies employed on making concertina barbed wire coils which are delivered each night to TRICAR DUMP. "D" Company furnished Working Parties. Enemy shelled OOST-DUNKERKE cross roads about 9.30 p.m. About 10.30 p.m the Adjutant, 2/Lieut F.M. NICHOLAS was killed and 1 OR wounded by Shell fire. Captain S.H. HOLLEY took over duties as Acting Adjutant.	M
" "	29th		Work as previous days. Funeral of the late Adjutant, 2/Lieut F.M. NICHOLAS. The body covered with the Union Jack, was conveyed by Wagon to COXYDE, followed by the Officers and men of the Battalion. The body was interred at the COXYDE Cemetery, the firing party being found by the Battalion.	M
" "	30th		Work as on previous days. Divine Service.	M

J.H. Whitehead
Comdg 2nd Bn The Manchester Regiment
Lieut Colonel

Army Form C. 2118

2 Manchester Regt
Vol 39

WAR DIARY or INTELLIGENCE SUMMARY

(Erase heading not required.)

Instructions regarding War Diaries and Intelligence Summaries are contained in F.S. Regs., Part II. and the Staff Manual respectively. Title Pages will be prepared in manuscript.

Place	Date 1917	Hour	Summary of Events and Information	Remarks and references to Appendices
NIEUPORT	Oct 1		The Battalion proceeded from OOST-DUNKERKE to NIEUPORT by light railway. Bn HdQrs, "B" + "D" Coys in the first train which left about 7-30 P.M. "A" + "C" Coys in the second train left about 7-45 PM. Relieved the 5/6th Royal Scots in the ST GEORGES SECTOR (Left sub-section) relief being completed at 12-5 AM. 2nd "A" Coy on right. "B" Coy on left. "B" Coy in support and "A" Coy in Reserve. Casualties 2 ORs wounded by shrapnel.	G
do	" 2		Enemy shelled NIEUPORT in the vicinity of Bn HQ (SARDINERIE) during the day. Casualties NIL.	G
do	" 3		Bn in trenches ST GEORGES SECTOR. Casualties 10 R wounded shrapnel. Work on trenches.	G G
do	" 4		Bn in trenches Left subsector ST GEORGES SECTOR. Casualties NIL. Work on trenches.	G
do	" 5		do. Work on front line	G
COXYDE	" 6		Bn relieved by 10th Bn Manchester Regt. relief commencing 9-30 AM and marched to CANADA Camp COXYDE. Posts vacated by 11th Border Regt.	G
ADINKERKE	" 7		Bn at Canada Camp COXYDE. Left at 2-15 PM and marched to ADINKERKE, where after dinner had been served, barges were boarded, and Bn proceeded via DUNKERKE and ST POL (to PETITE SYNTHE) arriving about 11-30 pm.— CHAPEAU DU ROUGE, ROSENDAEL then marched via DUNKERKE and ST POL (to PETITE SYNTHE)	G

1875. Wt. W593/826 1,080,000 4/15 J.B.C. & A. A.D.S.S./Forms/C. 2118.

WAR DIARY
or
INTELLIGENCE SUMMARY

(Erase heading not required.)

Army Form C. 2118

Place	Date	Hour	Summary of Events and Information	Remarks and references to Appendices
PETITE SYNTHE	Oct 8		Bn in billets PETITE SYNTHE. General clean up after the tour in the trenches	6t
do	9		do. Training carried on.	6t
do	10		do	6t
do	11		do	6t
do	12		do	6t
do	13		do "A" + "B" Coy Bathed	6t
do	14		do "C" "D" " "	6t
do	15		do	6t
do	16		do Bn attempted a demonstration of the discharge of gas by letting loose	6t
do	17		do	6t
do	18		do	6t
do	19		do	6t

WAR DIARY or INTELLIGENCE SUMMARY

Army Form C. 2118

Place	Date	Hour	Summary of Events and Information	Remarks and references to Appendices
PETITE SYNTHE	Oct 20		Battalion in Billets PETITE SYNTHE Training and recreation carried on.-	G.T
do	" 21		do Church parades.-	G.T
do	" 22		do Training and recreation carried on.	G.T
do	" 23		do do	G.T
do	" 24		do do	G.T
do	" 25		do The Bn proceeded by route march leaving PETITE SYNTHE at 2.35 P.M.-	G.T
L'ERKELSBRUGGE			to L'ERKELSBRUGGE area	G.T
do	" 26		The Battalion proceeded by route march to ARNEKE North East "C" area leaving L'ERKELSBRUGGE at 10.5 A.M. Complete in Billets 1.30 P.M. The 32nd Division in reserve.	G.T
ARNEKE.				
ARNEKE	" 27		Bn in Billets ARNEKE Area "C". General clean up and Inspection by the Commanding Officer.-	G.T

WAR DIARY
or
INTELLIGENCE SUMMARY.

Army Form C. 2118.

(Erase heading not required.)

Place	Date 1917	Hour	Summary of Events and Information	Remarks and references to Appendices
ARNEKE	Oct 28		Batts in billets ARNEKE "C" Area. The Bn having been warned that it might have to move at short notice, training was left to the discretion of Company Commanders. This was carried into: Church parades, training carried on during the afternoon.	Gr.
do	29.		Battalion in billets ARNEKE Area. Training carried on. New formation of the attack	Gr.
do	30		do. Training was interfered with by the rain.	Gr.
do	31		do. Training carried on. Practicing the Attack.	Gr.

E. Vaughan Lt. Col.
Comg 2 Bedfords R.

2 Manchester
Vol 40

Army Form C. 2118.

WAR DIARY
OR
INTELLIGENCE SUMMARY.
(Erase heading not required.)

Instructions regarding War Diaries and Intelligence Summaries are contained in F. S. Regs., Part II. and the Staff Manual respectively. Title pages will be prepared in manuscript.

Place	Date	Hour	Summary of Events and Information	Remarks and references to Appendices
	Nov			
ARNEKE	1st		Battalion in Billets, "C" AREA. New formation of attack practised. Major General L. Shuta, G.O.C. 32nd Division inspected the Battalion Training Area and watched the Battalion in Training. Lieut Colonel E. Vaughan D.S.O. took over command of the Battalion from Major L.P. Whitaker M.C., 1st Bn The Dorset Regt.	Ex
	2nd		Battalion in Billets, "C" AREA. New formation of attack practised.	Ex
ARNEKE	3rd		Battalion in Billets, "C" AREA. The 5/6th Bn The Royal Scots and the Battalion practised the attack under Brigade arrangements.	Ex
"	4th		Battalion in Billets "C" AREA. Church Services were held in the morning. The Commanding Officer inspected A and D Companies Kits and the "Second in Command", Major E.R. Thorne inspected the Kits of "C" and "D" Companies.	Ex
"	5th		Battalion in Billets "C" AREA. Training carried out followed by practice of Company and Battalion attack. Battalion carried out Night Operations on like lines.	Ex

Army Form C. 2118.

WAR DIARY
or
INTELLIGENCE SUMMARY.
(Erase heading not required.)

Place	Date	Hour	Summary of Events and Information	Remarks and references to Appendices
ARNEKE	Nov 6th		Battalion in Billets "C" AREA. Battalion carried out New Formation of Attack training.	&c
-"-	7th		Battalion in Billets "C" AREA. Training of the Battalion on the New Formation of Attack carried out.	&c
-"-	8th		Battalion in Billets "C" AREA. Training of the Battalion in the New Formation of Attack carried out.	&c
-"-	9th		Battalion in Billets "C" AREA. The Battalion took part in the Brigade Scheme of Attack. Captain J.R. Murphy rejoined the Battalion from England and was posted to "C" Company.	&c
-"-	10th		Battalion in Billets "C" AREA. Training carried out followed by general clean up of equipment etc.	&c
-"-	11th		The Battalion marched to "B" Camp OUDEZEELE AREA, passing Starting Point at 11·45 am and arriving in Camp about 3 pm.	&c
OUDEZEELE	12th		Battalion in Tents, B Camp OUDEZEELE AREA. The Battalion marched to TUNNELLING CAMP near POPERINGHE passing Starting Point about 8 am and arriving in Camp about 2 pm.	&c

Army Form C. 2118.

WAR DIARY
or
INTELLIGENCE SUMMARY.
(Erase heading not required.)

Instructions regarding War Diaries and Intelligence Summaries are contained in F. S. Regs., Part II. and the Staff Manual respectively. Title pages will be prepared in manuscript.

Place	Date	Hour	Summary of Events and Information	Remarks and references to Appendices
TUNNELLING CAMP POPERINGHE	Nov 13th		Battalion in Tents and Huts at TUNNELLING CAMP. The morning spent on general clean up of equipment etc., and the afternoon work on the drainage system of the Camp; roads leading to the tents and Duck boards running throughout the Camp was carried out.	
- . -	14th		Battalion in Tents and Huts at TUNNELLING CAMP. Work continued on the cleaning up and improvements of the Camp.	GT
- . -	15th		Battalion in Tents and Huts at TUNNELLING CAMP. Work and training continued. The G.O.C. 32nd Division visited the Camp.	GT E.N.
- . -	16th		Battalion in Tents and Huts at TUNNELLING CAMP. Officers and N.C.O's visited the Town Hall, POPERINGHE to view a model of the front line system. Training continued The Corps Commander and Staff inspected the Camp and confidentially the whole of the Brigade on the way the improvements had been carried out under such adverse conditions.	E.N.
- . -	17th		Battalion in Tents and Huts at TUNNELLING CAMP. Training in attack practice carried out by the Battalion.	GT

WAR DIARY
or
INTELLIGENCE SUMMARY.
(Erase heading not required.)

Army Form C. 2118.

Instructions regarding War Diaries and Intelligence Summaries are contained in F. S. Regs., Part II. and the Staff Manual respectively. Title pages will be prepared in manuscript.

Place	Date	Hour	Summary of Events and Information	Remarks and references to Appendices
TUNNELLING CAMP POPERINGHE	Nov. 18th		Battalion in Tents and Huts TUNNELLING CAMP. Church Parade services were held during the morning. Officers and N.C.O's visited the model of the front line system exhibited at the Town Hall, POPERINGHE.	
- " -	19th		Battalion in Tents and Huts TUNNELLING CAMP. Training carried out during the day. The Battalion, in conjunction with the 15th Bn. H.L.I. carried out a Night Attack under Brigade arrangements.	G.T.
- " -	20th		Battalion in Tents and Huts TUNNELLING CAMP. Attack practice and routine training continued throughout the day. Night marching by compass on strong points. Battalion held a Cross Country Run, about 3 miles distance for the purpose of selecting a team to represent the Battalion in the coming Brigade run. Prizes of 20, 15, 10 and 5 Francs were offered and won by L/Cpl. R. Cooper, Pte. Wilson, L/Cpl. Macdonald and Pte. Carter respectively.	G.T.
- " -	21st		Battalion in Tents and Huts TUNNELLING CAMP. Attack practice and training continued. N.C.O's under Intelligence Officer on Marching by compass.	G.T.
- " -	22nd		Battalion in Tents and Huts TUNNELLING CAMP. Attack practice and training continued. A team of 20 representing the Battalion ran in the Brigade Cross Country Run, the	G.T.

Army Form C. 2118.

WAR DIARY
or
INTELLIGENCE SUMMARY.
(Erase heading not required.)

Instructions regarding War Diaries and Intelligence Summaries are contained in F. S. Regs., Part II. and the Staff Manual respectively. Title pages will be prepared in manuscript.

Place	Date	Hour	Summary of Events and Information	Remarks and references to Appendices
TUNNELLING CAMP POPERINGHE	Nov: 22nd	(contd)	result being :- 1st – 1st Bn The Dorset Regt, 2nd – 2nd Bn The Manchester Regt.	6-
" "	23rd		Battalion in Tents and Huts, TUNNELLING CAMP. The G.O.C. 32nd Division Major General C. D. Shute addressed the Brigade on the forthcoming operations.	6-
" "	24th		Battalion marched from TUNNELLING CAMP leaving about 2pm for POPERINGHE where it entrained. The Battalion detrained at BRIELEN and marched to CANAL BANK taking over Dugouts. "A" and "B" companies on east side of YSER CANAL "C" and "D" companies and Bn Headquarters on west side. Battalion complete in Dugouts by 7-0 pm.	6-
CANAL BANK	25th		Battalion in dugouts. Working parties furnished for making new tracks up to the front line; Ammunition carrying; Erecting and strengthening dugouts etc.	6-
" "	26th		Battalion in dugouts. Working parties again furnished.	6-
" "	27th		Battalion in dugouts. Working parties again furnished	6-
" "	28th		Battalion in dugouts. Working parties again furnished.	6-
" "	29th		Battalion in dugouts. Working parties furnished. The party furnished by "D" Coy sustained the following casualties; 2 other ranks killed and 4 other ranks wounded.	

Army Form C. 2118.

WAR DIARY
or
INTELLIGENCE SUMMARY.
(Erase heading not required.)

Instructions regarding War Diaries and Intelligence Summaries are contained in F. S. Regs., Part II. and the Staff Manual respectively. Title pages will be prepared in manuscript.

Place	Date	Hour	Summary of Events and Information	Remarks and references to Appendices
	Nov.			
CANAL BANK.	30d		Battalion in dugouts. Working parties furnished. At 7-40 am an S.O.S. message was received and orders to "stand to" immediately and await orders.	
			The Battalion "stood to" until about 9-30 am when orders were received that the S.O.S. was cancelled. Working Parties continued.	G—

E. Vaughan Lieut Colonel
Commanding 2nd Bn. The Manchester Regiment

Army Form C. 2118.

WAR DIARY
or
INTELLIGENCE SUMMARY.
(Erase heading not required.)

2nd Manchester Regt

Instructions regarding War Diaries and Intelligence Summaries are contained in F. S. Regs., Part II. and the Staff Manual respectively. Title pages will be prepared in manuscript.

Place	Date	Hour	Summary of Events and Information	Remarks and references to Appendices
	1917			
YSER CANAL	Dec.1		The Battalion in dug-outs at YSER CANAL C.25.Central. The Battalion moved at 12 noon to IRISH FARM being accommodated in huts and tents. In view of the forthcoming operations by the 97th Infantry Brigade, the Battalion was placed under orders to be ready to move at fifteen minutes notice to exploit any success gained by the 97th Infantry Brigade or to repel counter-attacks.	
IRISH FARM	2		Battalion in huts and tents at IRISH FARM – Church Parades during the morning. News came through in the early hours of the morning that the attack by the 97th Infantry Brigade had been successful, all objectives having been gained. Later a message was received that the 97th Infantry Brigade had been compelled to fall back and eventually the Battalion was placed under orders to proceed to BELLE VUE that night and be prepared to take over the defences of the Ridge on the following night. The Battalion moved off at 11.0p.m., and marched to BELLE VUE, and on arrival there constructed small temporary dug-outs.	
BELLE VUE.	3		The Battalion at BELLE VUE. The situation was reported very bad by the 96th and 97th Infantry Brigades and the Battalion was placed under orders to be ready to move at practically a moments notice. About 7.0 p.m., the enemy shelled BELLE VUE very heavily killing 2 and wounding 4 O.R. The Battalion moved up to the Left Sub-sector at 10.30 p.m.,	

Army Form C. 2118.

WAR DIARY
or
INTELLIGENCE SUMMARY.

(Erase heading not required.)

Instructions regarding War Diaries and Intelligence Summaries are contained in F. S. Regs., Part II. and the Staff Manual respectively. Title pages will be prepared in manuscript.

Place	Date	Hour	Summary of Events and Information	Remarks and references to Appendices
	1917. Dec.			
			and relieved the 15th Lancashire Fusiliers; "A" Company on the Left, "B" Coy in Centre "C" Company on the Right, "B" and "D" Companies being in support - relief complete at 4.0 a.m. The front was held by an organised system of shell-holes, Battalion Headquarters being at Pill Box No. 88. Estimated casualties were reported at 10 O.R.	
LEFT SUB-SECTOR.	4		Battalion in LEFT SUB-SECTOR. Situation normal. Three battle patrols were sent out during the night, each consisting of 1 Officer and 10 men. Casualties reported during the day 3 killed and 4 wounded. Lieut. Haynes reported missing.	
DITTO	5		Battalion in LEFT SUB-SECTOR - enemy shelled the Battalion Front very heavily in the early hours of the morning. To-night 2nd Lieut. HOLMES and 20 O.R., were ordered to capture the Mebus on the Battalion Front. The patrol went out at 7.30 p.m., but were met by heavy machine gun fire from the point in question, and after being out for some considerable time the patrol withdrew for further orders. Casualties of the patrol - 1 O.R. killed and 1 O.R. wounded. Battalion extended the LEFT COMPANY FRONT to the PADDEBEEK. Battalion relief carried out - the 5/6th Royal Scots relieving the Battalion in the LEFT SUB-SECTOR, Headquarters "A", "B" and "D" withdrawing to BELLE VUE and relieving the 15th H.L.I., relief being completed by 3.53 a.m., the 6th inst. "C" Company remained in supportof the 5/6th Royal	

Army Form C. 2118.

WAR DIARY
or
INTELLIGENCE SUMMARY.
(Erase heading not required.)

Instructions regarding War Diaries and Intelligence Summaries are contained in F. S. Regs., Part II. and the Staff Manual respectively. Title pages will be prepared in manuscript.

Place	Date	Hour	Summary of Events and Information	Remarks and references to Appendices
	1917		Royal Scots.	
BELLE VUE	Dec. 6		Total casualties 1 killed and 7 wounded.	
	7		Battalion (less "C" Company) at BELLE VUE. Enemy shelled our positions very heavily. "D" Company moved at 5.30 p.m. from BELLE VUE to GOUBERG SPUR in support of the 1st Dorsets. Trenches were dug by the Company under the supervision of the R.E. Carrying parties for rations, water, hot food, etc., for the Battalions in the line were furnished by "A" and "B" Companies. Casualties, 3 killed and 17 wounded - information was received to-day that Lieut. HAYNES was wounded and in Hospital.	
DITTO	7		Battalion (less "C" and "D" Companies) at BELLE VUE. Companies during the day were engaged in salvaging any Stores etc., lying about. Carrying parties again furnished for carrying rations, water, etc., to the Battalions in the Front Line. Casualties 7 wounded.	
DITTO	8		Battalion (less "C" and "D" Companies) at BELLE VUE. Companies engaged in salvaging and in providing carrying parties to the Battalions in the Front Line. Casualties 1 O.R. wounded.	
DITTO	9		Battalion (less "C" and "D" Companies) at BELLE VUE. A large amount of salvage in the shape of equipment, petrol cans, food containers, etc., was carried by the two Companies	

Army Form C. 2118.

WAR DIARY
or
INTELLIGENCE SUMMARY.
(Erase heading not required.)

Instructions regarding War Diaries and Intelligence Summaries are contained in F. S. Regs., Part II. and the Staff Manual respectively. Title pages will be prepared in manuscript.

Place	Date	Hour	Summary of Events and Information	Remarks and references to Appendices
	1917 Dec.		at BELLE VUE to the Salvage Dump at KANSAS CROSS. Enemy shelled BELLE VUE very heavily. Casualties 4 wounded. Battalion relieved by the 6th Somerset Light Infantry, relief commencing about 10.30 p.m. "D" Company withdrew from GOUBERG SPUR at 11.0 p.m., without relief as ordered. Battalion relief reported complete at 12.30 a.m., on the 10th inst.	
YSER CANAL.	10		Battalion took over dug-outs on the banks fo the YSER CANAL, being complete in dug-outs at 5.15 a.m., on the 10th inst. Battalion in dug-outs CANAL BANK. Battalion moved from CANAL BANK at 9.55 a.m., to huts at HOSPITAL FARM - complete in huts by 2.0 p.m. The rest of the day was spent in cleaning up and inspection of feet. The Battalion was placed under orders to be prepared to move at two hours notice.	
HOSPITAL FARM.	11		Battalion in huts at HOSPITAL FARM. The day was spent in cleaning up after the tour in the line and the inspection of clothing, etc - also in the checking of all stores.	
DITTO	12		Battalion in huts at HOSPITAL FARM. During the morning routine training was carried on; also the issuing of new clothing. The afternoon was spent in bathing and recreation.	
DITTO	13		Battalion in huts at HOSPITAL FARM. Bathing and routine training carried on. Working parties found for working in the Camp under the direction of the Camp Adjutant.	

Army Form C. 2118.

WAR DIARY
or
INTELLIGENCE SUMMARY.

(Erase heading not required.)

Instructions regarding War Diaries and Intelligence Summaries are contained in F. S. Regs., Part II. and the Staff Manual respectively. Title pages will be prepared in manuscript.

Place	Date	Hour	Summary of Events and Information	Remarks and references to Appendices
	1917			
HOSPITAL FARM.	Dec.14		Battalion in huts at HOSPITAL FARM. Routine training carried on and further working parties found.	
HOSPITAL FARM.	15		Battalion in Huts at HOSPITAL FARM. Routine training carried on and further working parties found.	
DITTO	16		Battalion in Huts at HOSPITAL FARM. The usual Church Parades were held in the morning and the rest of the day was devoted to recreation.	
DITTO	17		Battalion in Huts at HOSPITAL FARM. At 2.15 p.m., the Battalion moved to CANAL BANK being accommodated in dug-outs - complete in dug-outs at 4.45 p.m. Working party found.	
CANAL BANK.	18		Battalion in dug-outs CANAL BANK. The day was spent in settling the Battalion in dug-outs and in generally cleaning up. Working parties found.	
DITTO	19		Battalion in dug-outs CANAL BANK. Working parties found. Capt. S. WATTS to-day rejoined the Battalion from Course at 5th Army Infantry School. 2nd Lieut. A. F. Dale to-day left for the 14th Pioneer Company, R.E.	
DITTO	20		Battalion in dug-outs CANAL BANK. All available men were to-day engaged in working parties of various descriptions.	
DITTO	21.		ditto ditto.	

Army Form C. 2118.

WAR DIARY
or
INTELLIGENCE SUMMARY.
(Erase heading not required.)

Instructions regarding War Diaries and Intelligence Summaries are contained in F. S. Regs., Part II. and the Staff Manual respectively. Title pages will be prepared in manuscript.

Place	Date 1917	Hour	Summary of Events and Information	Remarks and references to Appendices
CANAL BANK	Dec.22		Battalion in dug-outs CANAL BANK. The day was spent in drawing Battle Stores and generally in preparing for the next tour in the line.	
CANAL BANK	23		Battalion in dug-outs CANAL BANK. The Battalion moved off at 3.15 p.m., to take over the RIGHT SUB-SECTOR, relieving the 11th Border Regiment, relief being complete at 1.0 a.m., on the morning of the 24th. "C" and "D" Companies were in the Line, "B" in support and "A" in reserve. Wiring parties found by the Battalion working on front line posts and flanks. Capt. Thwaytes to-night joined the Battalion in the line. 2nd Lieut. F. J. Cook to-day proceeded to the 14th T. M. Battery.	
RIGHT SUB-SECTOR.	24		Battalion in RIGHT SUB-SECTOR. Casualties:- 2nd Lieut. J. Rowley and 1 O.R. killed, 4 O.R. wounded. Two prisoners were to-night captured by 2nd Lieut. O. Cassidy. Wiring parties found by the Battalion for working on front line posts and flanks.	
RIGHT SUB-SECTOR.	25		Battalion in RIGHT SUB-SECTOR. German prisoner captured by "D" Company about 4.0 a.m. Casualties:- 1 O.R. killed, 5 O.R. wounded. Wiring parties found by the Battalion working on front line posts and flanks.	
RIGHT SUB-SECTOR.	26		Battalion in RIGHT SUB-SECTOR. Casualties- 7 O.R. wounded. Wiring parties on front line posts and flanks again found. The "S.O.S." was sent up by the centre Battalion of the Division on our Right. A heavy barrage was put down by the enemy on our outpost line and on	

WAR DIARY
or
INTELLIGENCE SUMMARY.

(Erase heading not required.)

Army Form C. 2118.

Place	Date	Hour	Summary of Events and Information	Remarks and references to Appendices
	1917 Dec.		artillery replied with a heavy counter-barrage almost immediately, the fire being well distributed along the Battalion front.	
RIGHT SUB-SECTOR.	27		Battalion in RIGHT SUB-SECTOR. Casualties 8 O.R. wounded. The Battalion relieved by the 5/6th Royal Scots, relief commencing at 5.0 p.m., and being complete about 9.30 p.m. The Battalion (less Headquarters and "D" Company) moving to the CORPS LINE and Headquarters and "D" Company moving to ALBERTA, the Battalion being complete in position at 11.30 p.m.	61
CORPS LINE & ALBERTA	28		Battalion in CORPS LINE and at ALBERTA. Casualties 5 O.R. wounded. Carrying and working parties for the front line found by the Battalion. The enemy shelled the CORPS LINE very heavily with 5.9s about three p.m. Casualties:- 3 killed.	
CORPS LINE & ALBERTA	29		Battalion in CORPS LINE and at ALBERTA. Carrying and working parties for the front line found by the Battalion.	
CORPS LINE & ALBERTA	30		Battalion in CORPS LINE and at ALBERTA. The Battalion relieved by the 16th Sherwood Foresters (39th Division) - relief commenced at 5.0 p.m., and being complete at 7.15 p.m. The Battalion proceeded to dug-outs at CANAL BANK being complete therein by 9.45 p.m. During the Battalion's tour in the line a large amount of salvage was collected and carried to the Salvage Dump for disposal.	
CANAL BANK.	31		Battalion in dug-outs at CANAL BANK. The day was spent in cleaning up generally after the tour in the line.	

WAR DIARY
or
INTELLIGENCE SUMMARY.
(Erase heading not required.)

Army Form C. 2118.

Instructions regarding War Diaries and Intelligence Summaries are contained in F. S. Regs., Part II. and the Staff Manual respectively. Title pages will be prepared in manuscript.

Place	Date	Hour	Summary of Events and Information	Remarks and references to Appendices
CANAL BANK	1918 Jan.1.		Battalion in dug-outs at CANAL BANK. At 11 a.m. the Battalion marched to ST. JEAN STATION where it entrained for AUDRUICQ. On arrival there the Battalion proceeded by route march to LISTERGAUX. The Battalion was reported complete in Billets at 6.15 p.m. Major W. F. Jefferies rejoined the Battalion from England to-day and took over the duties of Second in Command.	
LISTERGAUX	2		Battalion in Billets LISTERGAUX. The day was spent in drawing Stores, etc., and generally in getting the Battalion settled in their new quarters.	
ditto	3		Battalion in Billets LISTERGAUX. Routine training carried on. Capt. N. W. Humphrys and 2nd. Lieut. E. F. Lowther rejoined the Battalion to-day.	
ditto	4		Battalion in Billets LISTERGAUX. Routine training carried on. Lieut. J. W. Culley rejoined the Battalion to-day.	
ditto	5		Battalion in Billets LISTERGAUX. Routine training carried on. The Commanding Officer (Lieut. Colonel Vaughan) to-day proceeded to England on leave, Major W. F. Jefferies taking over command of the Battalion in Colonel Vaughan's absence.	
ditto	6		Battalion in Billets LISTERGAUX. The usual Church Parades were held to-day.	
ditto	7		Battalion in Billets LISTERGAUX. The Battalion paraded this morning for inspection by the Brigadier.	
ditto	8		Battalion in Billets LISTERGAUX. The inspection of the Brigade by the Corps Commander which was to have taken place to-day was cancelled owing to a heavy fall of snow and the severe weather conditions generally. Bathing and training under Company arrangements carried on.	
ditto	9		Battalion in Billets LISTERGAUX. Training carried on on the Brigade Training Area. Major W. F. Jefferies to-day proceeded to the 2nd Battalion, Royal Dublin Fusiliers, and the command of the Battalion was taken over by Major N. W. Humphrys.	

Army Form C. 2118.

WAR DIARY
or
INTELLIGENCE SUMMARY.
(Erase heading not required.)

Instructions regarding War Diaries and Intelligence Summaries are contained in F. S. Regs., Part II. and the Staff Manual respectively. Title pages will be prepared in manuscript.

Place	Date	Hour	Summary of Events and Information	Remarks and references to Appendices
LISTERGAUX	1918 Jan.10		Battalion in Billets LISTERGAUX. Routine training carried on.	
ditto	11		Battalion in Billets LISTERGAUX. To-day was celebrated by the Battalion as Christmas Day - dinners were served in the Y.M.C.A. Hut, AUDRUICQ, followed by a Concert and Entertainment.	
ditto	12		Battalion in Billets LISTERGAUX. Routine training carried on. Lecture given by the Divisional Gas Officer in the afternoon.	
ditto	13		Battalion in Billets LISTERGAUX. The usual Church Parades were held to-day.	
ditto	14		Battalion in Billets LISTERGAUX. Training was greatly interfered with owing to a heavy fall of snow.	
ditto	15		Battalion in Billets LISTERGAUX. Musketry practices carried out by the Battalion on the GUEMY Rifle Range.	
ditto	16		Battalion in Billets Listergaux. Training was greatly interfered with owing to rain and was carried on under Company arrangements.	
ditto	17		Battalion in Billets LISTERGAUX. Training was again interfered with owing to the weather conditions and carried on under Company arrangements.	
ditto	18		Battalion in Billets LISTERGAUX. Musketry practices carried out by the Battalion on the NORTBOULINGHEM Rifle Range.	
ditto	19		Battalion in Billets LISTERGAUX. Routine training carried on, followed by a Lecture to the men by the Brigade Major.	
ditto	20		Battalion in Billets LISTERGAUX. The usual Church Parades were held to-day.	
ditto	21		Battalion in Billets LISTERGAUX. The day was generally spent in preparing for the move on the following day.	

Army Form C. 2118.

WAR DIARY
or
INTELLIGENCE SUMMARY.
(Erase heading not required.)

Instructions regarding War Diaries and Intelligence Summaries are contained in F.S. Regs., Part II. and the Staff Manual respectively. Title pages will be prepared in manuscript.

Place	Date	Hour	Summary of Events and Information	Remarks and references to Appendices
LISTERGAUX	1918 Jan.22		Battalion in Billets LISTERGAUX. The Battalion moved off at 5.50 a.m. and marched to AUDRUICQ STATION where they entrained for ELVERDINGHE. The Battalion then proceeded by route march to DIRTY BUCKET CAMP being accommodated in huts - complete in huts by 3 p.m.	
DIRTY BUCKET CAMP.	23		Battalion in huts DIRTY BUCKET CAMP. Inspections held of rifles, kit, etc. 69 O.Rs. under Capt. S. Watts and 2nd Lieut. R. F. Whitmore to-day proceeded to the 173rd Tunnelling Company (attached).	
ditto	24		Battalion in huts DIRTY BUCKET CAMP. Routine training carried on. Colonel Vaughan rejoined the Battalion from leave.	
ditto	25		Battalion in huts DIRTY BUCKET CAMP. Routine training carried on.	
ditto	26		Battalion in huts DIRTY BUCKET CAMP. Routine training and bathing carried on.	
ditto	27		Battalion in huts DIRTY BUCKET CAMP. The usual Church Parades were held to-day.	
ditto	28		Battalion in huts DIRTY BUCKET CAMP. Routine training carried on. Colonel Vaughan to-day proceeded to Conference at II Corps School, PHILECOURT.	
ditto	29		Battalion in huts DIRTY BUCKET CAMP. An Inter-Battalion wiring competition was held this morning, the wiring squad of "B" Company representing the Battalion. After an exciting contest the Battalion squad tied with the 1st Dorset Regiment for first place. In the afternoon a demonstration in the use of Chinese dummy figures was given which was attended by the C.O., 7 other Officers and 20 N.C.Os.	
ditto	30		Battalion in huts DIRTY BUCKET CAMP. The Battalion moved off at 10.40 a.m. and marched to EMILE CAMP (BOESINGHE No. 2 area.) being accommodated in huts - being complete in huts at 12. 20 p.m. The Battalion being in Divisional Reserve was placed under orders to be ready to move at two hours notice. Capt. S. Watts, 2nd Lieut. E. F. Lowther and 69 O.Rs. to-day rejoined the Battalion from the 173rd Tunnelling Company.	

Army Form C. 2118.

WAR DIARY
or
INTELLIGENCE SUMMARY.
(Erase heading not required.)

Instructions regarding War Diaries and Intelligence Summaries are contained in F. S. Regs., Part II. and the Staff Manual respectively. Title pages will be prepared in manuscript.

Place	Date	Hour	Summary of Events and Information	Remarks and references to Appendices
EMILE CAMP.	1918 Jan.31.		Battalion in huts EMILE CAMP. Routine training carried on.	

R.M. Humphreys. Major.

Commanding 2nd Battalion, The Manchester Regiment.

www.ingramcontent.com/pod-product-compliance
Lightning Source LLC
Chambersburg PA
CBHW080924230426
43668CB00014B/2189